# Nothing Wanting

# NOTHING WANTING

*Asexuality
and the
Matter of
Absence*

KJ Cerankowski

University of Minnesota Press
Minneapolis | London

The University of Minnesota Press gratefully acknowledges the generous assistance provided for the publication of this book by Oberlin College.

Portions of "A Meandering Introduction, An Asexual Foray" were published in a different form in "Making Nothing Out of Something: Asexuality and the Rhetorics of Silence and Absence," in *The Routledge Handbook of Queer Rhetoric*, ed. Jacqueline Rhodes and Jonathan Alexander (Routledge, 2022). "An End to Ends" was published in a different form as "The 'End' of Orgasm: The Erotics of Durational Pleasures," *Studies in Gender and Sexuality* 22, no. 3 (2021): 132–46; published by permission of Taylor & Francis Ltd., http://www.tandfonline.com. Portions of "Redacted" were published in a different form in "The Feverish Saint: A Queer Crip Encounter with the Public Universal Friend," in *Cripping the Archive: Disability, History, and Power*, ed. Jenifer L. Barclay and Stefanie Hunt-Kennedy (University of Illinois Press, 2025).

Published by the University of Minnesota Press
111 Third Avenue South, Suite 290
Minneapolis, MN 55401-2520
http://www.upress.umn.edu

ISBN 978-1-5179-1642-8 (hc)
ISBN 978-1-5179-1643-5 (pb)

A Cataloging-in-Publication record for this book is available from the Library of Congress.

Printed in the United States of America on acid-free paper

The University of Minnesota is an equal-opportunity educator and employer.

34 33 32 31 30 29 28 27 26 25          10 9 8 7 6 5 4 3 2 1

# Contents

*This page intentionally left blank.*

# A Meandering Introduction, an Asexual Foray

The preceding page is blank. More accurately, the preceding page was blank until it was printed with the notification that it was intentionally left blank, a declaration that belies its own intention. The declaration fills the once-blank page, infelicitously declaring the blankness of a page that is no longer blank. The blank page is but a mere memory, only the once-possibility of a page soon to be marked.

I begin with a reflection on the no-longer-blank page as an illustration of this book's questions and obsessions: Was the page ever really blank? How do we make sense of a page that is not blank but declares itself to be so? What is the lie of blankness, emptiness, absence, or silence? My project here is to reveal presence where there is purported to be absence, to assert that refusals, gaps, silences, the neither here nor there, and other assumed nulls and naughts are places where living, existence, and activity continue—untidy, cheerful, awful, and awe-ful.[1]

When you hear someone shout, "Nothing to see here, folks," you can undoubtedly bet there is something rather exciting or embarrassing or perhaps even scandalous to see. The declaration of there being nothing to see is simply discursive smoke and mirrors, an attempt to convince the looker to turn away or to stop seeking altogether. Nothingness becomes a concealment, a production of absence that serves to deflect, distract, undermine, and avert. In fact, manufacturing absence and nothingness by erasing, eliminating, or ignoring a presence seems to be de rigueur in the maintenance of the status quo. The demand to look away is often tethered to a refusal to see, to acknowledge, or to experience that which disturbs and unsettles the norm.

Of course, the inversion to turning away is the gawking, gaping stare. To be on the receiving end of the look is to be immersed in an all-too-present encounter with one's differences while judgmental eyes bore into, rank, and value any failure, bumble, or deviance from the white, cisgender, nondisabled norm. In such a situation, a common reaction for the one being ogled may be a wish for the stare to be averted, to be released from the discomfort of the gape. Or, for those of us who have caught the looks enough times, our exasperation, pain, and anger produce the quick retort, "What are you looking at?" A way to face the stare head-on, the question usually tends to garner a result not too unlike when one declares, "Nothing to see here!" In the least contentious scenarios, the looker might respond with a clipped, "Nothing!," as the eyes shift and look away, as the person turns on their heels and flees the scene.

But to the gawker, I push the question "What *are* you looking at?" You are looking at something or someone, so the response of "Nothing!" will not suffice. To press on the question is to refuse erasure and to resist the declaration that one look away under the pretense that there is nothing to look at. It is to instead demand, as Eli Clare writes, that "the gawking, gaping, staring finally turns to something else, something true to the bone."[2] It is another way of saying, "Look at me," rather than, "Don't stare."[3] Look. Be unsettled. By the queer body, the sick body, the disabled body, the racialized body, the colonized body. See what you have refused. I am reminded of a moment in Suzan-Lori Parks's play *Venus*, which tells the story of Saartjie Baartman, a Khoekhoe woman who was taken from her home in southwestern Africa near the Cape Colony to be toured around Europe as a "sideshow wonder" known as "The Venus Hottentot," often also referred to as "Sarah Baartman." In Parks's play, we learn an important lesson about voyeurism: The one who stares does not, indeed, see everything. As Saartjie Baartman stands on display, Parks notes, "The things they noticed were quite various but no one ever noticed that her face was streamed with tears."[4] The gawkers could not, in fact, see what was true to the bone as they erased her subjectivity and her emotional life. What may seem obvious but is worth stating nonetheless: Just because no one saw the tears does not mean she did not cry. A story of salt. An affective mattering. A sentiment. A sediment. A settlement. Sometimes what goes unseen is the thing that matters most.

To be clear, I am not suggesting that gawkers keep up their rude staring in order to see everything, in order to steal even the things that the one on display may want to keep for herself. Concealment can also be a valuable tactic of the oppressed.[5] Rather, I am urging that we all interrogate how, when, and why we look and what we are looking at or for. When we look, let us look with care, with an attunement to silenced histories and ongoing structures of erasure and elimination. When we sense, let us sense toward possibilities we know and carry in our bones, stories of pain and violence but also stories of beauty and pleasure, all of which we haven't been able to sense into because we were told to look away, urged to believe there was nothing to see, nothing to know, nothing to recognize as vibrant life and activity outside the colonial ordering of whiteness, heterosexuality, and properly (re)productive bodily capacities and relations. What might be made possible when we recover those erasures and eliminations, when we understand a silence not as a mere cover-up but as a missed reading, a misreading, or an intentional misdirecting?

Such misdirection is an extensive art form of the colonial apparatus, a technology of the machine that seeks to homogenize, normalize, and normativize life through elimination and constant redirection. By beginning with silence, attuning to absence, and—as I will ultimately argue—thinking asexually, we come to understand what is at stake in unsettling these intertwined colonial epistemologies and ontologies. As Karen Barad asserts: "The question of absence is as political as that of presence. . . . The void—a much-valued colonialist apparatus, a crafty and insidious imaginary, a way of offering justification for claims of ownership in the 'discovery' of 'virgin' territory—the notion that 'untended,' 'uncultivated,' 'uncivilized' spaces are empty rather than plentiful, has been a well-worn tool used in the service of colonialism, racism, capitalism, militarism, imperialism, nationalism, and scientism."[6] The void: the empty, destitute space to be claimed and filled. To be voided: cleared, emptied, nullified. The colonial apparatus: imagining a void while voiding, voiding in order to refill, a cover-up. As Adam J. Barker puts it, "Understanding settler colonialism by definition requires piercing [its] invisibility, revealing that which colonial power would obscure for its own interests."[7] In other words, colonial power depends upon us agreeing and believing that the page is actually blank, was always already blank—all in the service of convincing us of the nothingness of real material presences, of the impossibilities of actual existences, of the silences of long-buried screams.

## MOUNTAINS AND MOLEHILLS

There is a familiar adage leveled against someone who seems to be making a bigger deal of something than needs to be made: the accusation that they are making mountains out of molehills or making something out of nothing. This book contends with the inverse, when mountains are dismissed as mere molehills to be trampled and forgotten. But the quest to scale these rediscovered mountains can quickly become a dogged journey as the scope of a study of presence within absence has no bounds. So here I bring us to a point of focus—the absence or presence of sex. Sex is a category and activity that, as Mark Rifkin notes, cannot be disentangled from our understandings of the effects of colonization, particularly through the invention of perversity, deviance, and nonnormativity. Sex makes the person (literally and figuratively), defines relations, constitutes legal categories, and otherwise organizes settler societies.[8] The absence of sex—its morphological formation, its bodily and reproductive activity, its locus as a site of desire—then troubles the ordering of the body (what is a body without sex?), the constitution of the human (is sex not a natural human instinct?), and the value of desire (what greater desire is there than the sexual?). To put a fine Foucauldian point on it, sex, like power, is everywhere. And when it's not, well, we tend to look for where it might be hiding.

It is particularly notable that even queer frameworks, which often seek to interrogate and undo compulsory heterosexuality and heteronormativity, do little to disrupt compulsory sexuality and sexual normativity. When I refer to *compulsory sexuality,* I draw on Kristina Gupta's understanding of the concept "to describe the assumption that all people are sexual and to describe the social norms and practices that both marginalize various forms of nonsexuality and compel people to experience themselves as desiring subjects, take up sexual identities, and engage in sexual activity."[9] Compulsory sexuality is thus a normative—and, I add, colonial—structure that compels sexual desire and even sexual pleasure (in the right ways, at the right times, under the right circumstances, and to the right ends). I also place a caveat on Gupta's original definition to clarify that the compulsion is to experience oneself not just as a desiring subject but as a *sexually* desiring and *sexually* desirable subject. For, as I ask throughout this book, what might it mean to experience oneself as a nonsexually desiring subject but a desiring subject nonetheless?

My suggestion, then, is that even queer theory operates under the logics of sexual normativity, wedding itself to the belief that sex (as in any sexual desire or practice) is central to human existence and relationality. The absence of sex is usually interpreted as repression or closeting. Remarking on Michel Foucault's oft-cited quip, "There is not one but many silences," Benjamin Kahan argues that "despite its frequent citation, this pronouncement usually remains unheeded as queer studies reads silence in only one way: reading the 'absence' of sex as itself a sign of homosexuality. Queer readings tend to interpret 'absence' (preterition, silence, the closet, the love that dare not speak its name, the 'impossibility' of lesbian sex) as 'evidence' of same-sex eroticism, covering over our ability to read actual absences of sex."[10] Not only does Kahan point out the ways in which even radical queer attempts at reading against the sexual grain sometimes reinstate the epistemology of the closet where there may have in fact been no closeted homosexuality to begin with, but he also raises the question of absence itself. It is remarkably an absence of sex that Kahan is both looking for in its actuality and also accusing queer studies of filling, in a way, with an incorrect presence: a latent or hidden homosexuality. And while I, too, am drawn to exploring how we might recuperate celibacies and asexualities from within these absences of sex, I am also concerned about the ways in which absences of sex get reduced to other absences as well: no sex = no pleasure, no sex = no romance, no sex = no love.

While it is true that queer artists and writers have historically found ways to encode same-sex desire within seemingly innocuous, sexless interactions and desexualized character portrayals (see, for example, Vito Russo's classic *The Celluloid Closet*), my present concern is for the queer reader who has been trained to read so deep into the closet that any absence of sex becomes suspicious. Such a suspicious, perhaps even paranoid, reader becomes so distrustful of the possibility of asexuality that they begin to find sex where there may actually be an aversion to sex, a refusal of sex, or a way of loving and being otherwise that is asexual, aromantic, celibate, or nonsexual.

To make the case in point, let us revisit a well-rehearsed study of queer reading that has subsequently been taken up and reframed through asexual analytics. Nathan Snaza returns to Eve Kosofsky Sedgwick's famous queer reading of Henry James's novella *The Beast in the Jungle* in which she determines protagonist John Marcher's "secret" must be closeted homosexuality, a reading that Snaza argues "gives in" to paranoid reading and further defies Sedgwick's own axiom, "Some people like to have a lot of sex, others little or none."[11] Despite setting herself up for the possibility of a nonsexual reading of Marcher (a reading that indeed might be more surprising or reparative, as asexual possibility is made illegible through a paranoid analytic), Sedgwick instead reads Marcher's "failure to desire at all" as closeted homosexuality. Sedgwick's reading thus leads Snaza to ask why Marcher must "have a *sexuality* at all," as he suggests instead, "if Marcher 'fails to desire,' it is entirely possible that the only thing that needs to be said about that is this: he fails to desire." To attempt to explain that failure to desire, Snaza continues, "by shuttling it through a reading practice that takes as axiomatic that *one must (sexually) desire*" is perhaps not the best hermeneutic practice. Snaza then suggests that giving up on this "hermeneutic compulsion" can let us feel into more complex biopolitical questions in the text, and here I wholeheartedly agree with Snaza's critique of Sedgwick and the opening he presents toward new biopolitical questions when desire takes different shapes from the sexual, including a so-imagined failure. But Snaza also laments that "asexually oriented reading finds itself in the embarrassing position of focusing on moments where *there is nothing to interpret.*"[12]

In many ways, like Snaza, I too want to let sleeping dogs lie. A failure to desire might simply be nothing more than a failure to desire. But I want to also offer another possibility. I may be accused of mincing words here. It is true that Snaza writes, in multiple places, of asexual desires, pleasures and erotics that eschew the sexual, but it is also important to tease out the invocation of nothingness that embarrasses the asexually oriented reader.[13] Revisiting the axiom that one must (sexually) desire, I suggest that *sexually* may not be parenthetical. In other words, it is not necessarily that one must desire but that the preoccupation with *sexual* desire often forecloses other desires, leading us into a false binary: Either one desires sexually or one fails to desire at all. *Desire* becomes a narrowing shorthand for *sexual desire.* If we accept that any lack of sexual desire is a failure to desire altogether, we overlook the presence of nonsexual desires and may conclude that "there is nothing to interpret." The absence of sex yet again seems to be equated to nothingness.

In a similar vein, Elizabeth Hanna Hanson takes up Henry James to formulate asexual narrative structure as one in which we ought to expect nothing to happen. Hanson writes, "The stasis, the failure of event and of movement that characterizes asexual narrative is the product of an *absence of desire,* and this is why such a narrative is specifically asexual, not merely queer, modernist, or infused with an affect or behavior like laziness or sloth (although it may be any or all of these things as well)."[14] Hanson argues not only that we learn to interpret absence by way of asexuality but also that we take into account how asexuality structures the narrative itself and challenges linearity and resolution. (We will meander back to irresolution and its wandering middle later.) This focus on stasis is not to suggest that asexual relationships themselves are stagnant, but it is to direct us toward a new way of reading absences, in which expecting nothing to happen may be the asexual modus operandi.

But here's the rub: Hanson's claim, similar to Snaza's, is seemingly staked on the assertion that asexual narrative is absent of desire. I want to take a moment here to fine-tune asexual reading methods, to practice rereading absence. Asexual narratives, I contend, can be full of desires. There is, in fact, a lot that happens; it's just not always what we have been indoctrinated to expect to happen. Arguably, if we recall the diversionary tactics of the declaration of there being nothing to see, it would seem that the suggestion that we should expect nothing to happen should impel us all the more to look anew at what *is happening* instead. In the end, both Snaza and Hanson do ultimately move in this direction. Snaza names Marcher's desire after all: "a desire for the social recognition of a grievable relation not structured by sexuality."[15] And Hanson concedes that Marcher recovers a sort of desire in his old age: "wanting there to be something rather than nothing to supply him with meaning," or quite simply, his only desire is "the desire for narrative."[16] In other words, Marcher wants nothing specific, but he does want. And his wants contain within them negatives: something more meaningful than nothing, a recognition that is not tethered to sexuality. A Bartlebyan kind of want.

I invoke Herman Melville's "Bartleby, the Scrivener" here, another favorite of queer literary analysis, because I think Bartleby's preference "not to" is also instructive in thinking about absent desires. As Michael Cobb notes, much ink has been spilled over Melville's odd scrivener because "Bartleby is full of so much potential meaning, potential refusal of any definitive, perhaps sovereign meaning, that philosophers and literary critics regularly use him as a figure of paradoxically strong passivity—Bartleby is passive but saturated with very aggressive ideas."[17] Sianne Ngai suggests a similar paradox in that Bartleby's turning away is at once polemical and passive.[18] And Nicholas de Villiers focuses on the opacity and passive resistance of Bartleby's queer grammar (via Gilles Deleuze) in the open-ended "not to."[19] Passive, always passive.[20] And so full of potential. Full, not empty. In an effort to interpret that fullness, I want to shift the focus from the "not to" toward the declaration of preference: "I would *prefer* not to." I read this expression as an active insistence on a preference to not do. Bartleby is actually agentive in his refusal, hardly passive.

Plenty of feminist, queer, and decolonial thinkers variously take up Bartleby's refusal or other formations of a "politics of refusal" as agentive.[21] In the specific context of asexuality, Breanne Fahs and Ela Przybyło advocate for the radical potentials of an asexual politics of refusal, while Megan Milks challenges the limits of such a progress-oriented asexual politic.[22] Accounting for the absenting of Blackness in mainstream asexual movement discourse, Ianna Hawkins Owen posits a "declarative silence" as a refusal to be hailed, as an active, agentive choice to say nothing. Such silence, then, "is not static but dynamic: a silence that impresses with its intended presence."[23] A present silence. An impression. An action. Refusing—or saying "no"—is rarely a refusal of everything. Sometimes, refusing one thing means saying yes to other things. Building from this important work on active political refusals, I want to pivot again to the preference rather than focus on the refusal. To prefer not to is still to prefer. To want nothing is still to want. To not desire sex is not to not desire at all or to desire nothing. Put another way, to desire no sex is still to desire.

Like Bartleby, the asexual only appears to desire nothing. Asexuality has been defined by what it is not and by what it lacks—the Asexual Visibility and Education Network describes an asexual as someone who "does not experience sexual attraction," which inevitably leads to the question posed by Owen: "If the asexual is one who does not 'experience sexual attraction,' what is this 'sexuality' that asexuality defines itself against or in the absence of?"[24] What is the sexual something to asexuality's alleged nothing? The question of absence plagues asexuality: What does it mean to be asexual, to practice/do asexuality, or to desire or prefer not to if we understand asexuality only as absence, as nothing to interpret? In an attempt to redress Foucault's theories on sexual confession in regard to asexuality, Przybyło writes, "In the absence of anything to confess, it is that absence that must be confessed."[25] While it is true that asexual people have had to come out or confess their asexuality or their lack of sexual attraction, I, like Przybyło, am critical of any compulsion to confess anything, even if that anything seems to amount to nothing.

However, I am troubled by the premise that there is an absence of anything to confess. Asexuality is again evacuated.

To equate a desire not to (or a failure/refusal to desire sexually) with absence or nothingness is to essentially invert the adage with which we began this section. It is to make nothing out of something. I suggest that a hermeneutic that brokers happening and substance on often unnoticeable, insidious sex normativity and compulsory sexuality essentially makes nothing out of many somethings. I am particularly concerned with the oversights and misapprehensions of so-imagined sexual absences, where the constraints of normative ideologies of sexuality, including the design of discrete sexual orientation categories as well as prescriptions of healthy, human-defining ideals of sexual desire and practice, serve to erase asexual possibilities for desiring, pleasuring, or relating. That is, we need a hermeneutic of absence untethered from compulsory sexuality. To be clear, I am not attempting to recuperate asexuality as a substantive sexuality or sexual orientation, as I have no investment in reifying the (colonial) ordering of sex. Rather, I am concerned with the substance of asexualities: a range of nonsexual desires, a plethora of pleasures, a multitude of intimacies—spatial, temporal, material, and affective ways of living in the voids. Whereas many understand asexuality as a restriction, like a diet, a removal of something—sex—from one's life, I understand asexuality as expansive, bringing awareness to flavors one might not have otherwise known existed. Ultimately, I am less interested in the question of what it means to be asexual and more taken by an asexual attentiveness to the world, a mode of living that recognizes fullness and possibility where there was once deemed to be nothing. It is to recognize that wanting nothing is still wanting, but to also flip that emptiness to a fullness: nothing wanting, as in wanting for nothing, as in satisfied, not lacking, yet wanting so much more for everything and everyone that has been dismissed as nothing.

## ABSENCE MAKES THE HEART

If it is not obvious by now, I love a good spin on a classic aphorism. And I have no problem mixing low-brow pop culture with high theory; isn't there something to learn everywhere we look? And where better to find on full display the heteronormative and sex-compulsive organization of dating, sex, and romance than on reality TV dating shows? My queer take on these shows could constitute an entire other book, but there is one particular moment that caught my attention that I can't help but indulge here. In Netflix's *The Ultimatum*, a show premised on couples splitting up for three weeks for a trial marriage with someone else, cohost Nick Lachey offers some foreboding wisdom to the participants: "Absence can make the heart grow fonder or absence can make the heart grow absent."[26] On the face of it, he is suggesting simply that some space from their partner will either create a sense of longing or essentially result in a forgetting of the no-longer-present lover. But I want to dig deeper into this idea that the heart grows absent. What is an absent heart?

In *A Lover's Discourse*, Roland Barthes laments, "Absence becomes an active practice, a *business* (which keeps me from doing anything else)."[27] Far from being a mere void, absence occupies a life, takes up space in it, becomes something one works at, a practice that interrupts one's ability to get anything else done. (I can attest—the writing of this book suffered its own drawn-out delays in the all-consuming mourning of absented loves and lovers.) When the heart grows absent, it becomes busy. Busy with longing, with missing, with filling the absence left by the departed. For Barthes, the absent lover constitutes his own presence: "An always present *I* is constituted only by the confrontation with an always absent *you*."[28] I am present because you are not. I exist because you have left me to my own existence. You may exist somewhere, but not for me. The absence of the other creates a longing *I*, a desiring *me*. Something is always made present in the face of an absence. "For shimmer to capture the eye, there must be absence of shimmer. To understand how absence brings forth," writes Deborah Bird Rose, "it must be understood not as lack but as potential."[29]

Imagine an *I* constituted through an always-absent lover, with no desire for a lover at all. What else keeps that heart busy? There are many ways to stay busy with desire. The absent *you* may simply mean so much more potential for the desiring *I* to desire beyond the other, more than or other than a lover. Imagine what else may catch the eye, what else may shimmer for the heart. Absence is not mere loss or emptiness but the beginning of possibility. It is not my intent here to give an exhaustive account of the philosophies of absence.[30] Rather, I want to follow a thread of thought into the possibilities contained within absences to bring us to the multitude of possibilities for love, desire, intimacy, and pleasure contained within sexual absences.

Let's do so by way of silence, kin to absence. For feminist rhetorician Cheryl Glenn, silence is its own kind of beginning, a presence that arises out of absence. Drawing on Max Picard, Glenn writes, "When language ceases, silence begins. But it does not begin *because* language ceases. The absence of language simply makes the presence of silence more apparent."[31] Here, in Glenn's framing, we might conjure a "silent presence," wherein the absence of language, or the absence of noise and sound, makes the presence of silence apparent—a supposed nothing becomes something, not-language/not-spoken/not-sound/not-noise becomes the thing we call "silence." Silence may mark the beginning of possible sound, but it is also its own presence. Or, as Natasha Chuk succinctly puts it, "Silence has presence as much as it has absence."[32] And in its presence, silence becomes something we listen to, something that can be heard. In fact, pure silence, as in a complete nullification of sound, is nearly impossible. Susan Sontag claims, "A genuine emptiness, a pure silence, is not feasible—either conceptually or in fact." And from silence to absence, building on John Cage's quip about there being no such thing as silence ("Something is always happening that makes a sound"), Sontag suggests, "Similarly, there is no such thing as empty space. As long as a human eye is looking, still to be seeing something—if only the ghosts of one's own expectations."[33] Apparitions. Resonances. Traces. Silent presences. Absent presences. The recognizable residue of things allegedly not there.

Similarly, for mathematician and philosopher Brian Rotman, zero marks absence *and* it is imbued with the fullness of being the start of everything. A kind of vanishing point that is nonetheless a point, a perspective in and of itself, "zero then represents the starting point of the process; indicating the virtual presence of the counting subject at the place where that subject begins the whole activity of traversing what will become a sequence of counted positions." We begin at zero, a "trace of subjectivity, pointed to but absent."[34] In other words, zero, thought to be a sign of nothingness is both absent and present, a point to start from, a potential for the count, a beginning, a possibility, a trace of existence. Not too unlike the blank page with which we began. Robert Kaplan opens his history of zero with an invitation into the vastness of zero's world: "If you look at zero you see nothing; but look through it and you will see the world."[35] Let us look through the blank page, through (a)sexuality, through all the nothings into the somethings they entreat us into. Or, as John Cage puts it, "Something and nothing are not opposed to each other but need each other to keep on going."[36] Which is all another way of saying that the silence roars, the absence is palpable.

In *The New Celibacy*, Gabrielle Brown writes, "Just as silence is the basis for sound, for speech, for music, celibacy is the basis for sex."[37] Celibacy and its affinities—asexuality, abstinence, chastity, virginity (supposed sexual zeros)—take the position of zero: the base, the starting point, both something and not the thing, the foundation from which we move into sex or into desire, from nothing into something, from something thought to be nothing into something more, entire worlds. Asexuality, like silence, like absence, is a site of potentiality and possibility, rife with desire. To be asexual is not to be without desire but to be expansively desirous, to be free to want anything or nothing, to value nonsexual desires and pleasures as much as, if not more than, sex. And here, I must clarify that the potential of sex does not necessarily have to follow from asexuality; rather, asexuality marks its own presence, full of its own desires, its own beginning for reimagining intimacies, relationalities, and sexualities.

Asexuality asks us to contend with absence and silence by demanding that we pay attention not only to the ghosts, the shimmers, the "asexual resonances," and the traces but also to what is materially, substantively, and substantially there.[38] To be clear, to seek an unregarded presence in absence is not to vie for recognition within mainstream frameworks or to make space for asexuality in a litany of sexual orientations and identities that ultimately uphold the bounds of the respectable liberal human subject made legible through legitimated sexual desire and practice. Far from a cry for visibility for this "invisible orientation" or for asexuality's silence to be heard among the moans and groans of sex, I am calling for a radical shift in how we conceive of absence and presence, how we resist both colonial logics of erasure and also romanticized fantasies of a recovery of the "natural," how we relearn to pay attention to what seemed to be nothing, how we listen to silence, how we see the invisible, how we feel emptiness, how we read for absences.

## READING FOR ABSENCE

When I first began reading for asexuality, I wanted to bring asexuality out of the closet, to find asexuality as an expression of sexual identity or as a licit sexual orientation in an effort to prove that it exists, that it can be and has been represented, and that people should care about it. With a dearth of literature on asexuality to work with, I learned to read for its absence in a different way: I would look for analogous key terms like *celibacy* or *sexual anesthesia* or *frigidity* or *chastity* to see where they would lead me in uncovering a history of something like asexuality and making the case for embracing asexuality as a way of life. Indeed, through this work, along with many scholars who helped grow the field of asexuality studies over the last fifteen years, the necessary first steps were in making sense of asexuality as an identity or orientation, to stake its existence and lay claim to its legitimacy, to answer back to pathologizing narratives that insist sex must be at the center of a healthy, normal human life. In other words, we had to make the case (in the way many LGBTQ studies scholars, disability studies scholars, and critical race scholars have done and continue to do) that the focus of our study is not in need of a "fix" or "cure" and that it is in fact worthy of scholarly attention.

As the body of scholarship on asexuality continues to grow alongside an increase in asexual visibility and acceptance in social and political spaces, especially among younger generations who are embracing the nuances of asexual, demisexual, and aromantic subjectivities, there is more room to expand the conversation beyond asexual identity and community formation. The time has come to examine how asexuality—as a lens, a hermeneutic, and an analytical tool—helps us think differently, explore the unexpected, and chart queer possibilities for living beyond heteronormative and sex-normative power structures.

So, then, what might it look like to develop a hermeneutic of absence as a way to read for asexual or nonsexual possibilities without the trappings of a method centered solely on identity and representation? Moving in that direction, Ela Przybyło and Danielle Cooper propose a "queerly asexual reading strategy" that strives to find asexuality everywhere in resonances and touches of asexuality between past and present in an expansive understanding of what counts as asexual.[39] Yet, when they apply their own asexual reading method to their objects of analysis, they continue to look for resonances of asexual practice in a life lived, as an expression of sexuality in and through the body. For example, in their reading of Agnes Martin's life and work, they focus their asexual analysis on her public disavowal of sex and her "demonstrated disinterest in sex," ultimately arguing that she is queer not only because of her same-sex relationships but also because of her asexual proclivities.[40] Przybyło later goes on to claim Agnes Martin (and Yayoi Kusama, whose work this book will also wander and wonder through) as an asexual aromantic lesbian.[41] By "reclaiming her into a queerly asexual archive" in these ways, there is a sense in which there is still a want for her to be asexual.[42] Rather than focus on her (a)sexual life, I am more interested in asking how a "queerly asexual reading method" might direct questions about asexual resonance or possibility in the affective encounters with her paintings (which I dwell on in this book), what it opens up for the kinds of intimacies we might have with art and artist, and how an asexual analytic helps us imagine other ways of living and being.

Instead of looking to answer the question of whether or not a particular person is asexual, what else might we read for in the absence of sex? I have already suggested we need to learn to read absence beyond the possibility of closeted queer sex and that we also need to learn to read for substance, or material presences and entangled exchanges, within alleged absences. To do so, we might begin by taking to task the ways dominant narratives of sexuality affect the kinds of expression we understand as absent of sexual, romantic, or sensual feeling. Imagine how someone might report to a friend after a date that ended without a kiss or caress that "nothing happened," or how a partner, perhaps entangling themselves emotionally or erotically with another who they have not yet physically consummated the relationship with, might insist to their betrayed partner that "nothing happened." It is quite obvious that in both scenarios, things happened, even if physical sexual contact didn't occur. Or consider how the single person is often conceived as one who has failed to achieve couplehood or how the idea of being "just friends" reinforces what Michael Cobb calls the "supremacy of the couple" (addendum: *sexual* couple), degrading friendship as "just"—just not as important as sexual or romantic couplings.[43] As Elizabeth Brake also argues, amatonormativity, or "the focus on marital and amorous love relationships as special sites of value," undercuts other forms of caring relationships and intimacies.[44] Importantly, even the asexual but amorous couple may gain access to that "special treatment for lovers" awarded by amatonormative privilege, while aromantic people, those who choose not to seek out romantic partnerships, are still perceived as failures in the achievement of couplehood.[45]

I am primarily concerned with the points where compulsory sexuality and amatonormativity collide, such that a normative commitment to the couple is also a commitment to the productive and reproductive citizen whose fulfillment of duty and achievement of happiness is realized through sexual performance and pleasure. These compulsory narratives thus position sexuality under a particular narrative arc, a sequence of sexual pleasure: become "turned on," exchange sensual/sexual gratification (with the self or others), climax, bask in postcoital glow, repeat as desired or necessary. Sexual pleasure imagined as teleological, genitally centered, and toward a climax limits our ability to imagine sensual pleasures that are durational, nonteleological, and nongenital. And relatedly, the failure to recognize such nonsexual/asexual organizations of pleasure and desire also leads to a failure to read for other types of intimacies and relationalities that are not dependent upon the climactic consummated love affair.

This book is an experiment in reading against climax, wandering and wondering, instead, in the spaces where nothing is supposed to be happening. In *Intimacies,* Leo Bersani and Adam Phillips note that an American critic faulted the 2004 French film *Confidences trop intimes* (*Intimate Strangers*) for never reaching its "natural and desirable sexual climax." In the face of its presumed naturalness and desirability, the film, they argue, makes climax "irrelevant." Rather, they ask, "what would it be like to actively expect nothing to take place?"[46] This question leads them to remark on the appearance of Henry James's *The Beast in the Jungle* in the film, which then leads to their own analysis of the book, which leads me back to Hanson's ideas about asexual narrative structure. For Hanson, an asexual narrative is "one in which nothing happens" by way of stasis, nonevent, and wandering middles that refuse linear meanings and resolution.[47] But for Hanson, the nothing happening is defined by absence of desire.

I want to spin the question a bit differently: What would it be like to actively expect something other than sex or romance to take place? What would it mean to seek out all the happenings that seem to lead us nowhere as they take place in a "wandering middle" that refuses climax and closure or that makes such climax irrelevant? What might it be like to hang suspended in the anticlimactic or to bounce in the reverb rather than aim for the peak? On the reverb, M. Remi Yergeau writes, "Echoes can be orgasmic, literally and metaphorically. . . . In many respects, echoing might be read asexually or demisexually, as interbodily attractions that do not take others or even entities as their objects of desire."[48] Echoes depend on space: A reflection of sound waves off the surfaces of a largely empty room is more likely to occur than in a crowded room. Echoes need silence and absence in order to make sound bounce and repeat. Our ears receive the echo in the space of delay, a time-space absence that results from an intimate entangling of our bodies with the objects, surfaces, and bodies that swap sound waves. What we learn from the echo is the value and pleasure of circular continuation, the refusal to climax, the denial of a productive end. In reading asexually, in listening for silences that make the echo possible, we not only find hints of asexual possibility but also unveil the fullness of life's desires, pleasures, beings, becomings, and being-withs.

In the reverb, we discover new intimacies, new ways of being present to others and the world. Let's echo back to *Intimacies*. Bersani and Phillips begin their exchange with a quotation from Phillips himself: "Psychoanalysis is about what two people can say to each other if they agree not to have sex."[49] The analytical encounter may not always be sexual, but it is always intimate. In fact, it depends on the "no-sex contract," which makes possible "a new way of being present to another person."[50] In a way, asexual intimacies, like Bersani and Phillips's understanding of psychoanalysis, are about new ways of imagining presence in the intimacies and desires that manifest within apparent vacancies of romantic or sexual expression, a way of recognizing what else can happen between two (or more or less) people (or beings or objects) when sex is not part of the contract. Instead of construing a lack of sex as a failure to attain true intimacy, we can shift the valuation of intimacy from one based on sexual contact to one based on the commingled affects and expressions of love, connection, and emotional bonding—the moments that may be overlooked if there is no sexual payoff. Just when you may have thought there was no spark there, that nothing was happening or going to happen, you might realize that a lot has been happening all along—encounters with the other, affective ties, romantic feelings, nonsexual touch. We just need to shift our expectations and retune our senses.

In developing this interpretative method for absence, I take direction from Kevin Quashie, who writes of the importance of quiet (not just as stillness or silence but as metaphor for the entirety of one's inner life) to Black life. Though I don't quite align with Quashie's characterization of silence as absence and quiet as presence, I do think Quashie's quiet theorizations offer a way into (re)thinking and noticing absence and silence. Quashie proposes an attunement to an "aesthetic of quiet," one that "requires a shift in how we read, what we look for, and what we expect, even what we remain open to. It requires paying attention in a different way." For Quashie, "the key is to let the unexpected be possible."[51] I interpret Quashie's call for reading anew for Black possibility as a way to read against mastery, which Julietta Singh describes as "vital to this process of imagining otherwise and dwelling elsewhere, to the relentless exercise of unearthing and envisioning new human forms and conceptualizations of agency."[52] Just as Quashie asks us to let the unexpected be possible, Singh asks us to read vulnerably, to "remain unremittingly susceptible to new world configurations."[53] To shift our reading in this manner is to refuse mastery over any narrative, to recognize that matter—the stuff of narrative—can never be mastered in its vibrant instability, that different things come to matter in many ways. It is to explore the unexpected possibilities of being human otherwise and undoing the human altogether, to track webs of relations and intimacies beyond the sexual, between and beyond the living and nonliving, the human and more-than-human.

I am writing (with abandon) toward abandonment, toward abolition. Calvin L. Warren writes, "To abandon the human does not mean one accepts the terms of inferiority or worthlessness."[54] To the contrary, it is to name and refuse how the deployment of the human continues to enforce inferiority and worthlessness. It may undoubtedly seem to be a perilous time (perhaps it always is) to put forth an antihumanist argument while human rights are facing global rollbacks, but it is the very construction of humanity that allows such rights to be distributed and revoked. A radical abolitionist approach to the human asks and requires us to live in integrity with each other and the planet. Like Warren, I also argue that reframing absence, silence, and nothingness is not about "celebrating the emancipatory potential of nothing" but about recognizing how intertwined liberal humanism is with the manufacture of the category of nothing.[55] To see through nothing into whole worlds of possibility is to simultaneously abandon the human, to know "that one must embody a nothing that the world works tirelessly to obliterate."[56] As such, I suggest an asexual analytic must also already be queer, decolonial, antiableist, and antiracist. The keys to this analytic lie in the possibilities to undo norms around sex and health, capacity and the human, desire and belonging—to be vulnerable to one another beyond the sexual. Let us dwell in the spaces we were only meant to pass through; let us listen for the echoes of the canyons, recognize the fullness of the voided; let us meander everywhere and nowhere.

## FOREST FOR THE TREES, A MEANDERING METHODOLOGY

A mossy patch in the Hoh Rain Forest of Olympic National Park is part of an experiment to create the quietest place in the United States—one square inch, marked by a small red stone, insulated from the roar of traffic and hum of airplane engines, a pocket of quiet in a world polluted with noise. Some might venture there to listen, to know what true silence sounds like, to experience what it is to hold one's breath and hear nothing (except perhaps the excited patter of one's own heartbeat), to feel the still, sleeping earth in one's bones. Silence is something we listen for and feel for here. We want to know the sound of quiet, the stillness of being without noise, the beginning of possible sonance. The forest—like silence, like zero—is a space of contradiction. It is a respite for quiet retreat amid a thick hum of plant and animal life, where one might go to be alone among so much existence, where growth arises from decay, where life composes from death's decomposition. An endless cycle with no clear origin or end, an always everywhere of living and dying. The forest refuses to end.

The forest is also a place of romantic fantasy and desire. As an imagined wilderness, it is an easy metonym for a constellation of arguably premodern, precolonial, preindustrial longings, fantasies of the pristine, romantic attachments to lush untouched nature. The unspoiled rainforest is where we find the fantasy of the human pitted against nature as the one who disrupts it or is threatened by it, rather than entangled with it. The very idea of a "quietest place" in a world always already saturated by visual, aural, and tactile noise is itself a fanciful longing for an impossibility in that burning desire for the hush.

A jaunt through this quiet, contradictory patch of forest is a scavenger's journey, a forager's quiet hunt, a queer writing methodology that "refus[es] coherence" in order "to make seemingly disconnected worlds collide."[57] *Nothing Wanting* embraces the unexpected by employing what I call a "meandering methodology," a methodology that is inseparable from and crucial to the book's argument. This book essentially argues that colonialism and capitalism—as ongoing global technologies—structure sexuality, pleasure, and intimacy through the construction and management of the human and through teleologically oriented time (progression, reproductive futurity, climax/ orgasm). I thus employ asexuality as one entryway into plotting otherwise against these logics. I do not mean to claim that asexuality as a sexual orientation is somehow inherently decolonial and anticapitalist; rather, I suggest that asexuality, as a lens through which to view the world, can help us wander more, refuse ends and endings, and deconstruct normative orders of sex and pleasure, space and time.

On the philosophical treatise, Walter Benjamin writes, "method is a digression." In this digression, Benjamin names the importance of "irregular rhythm," describing how "tirelessly the process of thinking makes new beginnings, returning in a roundabout way to its original object. This continual pausing for breath is the mode most proper to the process of contemplation." In other words, I digress, again and again. Importantly, philosophical contemplation, even in these pauses and digressions, does not lack momentum but, according to Benjamin, constitutes a mosaic in which the brilliance is found in the fragments of thought.[58] This book is a pasting of fragments, a collision of things that grabbed me and called me back to them as I scavenged, creating a collection of objects that struck me as providing new ways of approaching absence through gender, sexuality, and crip theorizing. The method is also a practice of juxtaposition, an experiment in placing disparate objects next to one another, scrutinizing the unpredictable places where they knot together. There are inevitable gaps, absences shaped by the constraints of finitude. But I have attempted to be as thorough as possible in each touchpoint in this motley gathering of objects that resist easy categorization or connection with one another as they cross genres and eras, traverse continents and cultures. I weave them together in a recurring entanglement of overlapping themes, a kaleidoscopic patterning of the strange and unexpected. I have been especially drawn to texts and films that are unsettling in their weirdness or absurdity in order to ask how and why they disturb as they dissolve the boundaries between human, animal, and plant, living and nonliving matter, as well as undo notions of normative embodiment and sex (as in both the sexed body and the practice of sex). Together, they form their own queer ecologies, ways of attending to unexpected entanglements of thought and affect, to the organic shapes of making and unmaking, to the geometries of desire and being with and without. My own small repository felt in the shimmering in-betweens.[59]

I draw on an eclectic, global archive that also challenges the boundedness of time and nation, for, as Bruno Cornellier and Michael R. Griffiths remind us, "settler colonialism is not merely a global phenomenon, it is also constitutive of the global."[60] It is an everywhere structure that has shaped and continues to shape our world in a global race toward some imagined, supposedly better future. Modernity's progress narrative is a never-ending demand for an arrival we will never achieve—we can always keep progressing in the ongoing structures that continually demand greater ends, as the fantasy of a pristine past and simpler times grows ever more desirable (and further away) in the exhausted imagination. To go somewhere, one must leave one defined point and arrive at another. Departures and arrivals reinforce the boundaries of place and body. Even the possibility of detention, the structural enforcement of remaining in-between, relies on the logic of here, there, and nowhere in between. To simply continue is a resistance to the continuing demand to arrive. Following Kim TallBear, let us "resist lineal, progressive representation of movement *forward* to something better, or movement *back* to something purer."[61] Let us lean into ongoingness in the refusal to end or to arrive and in the refusal to even steer toward an endpoint.

The chapters of this book might better be conceived of as waypoints—pit stops as I wandered into different gaps, stalled out in the in-betweens, paused to ponder, sat with a piece of art or film, poem or novel, or frantically wove a web between the different arts. One might imagine these waypoints on a map of nowhere to nowhere, a scavenger's journey on a recursive circuit, a series of echoes, a forager's foray into the filamentous, a constant retreat and extension, a perpetual circling back as a refusal of neoliberal demands for arrival and achievement. Each waypoint ventures into a kind of absence, plays between metaphorical and actual voids, connects to elements that orient us in an intimate weaving of asexual intimacies and tangled ecologies—mycelial networks, boundless sky, complexly inhabited wildernesses. The form and content follow the method; fragments fell into place the way they did, but they could have fallen into place in any number of other ways. A waypoint emerges within another waypoint, notes notate other notes, layering, peeling, remaking form and (formless) formation.[62] Such movement in thought and text is also a neuroqueer structure—one that follows my own distractions, idiosyncrasies, and obsessive lingerings, one that refuses normative conceptions of order, formulaic argumentation, expediency, and efficiency.

As I move to question not only what counts as intelligence but also what it means to create knowledge, I find a kinship with Mel Y. Chen's "intoxicated method" that makes "a sincere attempt to embrace sensorium," to engage in "categorical blurring," and to value "partial knowing."[63] It is exhausting to be exhaustive.[64] Chen characterizes their book as a disavowal of "thorough aboutness," as they employ a "decolonized or decolonizing cripistemology."[65] My refusal of the neoliberal impulse of efficient and teleological scholarship dovetails with Chen's call for neurodivergent, slow, and agitated reading, writing, and thinking that defy accretion and accumulation.[66] Here, some things gather; here, they also fall apart. Just as Donna J. Haraway writes of play with string figures as a process of "dropping threads and failing but sometimes finding something that works, something consequential and maybe even beautiful, that wasn't there before, of relaying connections that matter," I invite you, reader, to approach reading in the way I write: as a fractal practice, picking up and dropping threads that make connections that matter to and for you (or fail to do so), as a venture into plotting elsewhere and elsewise (or refusing to plot or be plotted altogether), as a method of meandering rather than following a direct linear path or orientation, an encounter with the impossibilities of naming or demarcating place and space, as a way to think outside of the lines and boxes, as a call to dwell in expansive neuroqueer thought movements and designs— an unmapping, really.[67]

Unmapping is a way of practicing Chen's call for "unlearning," to expand what it means to know and what counts as knowledge.[68] Natalie Diaz declares that "not all knowledge is for everyone," but some knowledge, such as land and water knowledge, is "legible to and used by those who are willing to defy the map and look into the surround."[69] This book is my attempt to look into the surround, to make a square, mapped thing round and unruly. But, books, by their very nature, demand a seemingly linear structure. Bound by the structure of the book, this work is capped on either end, somewhat ironically, by waypoints that refuse ends—beginning with an end to ends, ending with a series of returns that hesitate to end. The end is the beginning; the beginning is the end—my attempt at a more circular design. You may read the book from cover to cover, in a more linear fashion, noting how each waypoint builds and rebuilds and harks backward and forward. Or you may simply let yourself wander in bits and pieces, take a foray here or there, refuse sequentiality.[70]

There is no masterful way to read here. Loose and lose yourself in the book.

Like the book, the language that composes it poses its own limitations and shortcomings. I often struggle to write and say what I want to say exactly how I want to say it; the words always feel partial, the sentences—intentionally or not—incomplete. Some words gain utility for stretches of time and fall out of favor at other moments. Many words have many meanings; I often use a specific word intentionally, playfully even, in all senses of its meaning, but sometimes I forget its multiplicity and there are happy, or sometimes not-so-felicitous, accidents where words collide. At some point, the words stop belonging to me, if they ever did. Even if I still feel bound by them as I seek the boundless. I want to challenge the boundaries of the book, of language, of the nation-state, of the category of the human, and of the body. Through an asexually motivated endorsement of the anticlimactic and undoing of ends and boundaries, I suggest we give ourselves permission to wander, to hang out in the middles, to refuse linearity and progress, and to ponder. To refuse mastery in reading and writing, to let writing and reading be a way to think and to circulate knowledge while refusing the neoliberal capitalist demand for an efficient and formulaic arrival to a definitive argument. Let there be many arguments and many more questions. Let's (re)claim the place of the no-places where it has been alleged nothing happens.

# An End to Ends

As a restless teenager in a sleepy suburb, when I was not sitting bored behind a desk in high school or slinging burgers at the local fast-food joint, my time was spent riding in cars with friends, blasting music over the car stereo with the windows down, feeling the wind in my hair, and wishing upon the stars to get out of that town as soon as possible. Music was an integral part of those late-night drives, and music became my comfort, my escape, and a wellspring of pleasure for me. One evening as I drove, a close friend of mine excitedly told me about the new experiences he had just earlier shared with his girlfriend. He was emphatic about the indescribable pleasures of sex—the wetness, the hotness, the intensity of orgasm. I was only half-listening to him, partly because, at the time, I had decided to live a celibate life and I had little curiosity about his sexual exploits, but mostly because he was talking over one of my favorite bass and drum interludes right at the moment when the tenor guitar brings in the melody with absolute perfection. When he finished his story, I pushed the "back" button to restart the song from the beginning, and I told him to listen. As soon as the tenor guitar began to sing, I turned to him and said, "This is probably the closest I will ever come to an orgasm." He laughed and said, "I think it's called an eargasm."

## ASEXUAL PLEASURES AND ANTICOLONIAL EROTIC TEMPORALITIES

We know from a growing body of scholarship that asexualities have been and continue to be spectacularized, fetishized, misunderstood, erased, and pathologized in a culture devoted, as Michael Cobb describes it, to the "supremacy of the couple."[1] And here I would more acutely specify the social devotion to the *sexual* couple or, at the very least, to sexual coupling. There's seemingly nothing sexy, after all, about a couple not having sex. Most people seek counseling or separation/divorce in response to the problem of a waning sex life in the couple formation. Let's be clear: It is the sexual couple who reigns supreme.

And for the individual who refuses the societal mandate to couple up or to engage in sex? They will likely be met with skepticism about the state of their health or their wholeness as a person. When someone declares their abstention from a sexual economy, everyone from talk-show hosts and television personalities to real-life medical professionals to friends and family want to know what could possibly have happened to that person to make them not want sex. In other words, the general wonder is, what exactly is wrong with someone who does not want sex? Particularly, in Western societies, the normative framework for sexual expectation has been designed through the inherited legacies of colonization and its attendant policing and management of gender and sexuality. This inherited sexual value system then determines which bodies may be regarded as healthy, desirable, and desiring subjects according to dominant constructions of race, ability, age, and orgasmic potential. People who exist on the margins of dominant normative categories are often either completely desexualized on one end of the spectrum or hypersexualized on the other. No matter which end of this spectrum one is pigeonholed into, it ultimately means a loss of autonomy and demands a reimagining of "what counts as sovereignty."[2] (Settler) colonialism is, in fact, one of the things that happened (and continues to happen) that makes sexuality diagnosable and containable.

Mark Rifkin, tracing the ways Indigenous, First Nations, and Two-Spirit writers have put forth "alternative visions of peoplehood and sovereignty through the representation of an Indigenous erotics," suggests that an erotics of sovereignty can offer new ways to "register the complex entwinement of unacknowledged survivals, unofficial aspirations, and the persistence of pain."[3] By Rifkin's formulation, we can both account for the violences and traumas of colonization and produce new ways of relating and finding pleasure in the wake of pain and its endurance, for colonization enacts not only a physical violence upon the colonized but also ongoing epistemic violence that continues to shape how many people collectively conceive of so-called normal and healthy sexualities. Or, as Nathan Snaza writes, coloniality is "a vast and immanently organizing 'event' that takes manifold eventalforms," but "the colonial world is but one possible pattern in the ongoing ontogenesis of worlds, a pattern that holds thanks to how, for many of the Earth's inhabitants, our everyday practices tend this world whether we attune to it or not."[4] In other words, we do not have to maintain this one dominant patterning; there is potential for a "pluriversal vastness of worlding" or a "World as Plenum."[5]

Following la paperson, we must shift our thinking of colonialism from "a past event that 'happened to' Native peoples and not generalizable to non-Natives" to instead understand it as "something that 'happened for' settlers," that is "happening for them/us right now," or, following Snaza, as a world that is continually tended, even unconsciously, by many, though it need not be, as there are other worlds to tend and attend to.[6] Or as Eve Tuck and C. Ree describe colonialism: "an ongoing horror made invisible by its persistence—the snake in the flooded basement."[7] Which is to say, by recognizing the insidious ways settler colonial ideologies and "tendings" persist in our internalization and enactments of dominant culture, we recognize settler colonialism as a "set of technologies" that can both help us "forecast colonial next operations" and "plot decolonial directions."[8]

With access to such forecasting and plotting, we might begin to shift and work toward healing and repatterning the traumas of colonization that continue to haunt our genders and sexualities. As Kim TallBear frames it: "*Decolonization is not an individual choice.* We must collectively oppose a system of compulsory settler sexuality and family that continues building a nation upon Indigenous genocide and that marks Indigenous and other marginalized relations as deviant."[9] As a white settler, I must recognize the ways in which settler technologies have worked and continue to work for me, even as I find myself marginalized as a queer and trans subject. It would be all too easy for me to simply write about heteronormativity, sex normativity, and amatonormativity as if they are ahistorical power structures that operate in our society today, but from my vantage point in the United States, I cannot help but track state biopower and the regulation of gender and sexuality through the inheritance of the (settler) colonial violences upon which the country is founded. The settling of land and the settling of body are inextricably tied. For my purposes here, I think with Indigenous and decolonial scholars in order to plot a coalitional, anticolonial direction that pushes back against the ways in which colonialism, heterosexism, white supremacy, and capitalism have shaped and continue to shape dominant conceptions not only of sexuality but also of pleasure—how it is valued, what counts as pleasure, and for whom pleasure is allowed.[10]

My rethinking of pleasure is a movement toward anticolonial futures, to oppose and refigure dominant white settler configurations and managements of sexuality and pleasure. To be clear, I am not trying to write here *about* Indigenous people or Indigenous genders or Indigenous sexualities. Nor am I arguing that asexuality is inherently more decolonial or anticolonial or has particular Indigenous roots. Rather, I am engaging with Indigenous and decolonial thought in tandem with asexuality in order to think and plot/unplot outside of and against normative, colonial logics of sex and pleasure. By rereading what might be regarded as white Western depictions of sexuality, gender, and pleasure, I am offering alternative ways of approaching these representations through queer, anticolonial, and asexual lenses. In particular, I am interested in uncovering formations of pleasure that are absented by dominant logics that remain invested in the teleology and import of orgasm. Accordingly, I explore how an interrogation of the normative shapings of pleasure, especially in the realm of the nonsexual or asexual, can help us imagine and experience pleasure differently.

I am particularly invested in what happens when nonnormativity becomes marked as a perversity of desire rooted in a kind of absence—that is, for one to be figured as incapacitated of desire or to be deemed undesirable. Transgender, intersex, and queer people, people of color, Indigenous people, and disabled and chronically ill people have been routinely desexualized or cast as asexual subjects.[11] Further, people who choose an abstinent, celibate, chaste, or otherwise asexual lifestyle are often suspiciously regarded as immature, potentially ill and in need of treatment, ascetic to a fault, or just plain liars.[12] Such an attitude is reflective of compulsory sexuality and sexual normativity, which deem sexual desire as innately human and as necessary to survival as the need for nutritional sustenance. Just as María Lugones argues that the gender systems of colonialism and global, Eurocentered capitalism produce compulsory heterosexuality, I am suggesting that they also simultaneously produce compulsory sexuality as part of the imagined natural and desirable order.[13] As Sigmund Freud asserts: "The fact [*fact!*] of the existence of sexual needs in human beings and animals is expressed in biology by the assumption of a 'sexual instinct,' on the analogy of the instinct of nutrition, that is of hunger."[14] Asexuality, then, is not a mere loss of appetite but a refusal to nourish the body. And especially postsexual revolution, let us not forget that we are taught not only that we should all desire, need, or crave sex but also that we ought to do so in such a way as to liberate ourselves from the repression of sexual shame and prudishness (calling all queer people and women, in particular, please step up to access your sexual liberation and unlimited orgasmic potential). And what greater way to feed the hunger and to liberate the body than to relish in our sexual pleasures, know what turns us on, and pursue those pleasures, turn-ons, and fetishes to their alleged natural end, the climax of pleasure's course: the orgasm?

But what of pleasures, sexual and otherwise, that have a different duration, that never climax or that perhaps reach a different peak, those that delight us for brief moments or those that provide endless and ongoing joys and pleasantries? How might an attention to such pleasures help us plot otherwise? Rifkin explores how settler colonialism expands into temporality. In an effort to go "beyond" settler time, Rifkin moves away from the notion of absolute time, dabbling instead in the philosophies of relativity and simultaneity in order to conceptualize a temporal multiplicity that allows for "temporal sovereignty" that resists the ways in which settler time continues to erase the existence of Indigenous peoples and also ongoingly shapes life for all people.[15] Settler time demands a progress narrative involving the conquering and erasing of the supposedly uncivilized Native, propelling civilization into an imagined modernity. While such a temporal frame is organized around a movement toward an ever-progressing modernity, it simultaneously constructs a teleological narrative that "ends" the existence of Native peoples, or as Patrick Wolfe puts it: settler colonialism relies on a "logic of elimination."[16] But temporal sovereignty is more than a reclamation of presence; it is a demand to recognize the different shapes and experiences, collective and individual, of time.

Temporal sovereignty, a revision of settler time, moves us away from teleological settler progress narratives, so we might instead imagine different ways to orient ourselves in time: "To speak of temporal *orientation* suggests the ways that time can be regarded less as a container that holds events than as potentially divergent processes of becoming."[17] Such a temporal orientation, Rifkin argues, allows for a different way of connecting our experiences and sensations to our temporal surroundings. Temporal sovereignty makes space for cyclical or "spiraling time" and for nonlinear understandings of history that dissolve the mirage of a past that can be separated from a present and future.[18] The way I understand it, Rifkin leans toward the quantum, in which temporal sovereignty becomes another way to enter into Snaza's pluriversal worlding. It is, also, perhaps, a permission to wander and meander, to move sideways, forward and backward, in circles and spirals, a helical logic, a mycelial impulse.[19]

I wonder then if temporal sovereignty might necessarily be connected to erotic sovereignty. We must imagine the temporalities of pleasure differently in order to imagine and pattern pleasures within our own ways of becoming. If we draw a parallel in the construction of erotic time as one that also demands telos, an orgasmic end point based on a dominant procreative imperative to which pleasure, too, becomes attached, then what of those poor souls who never orgasm, or simply do not prefer it, or those who do not care much for sex and all its attendant pleasures? What of those misdirected youth who are too caught up on the pleasures of an eargasm to realize the greater potential of orgasm? How can we bring these suffering people leading lackluster lives into the fold of all the wet, explosive satisfactions that all healthy humans are supposed to be so hungry for?

Because asexuality is often regarded as absence, as a lack or a failure of nourishing and maintaining the body in a culture in which sex is considered the greatest intimacy or even the endgame in an erotic pursuit, those who do not have sex or who do not experience sexual attraction may be thought to be missing out on or renouncing life's greatest pleasures in addition to refusing to follow an imagined linear organization of proper sexual maturation, as if celibacy or asexuality are stages to grow (up) out of. Benjamin Kahan argues that celibacy is typically understood as a disavowal of pleasure, but, he suggests, although it can sometimes be an ascetic practice, it can also be a pleasurable practice. Kahan understands celibacy as an organization of pleasure rather than as a failure, renunciation, or even ascesis of pleasure. I similarly think of asexualities as an organization of pleasures that are particularly made apparent when sexual pleasure is forgone, or even perhaps an organization of pleasures that blurs the lines between the sexual and the nonsexual, allowing us to sit with both sensual and sexual pleasures without demanding they reach a genital climax, thus moving us out of the teleological structures of erotic time into something akin to a sovereign erotic temporality. In beginning to theorize the possibilities of asexual pleasures, Kahan draws on Leo Bersani's phrase, "nonpurposive pleasures" to suggest an opening for pleasures that are based in movement rather than in drives or purpose.[20] To move without purpose is also to meander, to seek pleasure without aim, to stay in motion in and through time, endless, aimless. Imagine instead a spiraling pleasure, an echoing pleasure, a haunted joy in the present remembrance of a pleasure past, pleasures with no end or pleasures so fleeting there is no time for a culminating closure, pleasures that don't demand to be classified as sexual or not, normal or not. How, then, might asexualities help us further imagine anti-climactic pleasures, enduring pleasures, blips of pleasure, or pleasures that eschew climax or approach climax differently? In the absence of sex and in a revision of erotic temporality, which other pleasures are made present?

## EROS WITHOUT TELEOLOGY AND THE PLEASURE OF PLEASURE

I am sitting in an airplane on a long flight across the country, com-pletely enrapt with and enraptured by Maggie Nelson's *The Argonauts*. My brain, my heart, dare I say my soul, are all abuzz with a literary pleasure. To be certain, Nelson's text is not perfect and it may even elicit bouts of literary displeasure. (I would be remiss, in a piece of writing situated in conversation with decolonial scholars plotting anti-colonial directions, to not mention the fact that Nelson describes wanting to find a longer name for her child, Iggy, and eventually set-tles on the Native American name Igasho, tribe unknown, based on her misremembering that her partner is part Cherokee. Aside from recounting being given a blessing for the choice of her baby's name by a lactation consultant who belongs to the "Pima tribe from Arizona," otherwise known as the Akimel O'odham, which Nelson incorrectly identifies at the "Othama tribe," Nelson writes nothing more on the matter, and in the end, the spectacle of two white Americans choos-ing a Native American name for their child remains.)[21] But in the most beautiful lyrical moments, I experience a deep satisfaction as I swallow the words inside my closed mouth, holding back their ut-terance lest my neighbor dart even more sideways glances my way. I swish the words around my tongue and teeth, letting them drip deep down into my throat where they travel into my body, across the blood barrier into my limbs, my veins, my beating heart. The pleasure of reading good writing is an erotic one. The pleasure of reading about erotic pleasure, perhaps even more so. A move between *plaisir* and jouissance, an erotic of reading that is both active and nonorgasmic, a different kind of "bliss."[22]

In the section I am reading, Nelson is recounting the pleasure she experiences when breastfeeding her infant son. She is afraid to in-dulge in it, but she wants it so badly. I cannot say I fully understand.

I have heard people tell such stories of the erotics of birth and breast-feeding, but my body does not twitch or tingle one bit at the thought. I do not imagine my body to be one capable of creating new life; I do not have breasts for suckling, let alone fondling. I removed them in part because they brought me no pleasure, more displeasure. But I am moved by Nelson's battle; it stirs something deep inside me. She asks: "How does one go about partitioning one sexual feeling off from another presumably more 'real' sexual feeling? Or, more to the point, why the partition? It isn't *like* a love affair. It *is* a love affair. Or, rather, it is romantic, erotic, and consuming—but without tentacles. . . . It is a buoyant eros, an eros without teleology." And she adds, "Even if I do feel turned on while I'm breast feeding or rocking him to sleep, I don't feel the need to do anything about it (and if I did, it wouldn't be with him)."[23]

An eros without teleology, being turned on without needing to do anything about it. Feelings and desires that toe the line between the sexual and the nonsexual, between the erotic and the platonic. How do we partition them? *Why* do we partition them? If we decenter the orgasm—the thing that drives one to do something (that thing) about such feelings—then do we remove the partition? These are the pleasures I want to make room for: the erotic, the romantic, the asexual, the nonsexual, the sensual that do not demand we "do anything about them," that do not require us to reach their orgasmic end, that do not ask us to understand them under the hierarchical peak of orgasm, or what Cynthia Barounis calls the "orgasmic imperative."[24] In *Orgasmology*, Annamarie Jagose builds on Stephen Heath's argument that ultimately suggests that the orgasm has become "the standard unit of measurement for sexuality," consequently producing "the normative sexual subject."[25] Crucial to Heath's argument is recognizing that the production of the normative sexual subject is also the production of the modern sexual subject, who should perhaps be both productive and reproductive.

The orgasm, then, as a measure of modern sexual subjectivity, becomes necessarily tied to the logics of colonization—orgasm, at the right time, in the right way, with the right person defines one's bodily capacity as well as the success, pleasure, and desirability of the modern sexual subject in colonial time, whisked successfully forward into an ever (re)productive modernity.[26] Jagose instead suggests if we can "see past" what we "presume to know about the object or event of orgasm," we may "reorganize axiomatically or even complacently held knowledges about not only sex, sexual orientation, and sexual agency but also the social contract, democracy, capitalism, modernity, affect, and history."[27] Could it be that revaluing orgasm, promoting nonhierarchical queer (a)sexual desires and affects can do all that—challenge capitalism, disrupt the social contract, reorganize modernity, plot against colonial logics, turn our world upside down and inside out? Well, that sounds like a lofty aim, but I suspect it can at least help us envision a myriad of ways we might rail against systems of capital and a "sex sells" ethos, along with the racist, ableist, and colonial sedimentations of history that have defined normalcy and health, thus opening up space for a shift in how we experience our bodies and the pleasures they afford us in time and space, propelling us toward a sovereign erotic temporality.

I want to stake a claim for an erotics of pleasure, of orgasm even, that does not rely on a teleological model of building tension until one arrives at the release, the orgasmic explosion, the muscular twitch of dissolution, that tiny little death. "There is," as Nathan Snaza writes, "not one orgasm, but many, and a political redirecting of the body's pleasures might take the form of experiments to not recognize pleasures in the ways we are told by common sense are at play."[28] Snaza builds this political redirection of the body's pleasures on derecognition, a refusal to be made recognizable by the settler state: "Bodies and pleasures may be operative in corporeal, experimental, affective, and directly political ways without cohering into anything recognizable by the state."[29] What could it mean, politically, to make orgasm unrecognizable, to give it many different shapes, to name pleasures that not only decenter orgasm but redefine it—knowing, dying, spending, coming as a pleasure, a bliss, that is never fully known, dead, spent, come and gone?[30]

To be certain, it is not that people do not already experience nonsexual pleasures. It is not that people do not already experience nonorgasmic sexual pleasures (whether intentionally or frustratingly unintentionally). Rather, it is about how some types of pleasure—particularly sexual orgasmic pleasures—are generally considered more pleasurable than others. And in the absence of that most pleasurable of pleasures, other imagined lesser nonsexual pleasures are forgotten. Attention to asexual pleasures brings out the joys of "eargasms," "emotional boners," and the pleasures that come with eating snow—a "snowgasm" perhaps. These nonsexual pleasures play with the terms of sexual expression and orgasm not only to revise and expand the terrain of what might be deemed "orgasmic pleasure" but also to highlight the sensualities and intensities of asexuality that are just as present as the sexual pleasures that are privileged and given import as the "greatest" of human sensations. But as these examples will show, there are many pleasures that exceed sexual bliss, or at least may be felt differently but with intensity.

As a teenager, when I drove around with my friend, I could imagine no greater pleasure than what I was experiencing in that moment from the perfect constellation of sounds and tones—though I must confess I have since experienced other pleasures as great or greater. When I think back to my friend's suggestion of an "eargasm" to describe my intense pleasure in the music, I cannot help but think of Jodie Taylor's conception of "musico-sexuality." Taylor makes a queer proposition that music itself *is* sex, which is to say that music provides a way of "shifting sexuality out of a reproductive sphere and aligning it with purely pleasurable intimacies."[31] Building on Suzanne Cusick's work in queer musicology in which she suggests that music, as something we do, may be the most intense way some people express and experience a "circulation of physical pleasure," Taylor argues that Cusick's framing provides a "subversive way of theorizing the interconnectivity of music and sexual identity beyond genital-associated sexual pleasures."[32] Similarly, Ben Davies develops what he calls an "auricular erotics" that is nearly synonymous with "sexual listening." Because listening is the active counterpart to hearing's passive receptivity—not unlike Roland Barthes's distinction between the more passive pleasure of text and the more active jouissance of textual encounter—Davies similarly links listening to sex because, like music, it is something we do, a dangerous elision between active, penetrative action and sex itself.[33]

In short, at the heart of Taylor's, Davies's, and Cusick's projects is an expansiveness in determining which types of pleasures count as *sexual* pleasures, thus expanding what counts as sex. For them, music and listening, then, may just *be* sex. To the contrary, I want to move in an inverse direction, to interrogate why there is a compulsion to expand sex into other pleasures and to move other non-genitally associated pleasures into sex in the first place. Why not let music be its own pleasure—sensual, even physical—without needing to turn it into sex? Can music not be pleasurable without it also being sex?

While it is true that for some people, as Taylor indeed reports, the ear functions as an erogenous zone with direct connection to sexual pleasure, can we not also think more expansively as to how we might conceive "the erotic potential of the ear"?[34] Let us let the "purely pleasurable intimacies" of music also hold the potential of asexual pleasures and nonsexual erotics. Rather than a polymorphous perversity one might hope to eventually grow out of, let us instead imagine a polymorphous sensorium of erotic pleasure that may, in fact, have nothing to do with sex. In this regard, I wish to highlight the joys and pleasures of asexuality in order to emphasize that an asexual lifestyle, orientation, relationship, or identity is anything but a stagnant, barren lack of pleasure. Rather than demanding a broadening of what sex is, to the contrary, revaluing orgasm in relation to the multitudes of pleasure made available to us actually broadens our understandings of pleasure, desire, and physical intimacies beyond sex.

But at this point you are probably left wondering what an "emotional boner" or a "snowgasm" is. Let us return, in a way, to music again. I am standing in a small divey music venue in San Francisco surrounded by a crowd of queer people. Animal Prufrock, formerly of the queer feminist duo Bitch and Animal, has just stepped onto the stage. The lights come on, the electronic tones of the Casio burst through the speakers in a simple, robotic melody, and Prufrock launches into a new song, crooning loudly and out of key about a hunger they feel when they're near someone. But it's not a "sex spell"; rather, it's a hunger in the heart. In the heart, they sing, is where they are hard for the other person. What they have, what the other person gives them, is an "emotional boner."[35]

People around me are laughing and hooting. I am laughing, and I am also moved. I hear the asexual joke, a metaphorical hard-on in romantic love, a hunger that needs not be sated with sex, that does not demand anything be done about it. I wonder about the crowd around me, as queer spaces so often reflect a hypersexuality, and not without good reason. Reclamation of a space in which one can express sexual desire without fear of violence or repercussion in an otherwise heterosexist and homophobic world has been pertinent and lifesaving. That relative safety and freedom of expression is what I love about queer spaces, but it is also what made queer spaces so difficult to inhabit when I was what I described as celibate, a period of orientation in my life that predated the language of asexuality. I always occupied queer spaces ambivalently. My gender, so queer and so out of place everywhere else, was mostly at home in queer spaces, even

while my periodic lack of interest in sex was not. So here I am, standing in a crowd of queer people, wondering if they hear the same joke
I do. For me, the sentiment is right on. I have an emotional boner for
the very idea of emotional boners. A hunger that does not need to
be satisfied with sex, a longing for someone that is not dictated by a
sexual spell, a heart feeling—a *hard* feeling—that does not want to
come, does not need to come.

The snowgasm brings us to the pleasures of the text again. I am
reading Eunjung Kim's essay "How Much Sex Is Healthy? The Pleasures of Asexuality." How appropriate my pleasure in reading of
asexual pleasure. Kim interrogates the ways in which we equate the
sex imperative to a health imperative. She analyzes a film I had never
seen before. I immediately go watch it. I cannot stop thinking about
it. In the film *Snow Cake*, directed by Marc Evans, Sigourney Weaver
plays the role of an autistic woman named Linda who has just lost her
daughter Vivienne in a car accident. Linda finds sensual pleasure in
watching flashing lights, bouncing on trampolines, and especially in
eating snow. There is one scene I watch over and over again. In a conversation with a man named Alex (played by Alan Rickman), Linda
asks, "Have you ever had an orgasm, Alex?" He replies, "It has been
known." Then Linda says, "Vivienne once described an orgasm to me.
It sounds like an inferior version of what I feel when I have a mouthful of snow. You should try it." I revisit Kim's analysis of Linda's behavior: "The snow-eating and trampoline scenes propose an equivalent to sexual pleasure experienced by the asexual Linda, giving the
film a way for sexual and non-autistic audience members to imagine
Linda's pleasure."[36] Almost, but not quite, I think. Kim's analysis
is framed as an accommodation for allosexual (or nonasexual) and
neurotypical (or nonautistic) viewers, but why should they only be
able to imagine Linda's pleasure in relation to orgasm? Why does the
audience need a measure of equivalency to sexual pleasure in order
to understand, to perhaps even feel, or to share Linda's pleasure? For
Linda, a mouthful of snow is the greatest pleasure, and she believes
it to be even superior to sexual orgasm, hardly equivalent. She even
tells Alex he should try it, suggesting that he too might find great
pleasure in a mouthful of snow. If an orgasm is inferior to what Linda
feels when eating snow, then the snow-eating cannot be equivalent to
an orgasm. It must be something else. It must be as pleasurable as . . .
well, a mouthful snow. It is a pleasure unto itself. I want only Linda's
pleasure in the snow, I want only pleasure in Linda's pleasure.

When I tell a friend about this film and my desire for pleasure for pleasure's sake and for pleasure in the pleasure of others, my friend reminds me of a scene in the quirky French film *Amélie*, directed by Jean-Pierre Jeunet, in which title character Amélie Poulain delights in the tactile pleasure of submerging her hand in a cache of grain. I, of course, immediately go and rewatch the film. I first take notice that each time we meet a new character, the narrator provides us with a list of their likes and dislikes. For example, Amélie's father hates urinating next to someone in a public restroom and likes peeling large strips of wallpaper from the wall and cleaning out his toolbox. Her mother dislikes when strangers touch her hands and likes polishing the floor and cleaning her purse. We are introduced to Amélie's likes by first moving through a scene portraying a clearly bored and somewhat amused Amélie lying on her back while a man moves on top of her. The narrator informs us that Amélie currently has no boyfriend: "She tried once or twice, but the results were a letdown. Instead, she cultivates a taste for small pleasures—dipping her hand into sacks of grain, cracking crème brûlée with a teaspoon, and skipping stones at St. Martin's Canal."[37] Despite the narrative framing in this particular moment, I want to note that while Amélie currently cultivates these pleasures in lieu of sexual relationships, it is important to recognize that she has an ongoing history of delight in tactile pleasure, from her heart racing at her father's meted out touch during childhood to her adult exploits in trying to bring pleasure to others through matchmaking and returning lost objects. This is all to say that these asexual delights should be thought of not as replacements for a failed sexual coupling but instead as possibilities of different, but just as valuable and pleasurable (sometimes more pleasurable), experiences.

Importantly, most of the likes—or pleasures—we learn of the characters involve doing, touching, and sensing, in mundane, rather anticlimactic activities. They are actions and active pleasures, but that action need not mean they *are* sex. Rather, they are sensual pleasures that quite honestly give me pleasure in imagining the pleasures derived from the acts. I want, again, simply the pleasure in the tactile and sensual pleasures of the characters. This study of pleasure in the pleasure of others brings me to wonder also of the possibility of experiencing even nonsexual pleasure in the sexual pleasures of others. In another scene, we find Amélie standing on a rooftop overlooking the city of Paris. The narrator tells us that in these moments of solitude, she amuses herself with "silly questions" like "How many couples are having an orgasm now?" After a montage of orgasmic couplings, Amélie turns to the camera and, with delight, reports, "Fifteen!" For Amélie, there is a kind of pleasure in acknowledging, taking stock, and tabulating the pleasure of others. I read this moment as a non-sexual pleasure in the pleasure of the other, even if the other's pleasure is of a sexual nature. Amélie's pleasures, Linda's pleasures, and my own pleasure in their pleasures let us engage actively in pleasure-making without equating that making of pleasure with the making of love, or sex. Pleasure for pleasure's sake, in "relation to itself," a "reverberation in the body and soul," an *ars erotica* that need not draw upon an Orientalist fantasy or be deflected back into sexual practice but resists a Western telos nonetheless.[38] Pleasure that exists for the sake of feeling its delights, pleasures that shift us away from the centrality of orgasm into new erotic temporalities, pleasures that help us plot new erotic directions.

## REVALUING ORGASM THROUGH ASEXUAL PLEASURES

The multiple ways of experiencing intense sensual pleasures I have so far recounted challenge the primacy of sexual orgasm and suggest that maybe sometimes cake *is* in fact better than good sex. Here, I am riffing on the importance of cake in the asexual community. There are several origin stories as to why the offer of cake became a way to greet new members on the Asexual Visibility and Education Network online discussion boards, or why asexual events often include cake. One obvious reason is the long-running joke that cake is better than sex, and asexual people, it should seem, would always rather eat cake. Despite my continued playfulness on the concept of orgasm when discussing asexual pleasures, I would like to suggest there is a difference in the duration of orgasm and the duration of "eargasms," "snowgasms," and "emotional boners." The latter are anticlimactic. They may be ongoing, potentially without end as long as one has music in the ears, snow in the mouth, or an emotional longing for another. Or they can be mere blips of pleasure, momentary returns of pleasure in the passing of a music note, in the moments between when the snow enters the mouth and melts into a cool trickle down the throat. The orgasm, in contrast, is the explosive endpoint, the climax of sexual pleasure, the telos of the erotic (it may, of course, repeat, but it is a repetition of endings). In *The Problem with Pleasure*, Laura Frost writes, "In the same way that an orgasm-centered theory of sexuality does not account for vast registers of eroticism, the idea of pleasure as a performance that has ended or a dam that has burst imposes false borders on the experience."[39] If we remove the partition, tear down those false borders, then we recognize that pleasures can have many durations; they can fold back on themselves—we can fill our mouths with snow over and over again; we can replay that favorite song; we can slowly savor each bite of cake and we must stop only when our stomachs are full, long, I hope, before they explode. These are pleasures that do not necessarily meet a climactic end but rather persist or pace themselves through time and on the body differently. Yes, yes, let us savor those nibbles of cake, from time to time, again and again. No end in sight. Always the possibility of another bite.

Asexual pleasures, then, bring about a durational affect, an experience of pleasure that potentially has no endpoint. They allow us to dwell in middles, to wander aimlessly, to meander in delight, to simply experience the experience, whether in its fleeting moment or in its enduring plenitude. The indefiniteness of asexual pleasures catapults sensual experience into a queer time of ecstasy, thrusting (pardon the pun) us out of the logics of linear time and, consequently, out of the logics of teleological settler time.[40] José Esteban Muñoz describes the different temporality of queerness: "Queerness's time is a stepping out of the linearity of straight time. . . . Queerness's ecstatic and horizontal temporality is a path and a movement to a greater openness to the world."[41] To be sure, Muñoz is writing about queerness here, not asexuality. Sometimes, I take what I view as asexuality's decided queerness for granted, but there has been and continues to be much debate about queer and asexual alignments. See, for one, my comments above about the alienation of asexual people in hypersexual queer venues. Further, even queer people hold onto a lot of stereotypes about asexuality as abnormal or unhealthy, a sign of repression, or a willingness to starve oneself, so to speak. And even queer people may reinforce colonial frameworks through what Scott Lauria Morgensen defines as "settler homonationalism."[42] Queer people too, must learn to plot otherwise.

In order to connect Muñoz's ideas about queer ecstatic time to asexual pleasures, I want to focus on how queerness operates ideologically, resisting logics of heteronormativity, and how, in its resistant logics, to be in the time of queerness must mean that one must also be willing to move into anticolonial temporalities, that a truly queer relationship to time must mean an unsettling of settler time.

If an inquiry into desire, pleasures, and intimacies can shift our perspectives on what we deem normal, normative, and healthy, then I consider that to be a queer inquiry that challenges dominant logics of colonial cisheteropatriarchy. As Kim TallBear notes, "Recognizing possibilities of other kinds of intimacies—not focused on biological reproduction and making population, but caretaking precious kin that come to us in diverse ways—is an important step to unsettling settler sex and family. So is looking for answers to questions about what intimacies were and are possible beyond the settler impositions we now live with."[43] Against settler imposition, we can look for other intimacies as well as other pleasures.

I think of asexual pleasures as moments of somatic, emotional, intellectual, and spiritual pleasures of varying lengths, like orgasms in a way, but they diverge from the logic and linearity of straight time and settler time. They exist outside of sex normativity's sequencing of pleasure: becoming turned on, exchanging sensual and sexual gratification, culminating in orgasm, and basking in postcoital glow. If asexual pleasures are located in a kind of ecstatic time that reveals new expressions of queer affects through nongenital, nonsexual, and nonorgasmic pleasures, then such pleasures may indicate "a movement to a greater openness to the world" in that they allow for an organization of pleasures that pushes back against straight and even queer imperatives to achieve orgasm as the closure of the sexual act.

Audre Lorde writes that "the erotic is a measure between the beginnings of our sense of self and the chaos of our strongest feelings."[44] In this sense, the erotic necessarily dwells in the in-between, a durational space-time between the two expansive points of the self and affect, perhaps also a process of becoming, to return to Rifkin's formulation of a divergent, ongoing temporal orientation. An asexual or nonsexual erotic, then, is necessarily of a different duration, asking us to sit with our pleasures, to enjoy them indefinitely—in the in-between, the meandering middle—to not need to do anything about them. It is also about a new capaciousness in the face of imposed absence—for example, TallBear notes that her "indigenization of the erotic does not privilege sex among intimacies. There are many ways to relate."[45] To move against erotic settler impositions is to unsettle both time and space.

Within asexuality studies, Ela Przybyło also draws on Audre Lorde to imagine asexual erotics that resist compulsory sexuality's tethering of sex and intimacy, though Przybyło positions her concept of an asexual erotic as oppositional to what she interprets as a Freudian erotic that is necessarily always imbued with sex rather than a more complicated libidinal drive toward life. But in living, we might indeed find a different (i.e., nonsexual) kind of drive toward duration. My imagining of an asexual erotic here is one that helps us better understand the expansive possibilities of nonorgasmic and asexual pleasures in a way that demands a refiguring of the space-time experiences of the body's sensations and drives toward life as an erotic ongoingness. Whereas Przybyło is primarily drawn toward Lorde's examples of dancing, building a bookcase, and writing a poem as mundane acts that open up spaces for erotically charged, nonsexual intimacies, I am more interested in Lorde's affective and temporal refigurings of the erotic that create space for existing in intimacy not only with others but also with ourselves in a bounty of pleasures through becomings and undoings of normative constructions of the body's desires and of desirable bodies.[46]

Such a formulation might then blur the lines between what counts as sex, but importantly, it also allows for the realization that we do not necessarily have to call all erotic pleasures and intimacies "sex" (or orgasmic, for that matter). Is gentle caressing of the skin on the back or the stomach a sexual act or an asexual act if it brings about pleasure that is as great as or perhaps better than orgasm? Are kissing and cuddling—not as foreplay but as isolated practices (or perhaps even as foreplay)—sexual acts if they bring about great satisfaction in and of themselves? Can't the erotic pleasure in the ear while listening to music be penetrative in a nonsexual way? Perhaps it is different for everyone. For some, such pleasures may indeed be decidedly sexual; for others, they may be just as valuable and intense but have no sexual or genital bearing. Maybe music is sex sometimes, but a lot of the time, music is just music that is pleasurable.

## FROM PRESCRIBING PLEASURE TO DESCRIBING PLEASURE'S POSSIBILITIES

When I was in my early twenties, I went through a period of denying myself many of life's pleasures. It is a longer story of exactly why I made this choice, linked to various ways in which I was trying to regain control of my emotional and psychic body that had in a way been stolen from me through years of abuse as a child. Being able to regulate what went into my body and how I used my body felt like an important way for me to create a sense of autonomy in my being.

During those years, I did not use any intoxicants, including drugs, alcohol, and caffeine. I followed a severely restricted diet that bordered on disordered eating. I did not have sex in any form, which is another way of saying, I did not have an orgasm. But I did allow myself the pleasures of books, music, and (excessive) physical exercise. In that time, I became significantly underweight and I stopped getting my period. A concerned friend of mine insisted I see an herbalist, and to appease her, I went to see him. After an assessment, he told me that I was not able to gain weight because my energy was blocked due to a coldness in my body. He told me I needed to eat more hot foods and meat (I was following a raw vegan diet at the time). Then he told me he was going to use acupuncture to make me get my period because all women need to have a regular menstrual cycle in order to maintain fertility. In that moment, he prescribed gender onto my body in a way that lined up with dominant understandings of people assigned female at birth. The gender that was prescribed to me was one of a reproductive womanhood attached to a reproductive futurity. I do not know if he cared if I experienced any pleasure in the process, but he wanted to make sure my body was fertile enough to produce a child, as, he seemed to believe, all females should.

If this doctor's visit is instructive in terms of how tightly gender is tied to sexuality and expectations of reproductive capacity, then I cannot help but also wonder how expectations around the capacity for or entitlement to pleasure might also be prescribed alongside gender. Paul B. Preciado suggests that we are living in a pharmacopornographic era, a biopolitical moment in which pharmaceuticals regulate the materiality of the body, especially around sex practice and gender. Testosterone is the drug that preoccupies Preciado's analysis of pharmacopornography, but I am also interested in what a pharmacopornographic analysis can reveal about the prescription of pleasure.[47] To understand how pleasure is literally prescribed today, we need only turn our critique to the creation and promotion of pharmaceuticals—so-called libido drugs—that promise to enhance sexual pleasure, to keep one's sexual appetite satisfied, to reinvigorate a waning sexual capacity, to set one back on the path to orgasm, and to otherwise fix one back into a settler sex economy.

First and foremost, these drugs suggest that people should want sex and they should want it just the right amount, in the right way, and, further, that orgasm should be achievable. Recall that the orgasm is the measurement for the normative modern sexual subject's capacitation; any failure thereof is a now a treatable dysfunction of sex. For men, the message is that they ought to experience a level of sexual attraction, desire, and arousal that enables them to be able to perform in a certain heterosexual, penetrative way in the bedroom. If they cannot, then they need help to get them back to the supposedly normal standards of masculine sexuality. To be unable to achieve an erection, after all, is a dysfunction of sex. Women, however, are simultaneously slut-shamed and prude-shamed, called "frigid" if they don't want sex enough (especially in the context of marriage) and called "sluts" if they have too much sex (especially outside the context of marriage). With such policing of female sexuality comes the policing of female orgasm. In *Diagnosing Desire*, Alyson K. Spurgas begins their book by clearly demonstrating contemporaneous beliefs derived from the supposed science of female sexuality that continue to perpetuate the mythos that female desire is always receptive and that the elusive orgasm is a female problem. When it comes down to it, gender becomes part of the diagnosis. To wit, I refer to "men" and "women" here, as the drugs are marketed explicitly to cisgender men and cisgender women. A more nuanced approach might be to address how these drugs are designed for people with penises and people with vaginas, but the reality is that drug companies are not including transgender and nonbinary people in their studies or marketing (I am not saying they should; I am simply acknowledging that they don't), so the pharmacopornographic prerogative is to prescribe these drugs for conditions determined to be treatable within the realm of defined sexual dysfunctions for cisgender men and cisgender women. In short, fixing sex is also a fixing of gender.

The snake in the flooded basement again rears its head, as the patriarchal and colonial ideals of the sexually obedient, reproductive, and appropriately capacitated nondisabled citizen work their way into how diagnosis and pharmaceuticals continue to uphold dominant norms of gender, sexual function, and pleasure. This brief foray into the prescription of pleasure is meant to simply demonstrate how insidious dominant logics of sex and gender are; rather than creating space for different experiences of pleasure, sex, not-sex, and desire, sexual science has become determined to reshape and fit the body's sensorium into its own fabricated boxes. Thus, again, we note how gender and sexual normativity regulate, at least ideologically if not physiologically, who should have which kinds of desires and, on top of that, who should be deemed desirable, meaning also who should have access to pleasure and which kinds of pleasure should be made accessible.

It serves us to recognize this biopolitical management of sexuality as deeply entrenched in settler colonial histories that had and continue to have direct effects, especially on Black and Indigenous people. Margot Canaday shows how this colonial policing of sexuality is exactly what aided in the building of a "straight state" that continues to prescribe sexuality and desirability through the "straightening" prioritization of whiteness, heterosexuality, cisgender identity, and nondisability.[48] Morgensen writes of the colonial violence that "marked Native peoples as sexually deviant populations to be subjected to a colonial education of desire."[49] Following this ascription of deviance and subjection to the colonial state, Morgensen also wonders how "discourses on sexual perversion tie Indianness *and* blackness to homosexuality, and how . . . they interlink."[50] Or in general, how did colonial discourses on sexuality link Indigeneity and Blackness to racism and dehumanization, working to both hypersexualize and desexualize, to manufacture fear of the supposed sexually threatening other while also deeming those racialized others as sexually undesirable in a white economy of desire and reproduction? When we interrogate these histories through a theoretical lens attuned to reading for asexualities and its attendant pleasures and displeasures, and when we examine how the biopolitics of the state regulates those pleasures, we must account for histories of racial trauma that continue to police which bodies should be desirable, how pleasure is prescribed onto certain bodies, how pleasure is stolen from marked bodies in a variety of ways, and if and how subjects are deemed worthy of accessing and experiencing pleasure.

This is to say that a revaluation of pleasure, a description rather than a prescription of pleasure, may function as one way to plot away from the teleology of orgasm, importantly allowing for a recuperation, through pleasure, of bodies stolen through the violences of colonization, racism, sexism, heterosexism, cissexism, and ableism. Additionally, for those who have had sexual pleasures stolen from their bodies through rape, abuse, illness, and chronic pain, recovering the value of nonsexual, nongenital pleasures can be all the more meaningful. This is not to simply regard pleasure as a point of resistance to the legacies of inherited pains and traumas but rather to create pleasure maps along pathways elsewhere, to carve our course out of the systems that continue to uphold dominant logics at the expense of oppressed and marginalized others. To feel pleasure not only as a way to survive but as a way to live on, to endure.

I have elsewhere written about how to recuperate a body that has been stolen through abuse and sexual assault.[51] I wanted to know how to put together the stories of the past, to find wholeness through the traumatic break. I must confess that part of that process took me personally astray from the celibate asexuality I inhabited for so long. Part of a recovery of my body included gender-confirmation surgery and the injection of the sex hormone testosterone into my body. With those technological interventions came a change in the sensations of my body, including a remapping of the nerves in my chest around my surgical scars and growth and change in my genitals that opened up possibilities for new sensual and sexual pleasures for me. But abruptly, that was all ripped away from me when I became suddenly ill. Following the onset of illness, I experienced complications that required surgical intervention. Despite the success of the surgery, I am left with tissue damage and chronic pain that makes many of the sexual pleasures I had newly discovered painful and impossible. It feels like sexual pleasure has again been stolen from me. And with that, I need to believe in and feel the value of my pleasures in music, language, film, and literature in order to live beyond that theft and damage to my body.

By reshaping our relationships to our bodies, to objects, and to others, I do believe an expansive approach to pleasure can be useful for everyone, even those who experience and value sexual pleasures and even those of us for whom settler technologies continue to work. It is my hope that putting an end to understanding orgasm as the end of pleasure helps those on the margins not only recuperate pleasures that may have been stolen from them through individual and systemic traumas but also helps us plot in anticolonial, antiracist, antiableist directions. Asexual encounters and asexual pleasures challenge us to think against that sex-normative progress narrative. Instead, we can delight in pleasure's brief instantiations and extended durations, imagine different ways of sharing pleasure and delight with others, and recuperate asexual intimacies.

My movement between pleasure and delight recalls how Ross Gay kept a log of experiences, encounters, and objects that delighted him day by day over the course of a year, writing his *The Book of Delights* with attention to small, everyday pleasures: a high five with a stranger, a flower growing from a crack in a curb, nodding his head in greeting to another Black person in public, or the sight of fire-flies blinking in the dark night. In an interview with Krista Tippett, Gay also speaks of how important it is to find these moments of joy and delight in times such as these, in the face of all of our impending deaths, but importantly in the face of so much state-sanctioned violence and Black death. His writing about delight is so important in this moment, and it is delightful, pleasurable, erotic even. Importantly, he notes that his delight grows when he shares it.[52] I want to share these pleasures and delights with you, reader, in hopes that they, too, will grow.

By focusing on and heightening these seemingly smaller pleasures, we expand our thinking about asexualities, reaching beyond the conceptualization of asexuality as a sexual orientation defined by a lack of sexual attraction. We find instead that asexuality reveals so much more substance, so much more possibility of pleasure, and different collective temporalities of shared delights. When we dislodge pleasure from an orgasmic center, we reveal how insidiously sex and its attendant pleasures continue to be regulated and governed in settler worlds along race and gender lines, marking some bodies as undesirable, undesiring, and thus unworthy or incapable of pleasure. But with asexual pleasures, we can account for the ways in which an entry into ecstatic time means the experience of ecstasies that differ from or exceed the orgasmic, that draw us out of settler time into lingering erotic temporalities. We can imagine pleasure differently and apart from the social imperatives that tell us that all we should want is to feel good and that the best way to feel good is to come and come hard. But maybe some of us, at least sometimes, just want to stay hard.

# Between

So much of my life is spent *between*. Between genders, between lovers, between time alone, between jobs, between bouts of illness, between bouts of wellness, between cities and nations. I do so much living in the in-betweens; so much happens. But often, the between, like the border, is characterized as something we simply pass through on the way to all the living we must do elsewhere, in some place that is nameable, mappable. If we pause and reassess all the ways we reside in between-spaces, we might start to revise our very definition of *between*. We might move from *between* as a nebulous zone that exists somewhere on a pathway from one defined point to another and instead conceive of *between* as a space of existing that undoes and blurs the very concepts of endpoints or defined and bordered spaces. In some sense, all spaces are between-spaces. The bordering and demarcating of space, place, and time is a "fabrication of the world."[1] While it is true that borders—national, social, physical—persist and restrict the movement and existence of certain bodies and subjects, we can also approach borders as sites to experiment in living, thinking, and patterning differently. I do not wish to ignore or erase the very real violence of detention and enforced disappearance of migrants, immigrants, and those deemed noncitizens by the state; rather, I am highlighting how this violence is made possible by the maintenance of borders, by the ongoing fabrication—or tending—of a gridded and fenced world. I suppose the question I am asking here is if a reimagination of the border might offer pathways toward the abolition of borders, the means to fabricate and tend to different, open worlds, and, importantly, modes to live within and with borders in the meantime. Sandro Mezzadra and Brett Neilson suggest that employing "border as method" can offer "productive insights on the tensions and conflicts that blur the line between inclusion and exclusion," which can lead to "another kind of knowledge production."[2] What other kinds of knowledge might we produce, or which other worlds might we make possible, from the positions and perspectives of living in the between, of staying in the delay, of refusing the pressure to make an arrival (or a departure)? To explore these questions, I follow the cuts—the excisions of flesh, the splice of the film, the action that moves us from one scene to the next, a practice that adds, that leaves a mark, and connects, as much as it subtracts and takes away. Julietta Singh suggests, "Every narrative we engage is a series of cuts, every act of education marked by its infinite and oftentimes violent erasures." The cut is a violence but it is also a composition—always partial, always full of gaps, even when it may appear to be a "seamless flow."[3] The whole is always full of holes, and in those holes, possibilities for remaking, unfixing, and living differently.

## ///

Cut to Tina: fingernails caked with dirt, face freckled, eyes deepset in the arch of thick brows, uneven teeth a dull yellow-brown beneath the curl of her lip, the nostrils of her keen nose atwitch. Each time Tina sniffs, the camera closes in tighter on her nose and mouth, snoutlike in its movement, revealing something maybe a bit animal in the crinkle between nose and lip, in the *sniff sniff sniff.* "You there with the cap," she calls out. Hold the long shot on Tina, posted in a ferry terminal along the Swedish coast on the Baltic Sea, a navy-blue uniform marking her as *tull,* customs enforcement, *tullverket* in Swedish. A teenage boy in a cap responds to her call. He is illegally carrying alcohol. Tina confiscates it. He leaves the frame, but we hear him call out, "Ugly bitch!" He says he "can't stand that kind" as he fades down the terminal hallway. We might mistake his ire and his words for that typical everyday display of misogyny some men perform toward the women who get in the way of their getting their way. But Tina has been bullied her whole life, called "ugly," called a "freak," called a "monster" since she was a child. She doesn't even flinch at the boy's words. Because Tina has heard it all before, she's taken it in and started to believe it about herself.[Foray 1] The fact of the matter is, Tina *is* different from all the people who surround her; she just doesn't know yet the extent of how different she is, how unhuman she is. Instead, she believes her difference marks her as nothing more than an "ugly, strange human with a chromosome flaw," a genetic defect that has not only shaped her physical appearance but also rendered her infertile. It will take a failed bust, a body cavity search that turns up nothing but confusion, and an intimacy built in the aftermath for Tina to learn that, in fact, there is no flaw in her.

Ali Abbasi's 2018 Swedish film *Border* (*Gräns*), tells the story of Tina, a customs officer in Kapellskär, Sweden. Her daily life appears rather mundane and routine. She lives with her boyfriend Roland in a small house in the woods. Roland does little to contribute to the household. He raises fighting dogs, who growl and bark at Tina every time she returns home, and he leaves town frequently to enter dog fights, where, Tina knows, he also meets up with other lovers. Tina seems apathetic to the whole situation; she long gave up on a sexual relationship with Roland because penetrative sex had proven too painful for her.[Foray 2] She seems to simply tolerate him in her home life where she has perhaps grown used to having him around rather than being entirely alone. Tina's elderly father lives in a nursing home, and she visits him with some frequency, but she otherwise seems to find the most fulfillment in her work. While she appears to have no close friends, she has at least earned some respect at work for her talents. Tina has an uncanny, almost supernatural, ability to sniff out crime, which comes in handy in her post as a customs agent. Tina can smell shame and secrecy; she knows when someone is hiding something, and she is never wrong.[Foray 3] Tina's life is on a loop: morning walks in the woods dotted with occasional enchanting wildlife encounters, a day's work at the ferry terminal, evenings at home in forced conversation with Roland, periodic visits to her father. Everything seems in order. Nothing changes; nothing seems worth changing. That is, until she meets Vore.

The film is adapted from John Ajvide Lindqvist's 2012 short story "The Border." I have chosen not to read comparatively across film and text, but I have included a foray, a series of digressions perhaps, into further possibilities offered by the short story (and some other intertexts), which can be followed through the foray notes found just before the endnotes in the back of this book. I have chosen to primarily focus on the film, which seems to have had greater global travel through its sheer accessibility—I first encountered the film in an art house cinema in Vancouver, British Columbia, and have subsequently rewatched it on a couple different video-streaming platforms from my home in the United States. I watch the film with the aid of English subtitles (and read the story in translation), so all quotations from the film come from the translation provided in the 2018 North American release of the film. As my analysis attunes to gaps and border spaces, the irony of the gap in what is lost in translation is not lost on me.

From my situated perspective in North America, I have been curious about the way the film travels and takes up meaning in different national contexts. For example, when I first saw the film, my Canadian viewing companion and I were in the midst of multiple border crossings between the United States and Canada, as I was traveling back and forth between Vancouver, British Columbia, and Bellingham, Washington, for health care during a period of severe illness. Our experience of the film couldn't help but be inflected by the interrogations we faced at that border, the declarations we needed to make for the purchase of prescription drugs, the demands we faced to prove the legality of our possession and travel. Later, when U.S.-based scholars read early drafts of an essay version of this waypoint, they insisted I cite border studies scholars whose work focuses primarily and sometimes exclusively on the U.S.-Mexico border. No doubt when a national border and the borderlands are evoked in the U.S. American imagination, the preeminent point of reference is the U.S.-Mexico border. U.S. Americans can so easily forget that "the border" is not always *that* border. I do not dare risk imposing the specifics of U.S.-Mexico border surveillance or that particular subset of border studies on my analysis of this film (or on my experience at the U.S.-Canada border, for that matter). I do, however, provide some situational context for the film's location at the Sweden-Norway border.[Foray 4] Primarily, I am most interested in how the film gives us access to practicing border as method and thinking through the transnational and global flows of imperial power and the race and gender anxieties that give rise to global eugenics and the construction of the idealized human form.

While I am wary of universalizing meaning through the film, I am interested in what the film helps us imagine in terms of queer worldmaking. I suggest the film offers an opportunity to "unthink mastery" particularly around the formation of the category of the human as constructed through animacy and vitality and a disavowal of the animal.[4] Zakiyyah Iman Jackson, in a study of how the formation of the liberal human subject maintains both "the animal" and "the black" as abject features of the human, critiques a Hegelian universal humanity that opposes Man and Nature and relies on Reason to distinguish the human from the animal. Jackson writes, "This circuitous logic is one we inherit when a *difference* in Reason is interpreted as *absence or chaos*."[5] I am particularly interested in the notion that differences in reason are interpreted as absence of reason.[Foray 5] The animal is often described as "stupid" and lacking intelligence, but that intelligence is measured by a universal human standard. The different intelligences of animals are often reduced to base instinct, an absence of thought and knowing, a mere bodily function. But there are many ways the bodymind knows; there are different ways of reasoning, knowing, and being.[6] Humans that are deemed lacking in reason and closer to the animal are similarly debased. Singh notes that in claims to the human, "we have in this act of bringing some into the fold of humanity continued to produce others as abjectly outside." Even anticolonial discourse, she argues, in its attempts to resituate dehumanized subjects as human, "has produced a series of human, dehumanized, and inhuman 'remainders' through its claims to a universal human subject."[7] Indeed, there is much violence required in fixing and folding the "chaotic" other into the proper human form.

The human becomes a bounded category maintained by the standards of whiteness and universal humanity whose sex and gender can also be fixed into discretely bounded categories that are presumed to preexist in a body that dwells within and legally moves between national boundaries. But sex (and gender), as Paisley Currah demonstrates, changes. That is, sex is a category that is *done* by the state rather than simply being a thing one might *be*. The shape of sex and its management change depending on the governing body or state actors deploying and enforcing sex classification. In fact, even as social constructionist arguments demonstrate how the state produces sex, sex also plays a role in bringing the state into being: "Sex does do things, make things happen; it's not only an effect. In its work of setting out distinctions—and in the indeterminacy of those distinctions—it generates peoples, families, nations."[8] As the boundaries of the body and the nation are coconstituted, it is important to note that "if there were no possibility of anomaly, for infelicitous or deviant cases, there would be no need for a classification system."[9] Through a reading of *Border*, I take up the anomalies and deviant cases as refusals not only of classification systems and state regulation but also of the human itself. Here, I invoke Singh's call for a "humanimal dispossession," both in the sense of "dispossessing ourselves from the humanist subjects that we have become and in the sense of producing more intimate ways of engaging those who have been forcefully dispossessed." In doing so, Singh suggests, "we might begin the work of sculpting ourselves as different kinds of beings."[10] Or, in Calvin L. Warren's words, we might move toward an "ontological revolution."[11] I argue that for Tina, curing her sex and curing her gender become intertwined with curing her into humanity, or folding her into the human form. For Tina, it is only through humanimal dispossession and unbecoming human that she recognizes herself as a different kind of being with different ways of loving and communing that disrupt so-imagined commonsense categories of sex, nationality, and ethnicity that shape (and are shaped by) the world and its institutions.

As I argue throughout this book, the boundedness of body, nation, and place is linked to the boundedness of time and teleological progress—beginnings and endings, departures and arrivals. To go somewhere, one must leave one defined point and arrive at another. Departures and arrivals reinforce the boundaries of place and the borders that demarcate cities and nation-states. One of those earlier readers who I mention above also faulted this piece of writing for seeming to have nowhere to go and for failing to amount to something. But here I contend that such failure is precisely my point. In *Decolonizing Methodologies,* Linda Tuhiwai Smith writes of how Western classification systems continue to guide how we even begin to formulate our research questions and then how we follow those questions to knowledge formation by relying on presumptions of what constitutes human nature, morality, and virtue as well as what shapes space and time, gender and race. Plainly, Smith suggests, "ideas about these things help determine what counts as real," and I add, what counts as valuable, meaningful, and purposeful—what amounts to something, and what, in its failure to amount to something, amounts to nothing.[12] The demand for a particular kind of arrival of an argument is a demand for linearity in a perfectly packaged conclusion. Such a demand is also a (colonial) refusal to dwell in the trouble or to echo and reverb, to loop back and build upon, away from, and toward with no destination, to find meaning and knowledge in meandering, scavenging, and recursive exploration. No, this waypoint, like this book, refuses to arrive. Instead, we meander, sometimes circle back, dwell in the in-between, choose to amount to nothing, claim the place of the no-places. Why go anywhere when there is so much happening here?

*///*

Cut to Vore: face freckled, eyes deep-set in the arch of thick brows, uneven teeth a dull yellow-brown beneath the curl of his lip, scruff of facial hair across his chin. The first time Tina stops him, he is carry-

**FIGURE 1.** Missing film still.<sup>Foray 6</sup> Tina and Vore stand looking at each other in the ferry terminal hallway. Vore's brown leather duffle bag sits on a table between them, with Tina's hands poised over the bag, ready to search it.

ing nothing but an insect incubator. She smells something, but there is nothing to hold him on.<sup>Foray 3</sup> The next time he comes through the terminal, still smelling something and finding what appears to be nothing, Tina directs him to the back room for a deeper search. When the male officer emerges from the room, he pulls the latex gloves from his hands and shakes his head. He tells Tina she's the one who should have conducted the search, not him, because Vore— "She . . . he . . . she," the guard stammers—has a vagina, not a penis. Tina asks if that means "she" has had an operation, and the guard responds that he only noticed a scar on the tailbone, too far up to be from a genital reconstruction but a scar nonetheless. Tina startles at this information because she too bears a scar in the same place on her body, which she has always believed to be the result of a hard fall on a rock when she was a small child. Vore holds the key to unlocking the true story of the scar, which carries in it a history of medical experimentation, imprisonment, genocide, and a "fixing" of the body into the human.[13]

To be clear, I have no investment in reading trans or intersex onto either Tina's or Vore's body or into their identities (though some of their embodied experiences will ring eerily familiar to those with lived intersex and trans experience). On one level, such an endeavor might simply be considered impossible; Tina and Vore are not human, after all, so how could we ascribe them human labels, categories, or identities? But beyond a species technicality, I am not, in this case, interested in representation for representation's sake or toward some political end of increased visibility and proliferation of narratives of trans and intersex experience (though those things too have their import). Instead, just as I have already proposed the shift to an asexual analytic, I am interested in how reading *Border* through trans and intersex analytics helps us interrogate those interstitial and entangled relations between state surveillance, settler colonialism, gender, sexuality, and the production of the human.

To do so is to take up *trans-* as prefixal, prepositional, as movement, as a way of unpacking the constructedness of sex (and gender) itself, of the body, of the very idea of "human" as distinct and disentangled from animal, from plant, from the cellular, from earth and its elements.[14] And so too, it is to dwell in the prefix *inter-* of *intersex*, which, as David A. Rubin notes, "literally means 'among, between, in the midst of.'"[15] Which is to be, in a way, ambivalent, liminal, on the border, between. To think with *trans-* and *inter-* is to meander, to resist crossing from one point to another, to make multiple crossings in many directions, to refuse to arrive. To consider trans(gender) and inter(sex) as analytics, rather than identities, is to question "an illusory coherence to westocentric rationality and its globalizing structures of power," thereby allowing us to "rethink and rearticulate the biopolitics and geopolitics of sex, gender, race, and nation."[16] Or, as Toby Beauchamp frames it, a trans analytic can "intervene into the naturalization of race, disability, and citizenship."[17] Such an analytic then allows us to fixate on, interrogate, and undo what Rubin calls "principle dualisms" and Beauchamp calls "dichotomous frameworks" including not only man/woman or male/female but also binarisms such as nature/culture, human/animal, citizen/noncitizen, deviant/normative, or normal/abnormal, giving us further insight into the connected regulatory systems that surveil bodies across categories of existence.

In the act of fixating, we concentrate on, dwell with, become transfixed—that is, both pierced through and rendered motionless.[18] In our transfixations, we become unfixed in time and space, transitive, moving and living in the in-between. Or, as Marcelo Diversi and Claudio Moreira put it, "We live in the hyphen, we straddle the hyphen, we *are* the hyphen."[19] We might ask what matters in that slash or dash between allegedly fixed categories, what becomes in the gaps, cuts, and chasms. Rebecah Pulsifer suggests that *Border* offers an archive for a new materialism that examines representation for its "material performativity" rather than reducing representation merely to its "representational work."[20] Which is another way of saying that the questions I ask about the film are also a matter of mattering, of producing new ecosystems of possibility, expansive in their sexual, genital, and embodied imaginings. In particular, I move toward what Rubin calls an "ethics of uncertainty," a rethinking of difference toward cobelonging through a refusal of "hegemonic corporeal schemas."[21] Or, following Karen Barad, I explore how "ontological indeterminacy, a radical openness, an infinity of possibilities, is at the core of mattering."[22] In other words, what *Border* offers us is a way of imagining all that happens in the in-betweens, the spaces of indeterminacy and uncertainty that unsettle so many dichotomies, revealing how bodies matter in their materiality and in their significance beyond the universal human form. Tina and Vore offer us imagined possibilities of mattering and being through humanimal dispossession in their interstitial existence as not-human but also not-animal (spoiler: they are trolls), such that we might find space to imagine an otherwise world that combines an ethics of uncertainty with what Eunjung Kim calls an "ethics of queer inhumanism," an antiableist, antiracist ethic of "proximity and copresence" with objects, matter, and beings—a *trans*national *inter*subjectivity, even.[23]

Borders are interstitial zones (to state the obvious). But what does that mean for how we conceive of the interstice? Homi K. Bhabha describes the interstitial as a "living 'in the midst of the incomprehensible'" or "the transitive time of the body in performance."[24] For Bhabha, a willingness to dwell in and among the incomprehensible, to live into the *trans*itivity of time and body, makes possible an interstitial perspective that refuses a linear essentializing formation of nation as a unified whole without holes; it understands the nation as liminal, not just at its borders but within the nation itself. Such a perspective then allows us to interrogate how subjects are "formed 'in-between,' or in excess of, the sum of the 'parts' of difference (usually intoned as race/class/gender, etc.)," thus opening up the possibilities for cultural hybridities that make space for difference "without an assumed or imposed hierarchy."[25] Even as the nation defines and coheres itself along borders that mark it as bounded and discrete (parallel to the ways in which liberal humanism imagines the human as a discrete, bounded, autonomous subject), the space of the border is only a beginning point for cracking open the mythology of the fixity of the nation-space. The nation and the national subject are always already interstitial, vacillating, and transitive, entangled with matters of being and becoming and the attendant securitizations and surveillances that attempt to deflect our attention away from the greater possible imaginings that come with the rupture of, ambivalence toward, and refusal of hegemonic corporeality.

It is thus the task at hand to throw us back into the midst of, to dwell in the gaps, to fixate on (as in to fix, as in to correct, as in to undo) the notion that gaps are absences, silences, and emptinesses. The interstice is often regarded as a vacuous space, an in-between where nothing exists and little to nothing happens, even as bodies and objects regularly pass through, ostensibly in transit to the places where the stuff of life and living actually take place. But, like Dylan McCarthy Blackston, who writes of the political and theoretical potential in the "thick activity" of interstices, I am suggesting not only that much happens in the interstice but that these transitive spaces are also spaces of dwelling, where all the (untidy) activity continues, where living lingers, *inter*twines, and coexists in the midst of all that is uncertain and incomprehensible.[26] Tim Ingold similarly writes of dwelling as "the way inhabitants, singly and together, produce their own lives." Dwelling is thus necessary for "such activities as designing, building, and occupation" to take place at all.[27] We dwell in order to build and to make place and space. Dwelling is a counterhegemonic activity, and it is also an everyday activity. For example, writing on queer diasporic aesthetics as practices of contestation and imagination for pleasure and living otherwise in the ongoing violences of colonial modernity, Gayatri Gopinath asks us to dwell in the performative possibilities of the everyday as a way to "contest this violence by finding imaginative and pleasurable ways to dwell in the wake of forced containment and forced mobility." Aesthetic practices, these "everyday forms of dwelling" also unsettle binary oppositions and terms of movement/building/arrival, as they "offer a nuanced sense of the relation between staying and leaving, immobility and mobility, home and exile, dwelling and removal, indigeneity and diaspora, that refuses to privilege one of these terms over the other, but always attends to their co-constitutive nature."[28] Making is dwelling, and dwelling is making. Dwelling is living in and through the muck of it all. Dwelling is living.

Which brings us to the most paradigmatic of interstitial spaces, chock-full of thick activity where much happens but few people dwell or live in any permanent sense: the airport (or any transit terminal, for that matter). Beauchamp describes the space of the airport as one where "travel, borders, and bodies regularly converge."[29] In other words, it is both an interstice (a border space, an in-between) and an entanglement (a space of merging and convergence). And it is a space rife with biometric technologies. Biometrics, as Paisley Currah and Tara Mulqueen show, rely on the notion of a fixity of gender, even as sex changes based on state enforcement and securitization. Biometrics cannot account for the shifting body or the in-between body, and transgender people often "find themselves in the uncomfortable interstices between spatial and temporal registers, between stasis and change, between what one is and what one says or does."[30] Or, when attempts are made to integrate nonbinary and transgender people, such integration is arguably still "historically linked to practices of population registration, regulation, and classification" that utilize "colonial tools of surveillance."[31] Additionally, as Joseph Pugliese argues, biometric technologies are "infrastructurally calibrated to whiteness," meaning that some bodies (such as those belonging to people of color, disabled people, trans and intersex people) will "fail to enroll," baffling the system.[32] Beauchamp similarly traces the history of x-ray screening in airports in a collision of racism and gender normativity, moving from the perceived threat of the racialized "terrorist" through the diffractive impacts such a culture of suspicion has on the experiences of transgender and gender-nonconforming people who are subjected to the regulatory powers of gender under the guise of securing the nation. Borders and bodies are policed through an interweaving of threat simultaneously believed to be aimed at the nation and also at the bodies of the citizens who inhabit it. The transing of the nation, the crossing of borders, is thus sutured to race and gender.

What this entanglement reveals, rather than a cohesive and secure nation, is a series of fissures in state surveillance systems and biopolitical regimes. Take, for example, Mina Hunt's recounting of navigating the airport as a trans person engaged in multiple border crossings: the movement across national, state, or provincial borders, as well as across the borders of legible gender defined by biomedical and juridical systems. What Hunt learns is that her trans body baffles biometric surveillance systems, revealing that borders are indeed full of cracks (interstices within the interstice): "Borders, be they medical, juridical, or emotional, are not stable barriers; trans bodies haunt their peripheries—eroding the previously imagined solidity of boundaries."[33] In other words, it is not that nonnormative bodies can effectively undo state power but that they reveal the falsity of classificatory systems and lead us into points of refusal in the regime of conformity and regulation—little ruptures where we might expand our bodily imaginings. I think here of Gilles Deleuze and Félix Guattari: "Sometimes the borderline is defined or doubled by a being of another nature that no longer belongs to the pack, or never belonged to it, and that represents a power of another order, potentially acting as a threat as well as a trainer, outsider, etc." The anomalous one reveals the shapes of the border by nature of unbelonging, a kind of sorcery, for the sorcerers, the monsters, are "at the borderline of the village, or *between* villages."[34] And this is where we find Tina, her own sense of self eroding, even as she works to uphold the solidity of the border through her post at the ferry terminal. There we find Tina, living between many different kinds of villages.

### ///

Cut to Tina: the nostrils of her keen nose atwitch, *sniff sniff sniff.* Vore approaches Tina and drops his bag on the table in expectation of her suspicion. But for Tina (who is in many senses Vore's familiar, even if yet unbeknownst to her), Vore is not suspicious as a racialized or gender-nonconforming other who fails to enroll in the biometric systems of the ferry terminal. Rather, Tina is suspicious of Vore because her (nonhuman) mechanism of knowing—her sense of smell—tells her something is askew, something about Vore is piercing tiny little holes in the foundation of what she has come to accept in her role securitizing the ferry terminal.[Foray 7] But she finds nothing in his bag or on his immediate person. The ferry terminal is not equipped with the same x-ray technology we find in the airport, so if further investigation is deemed warranted (and Tina decides it is), then Vore must be searched more thoroughly. Into the private room he goes with a male guard. The male guard returns embarrassed (for himself or for Vore or for both of them, perhaps) because Vore has a vagina. Then there's the scar on the tailbone. Who is "she"? Who is "he"? Who is Vore? Tina wants to know, needs to know. Tina is never wrong when she smells criminal deceit and shame, but this time it seems that she is; Vore has baffled her olfactory system.[Foray 3] She apologizes to Vore, lets him know he has the right to file a complaint (he declines), and they part ways, but this will not be the last she sees of him. She is drawn to him, by his scent and by the mystery (and potential answers) he holds, and it won't take her long to seek him out.

In the meantime, Tina takes up a regular work schedule in the terminal. Most days of the week, she arguably spends more time there than in her own home.[Foray 8] One might say there is even a sense in which she dwells or resides in that interstitial space by nature of her occupation. And though she does not yet know it, Tina also "resides in the liminal space between human and nonhuman worlds."[35] In all the thick activity of these interstices, Blackston specifically argues for the disruption of the "fluidity of the transition from human to nonhuman," asking us to recognize instead how the interstitial space between human and nonhuman allows for "new sex terms, identity formations, racial attributions, and species categorizations" to take shape.[36] In this space, Tina surveils on behalf of a state that, she will soon learn, subjected her ancestors to invasive eugenics-driven medical testing and genocide. As she unlocks the secrets of her past and her being, she will find that conceiving of herself in new sex terms and species categorizations will be necessary to undo the ways she had been fixed into a national subjectivity by being fixed into the human, by being fixed into a woman.

### ///

Cut to Tina nude in a lush green forest.[Foray 9] She steps into a pool of water near a small waterfall, her breasts heave as she takes in the forest air. Tina has come to the forest to get away from her live-in boyfriend, Roland, whom she just overheard on the phone making plans to meet up with one of his lovers. Tina smells the other women on him, but she doesn't mind much because she's not having sex with Roland. They tried in the past, but it was too painful for Tina, so now she regularly dismisses his advances, opting out of sex entirely.[Foray 2] Tina instead indulges in other sensuous bodily pleasures in the moist earth between her toes, in the soft communion with woodland creatures like deer and fox, in the delight of the crunch of an insect between her teeth, in the wriggle of a worm on her tongue, and in the cool river waters that lap at her pockmarked skin.

Tina stands thigh-deep in the emerald water and turns her

head toward the sky—the camera's cut to a view from behind bears witness to the history of an incision on Tina's body: the slightest blemish, a small round ripple of skin on her tailbone. She will later learn from Vore, after she goes to find him at his hostel and invites him to rent her guest cottage, that this scar marks the place where her tail was surgically removed when she was a baby. Vore similarly had his tail removed when he was taken from his parents, upon whom humans had conducted medical experiments. Tina will later confirm this story with her adoptive father, who worked as a care-taker at a psychiatric hospital where Tina's birth parents and other trolls were being held for medical experimentation.[Foray 5] When her parents died, she was taken in as a baby, given the human name Tina (she had been called Reva), and raised as a human by the caretaker and his wife, who could not have children of their own.

The excision of the tail provides an entry into thinking through multiple registers of sex and its linkages to genitals and gendering, sexual capacity, and normative citizenship. In the nonconsensual surgical extraction of her tail, Tina's sex is "fixed" (corrected, put into place) by fixing her into the human form. The removal of the appendage brings her body into closer alignment with human rather than troll. She is then raised as a human girl who, when she grows into a woman, will simply be incapable of having children. But Tina's body subsequently transfixes (pierces, arrests, unsettles) the catego-ries of human and woman. If, as the ideology of compulsory sexual-ity indicates, to be human is to be sexually and orgasmically capaci-tated, then anorgasmia or an inability to enjoy or even have sex due to genital pain would be considered a debility or decapacitation.[37] Such a decapacitation then renders Tina an "unreal woman" in her temporary asexuality through her refusal of sex due to pain that in-capacitates her body's ability to engage in receptive sex, the action that would render her a proper, healthy, normal female human.[38] We find an echo of an argument made in waypoint "An End to Ends" that fixing sex is also fixing gender. The attempt to fix Tina into the human would require also fixing her into a "real woman" by curing her inability to participate in and desire receptive sex. But the tree hasn't healed, so why should she?[Foray 9] Or Tina's "healing" takes on a different shape and movement toward penetrative desire, rather than receptive desire. What Tina soon learns is that she is not in-fertile after all, and she is fully capable of pleasurable sex without pain.[Foray 2]

## A STACKED INTERLUDE

I have a friend who often jokes about being drafted unwillingly into the "game of man." Even if you don't want to play, you must at least mount something of a defense or you won't survive very long. Essentially what he is talking about is being hailed, inter-pellated as a man. We talk about those moments, after years of testosterone, that we notice we are pulled into the game more than we'd like. Hey, buddy. Hey, pal. Hey, *man*.

I once celebrated this friend's birthday with him on a New England beach during an uncharacteristically chilly and windy midsummer day. As we walked along the beach, I spotted a smoothed, intact purple and brown dappled shell lodged in the sand. I picked it up and carried it as we walked and talked, rub-bing it with my thumb like a worry stone. I slipped it in my pocket and did some research later. I discovered it to be the shell of a slip-per snail.

I learned that slipper snails, *Crepidula fornicata*, are protan-drous hermaphrodites, which means they are born male but may change their sex throughout their lives. They tend to live in stacks in the ocean. The younger male snails join the stacks at the top. The largest, oldest snails that live at the bottom of the stack had morphed from male to female as they moved down the stack. The snails in the middle of the stack (the ones living in the between) are between sexes, as their phallus shrinks and their reproductive opening forms.

I cannot stop thinking about slipper snails. I write about them and talk about them obsessively, in circles, how slipper snails provide a metaphor for thinking about the relationality of gender. How we become "man" or "woman" in relation to how the other sees us or makes us or needs us or wants from us. How I become a man in a particular way when a man says, "Hey, man." How I become ungendered when someone says, "Sir, ma'am, sir, ma'am. What are you?" I write about how I sometimes feel like men try to stack themselves on top of me, like they're trying to force me down to the bottom of the stack, trying to push me back into the female sex, like that's their way of "fixing" me for being the "wrong" kind of man.

I write about my own medical trauma. How testosterone and the complications of illness made my body a between-body. How

I have had my genitals fixed, as in repaired, to restore a functional (receptive) vagina. How I know all too well that fixing sex is a way to make the body "right," to affix the body to a gender and to affix a gender to the body.

When I think of the small heaps of slipper snails, perched on rocks where the water gently laps over and against them, I realize that what appear to be static piles are actually bodies in flux. So much living is done under, over, and between one another.

## ///

Cut to Vore reclining on his back in the lush green forest. Tina kneels over him, braced between his legs as he pulls down her pants. She leans back and gasps as a phallus rises up from between her legs. In my memory, her phallus looks like a mushroom. When I watch the scene back, it does bear some resemblance to a stinkhorn (*Phallus impudicus*), sometimes commonly referred to as dog stinkhorn because of its likeness to a dog penis.[39] But more mushroomlike is the way it grows between her thighs, reminiscent of a time-lapse video of a stinkhorn springing from the earth. I think it is no accident that the rise of Tina's phallus reminds me of a mycological fruiting. The mushroom, like Tina, lives between categories. Somewhere in that slash between plant/animal, fungi "make questions of our categories"; they are "slippery and transgressive—evading the binaries and the neat categorization of scientific taxonomy."[40] Of the stinkhorn, in particular, V Adams describes them as "nasty, fabulous, and somewhat alien queer kin" such that they "feel like a reminder of how disruptive, magical and strange the world—and we—can be if we let ourselves flourish beyond 'acceptable' tastes."[41] Mushrooms are perhaps beacons of the queer worlds already stretching out below and around us; they help us think away from the "acceptable" body, "acceptable" sex, and "acceptable" taste. Through the mushroom, we might expand our bodily imaginings of sex and gender as meandering forms, tendrilled like fungi, filamentous and filial, kinning and kenning. (For more on mushrooms, meander over to "Rot [Eaten] Rot" to take a mycological foray.) Tina, who already bears a relationship of kin and ken (an entangled, interspecies, inherited knowledge) to the forest and all that dwells, decomposes, and recomposes there, sprouts a troll phallus that, like the mushroom, may be deemed transgressive as it makes questions of her placement into the categories of woman

**FIGURE 2.** Missing film still.[Foray 6] A close-up of Tina's face hovering over Vore's. Vore's head is tilted back, eyes closed tightly shut, chin up, teeth bared as he grins in pleasure. Tina's eyes are gently closed, her mouth gaped open, almost as if she is going to bite down on Vore's chin.

and human.[Foray 10] As trolls, Tina and Vore live in the slash between human/animal; they trans- and inter- the categories of the human, of sex, and of gender.[Foray 11]

Vore pulls his own pants down and Tina is soon on top of him, penetrating him, thrusting, growling, and howling in pleasure. With Tina's boyfriend Roland out of town, Tina and Vore spend the next several days frolicking in the woods, snatching insects from the dirt and crunching them with delight between their teeth. Tina comes alive to herself (and to Vore) in new ways as they fuck among the mosses and trees.[42] Tina's pleasures expand as her bodily possibilities and capacities expand. By the end of the film, we will learn that in this time, they conceive a child together, a child whom Vore later sends to Tina to parent, with the plea for her and the baby to join him in a secret troll refugee community in Finland.[Foray 7]

It would be too easy to read this film simply as a story of sexual awakening or, worse, as a cure for apparent asexuality. Such readings overlook Tina's expansive erotic and intimate life that preexists and overlaps with her discovery of her sexual capabilities. Further, in Tina and Vore's conjugation, Tina refuses the hegemonic corporeal schemas of the human. She discovers her own sex in that interstitial space between human and animal. It is important not to misread Tina's coming into her trollness as a cure for her (or even *the*) human condition. Rather, it is a rescripting of the body toward more expansive genital sexual imaginings alongside Tina's already expansive sensual embodiment and relations with dirt, forest, insects, animals, plants. The film reveals what is made possible despite what was previously absented, erased, and unimaginable—a way to make the world look different by recovering what was eradicated in an attempt to cure and fold an unruly body into medical, colonial order. Christine Labuski writes how "genital imaginaries" are shaped by birth, allowing "what's between our legs" to determine "which of two extant categories will structure the majority of our lived experience." According to Labuski, these genital imaginaries can be just as rich and varied as they are impoverished, if only we are willing to move away from a "neat correspondence" of genitals and if or how they constitute an individual's erotic identity.[43] Building on the calls for new genital imaginaries and ontological revolutions, I am offering an undoing/transfixing of the human as a way to similarly create rich and varied genital sexual imaginings that stretch beyond binary taxonomies and categorizations in which impossible sex becomes differently possible. For as it turns out, much of Tina's pain arose from a governing system that tried to shape her and her sex into a subject and being that she is not and will never achieve in her becoming. As Vore tells her in response to her claim that she is damaged, "There is no flaw in [her]."

After their first sexual encounter, Tina and Vore lie side by side on the soft moss of the forest floor as evening falls. Tina turns to Vore and asks, "Who am I?" He tells her she's a troll, and he riffs on her belief of having a chromosome flaw, as he explains, "The chromosome change that gave you a tail enables you to smell what people feel and makes lightning chase you." Incidentally, Tina and Vore share another semblance of scars, Tina on her temple and Vore on his chest, where they were individually struck by lightning in the past.[Foray 9] I read Tina and Vore's shared relationship to lightning as another kind of intimacy with the matters of the more-than-human world. Barad describes lightning in sexually charged language as "electrical flirtation," "a crackle of desire," "a spurt of electrons," as it is part of the ecosystem of bioelectric codes that shape bodies.[44] Lightning is electricity, which Jane Bennett describes as "the stream of vital materialities called electrons." Electricity is always moving, sometimes predictably, sometimes not. The movement of electrons, electricity, and lightning depends on actions and interactions with other bodies.[45] In other words, lightning demands intimacy, an erotic (perhaps sometimes sexual but not always) commingling of the spark. We are electric entanglements.

These phenomena, "whether lizards, electrons, or humans," Barad writes, "exist only as a result of, as a part of, the world's ongoing intra-activity."[46] In this inter- and intra-activity, electrons, the stuff of lightning, are notably "made of virtual configurations/reconfigurings of disparate kinds of beings dispersed across space and time in an undoing of kind, being/becoming, absence/presence, here/there, now/then."[47] Barad describes electrons as inherently chimeras made up of their own emitted and swallowed photons.[48] How fitting, then, that lightning should chase the troll, a kind of chimera in its humanimal configuring and dispossession, in its undoing of the human kind.

Citing Norwegian and Nordic folklore and cinema, Pulsifer notes the troll's association with "uncontrollable forces of nature that have become increasingly threatening" (such as lightning, to name one), which leads to trolls being characterized as "mythical ecobeasts" that belie the "ecosystemic friction" between humans and the so-imagined natural world as they straddle both realms.[49] Similarly, Myra J. Hird, on thinking between the intersex and "transex" makeup of the natural world, makes the point that most of the "natural world" does not fit into a sex/sexual dimorphism that some humans have deemed "natural," which is perhaps a way of saying that we are a world of ecobeasts, humans included.[50] We might then understand trolls as othered others subjected to the violences of settler colonial nation-forming—creating fictions of human and beast, pitting the civilized world against the natural, threatening, unsettled world. For Tina and Vore, their scars—from the lightning and the surgical excisions alike—"both attach [them] to a past of loss and a future of survival."[51] In fact, the scar and its held histories reveal Tina not as a benefactor but as a survivor of settler state violence, the very state she deigns to secure by guarding its border from smugglers, "criminals," and suspicious others.[Foray 7]

In her role as customs officer, Tina straddles the line between survivor and inheritor of state violence and enactor of the state securitization that makes similar ongoing violences possible, including the erasure of gender variance and diversity by forcing and collapsing sex and gender difference into a reductive binary model based on

limited genital possibility. The treatment of Tina and her kind is a
further reiteration of the construction of the category of human and
the ways in which its attendant hierarchies and animacies entangle
race, sex, gender, and nation in terms of who is deemed lesser human,
inhuman, nonhuman, or unhuman, which determines whether one
is utilized for experimentation and exploitation or granted rights
and liberties through assigned value and worth. For viewers in the
United States or Canada, the story may seem all too familiar. In
the Scandinavian context, the film also arguably draws on Sweden's
mostly hidden history of racism and global colonization and brings
that history into a present-day context that includes continued struggle for undocumented persons living in Sweden, as well as a nation-
wide prevalence of Islamophobia and antisemitism and a rise in white
nationalism across Northern Europe. As such, the film uses the border zone between Sweden and Norway alongside the in-between figure of the troll to explore the historical ramifications of the perpetua-
tion of ideologies of border policing that rely on "protecting" citizens
through the maintenance of a white state that must fence out the racialized other.[52] And with its screening and easy availability beyond
the Swedish border, the film importantly reveals transnational and
global flows of imperial power and ethnonationalism and its attendant race and gender anxieties (especially in regard to immigration
and border crossings) and human idealization that upholds ongoing
eugenics projects.

In the face of these ongoing structures, *Border* gives us an opportunity to meander into worlds of inter- and intraspecies kin-
ships and intimacies, to delight in the pleasures of watching Tina
grow into expansively pleasurable worlds of possibility, and to also
straddle realms in the unsettling of the boundedness of place and
body, nation and temporality. Refusing an additive politics of liberal humanism that seeks to incorporate "dehumanized" others into
rights discourses by transposing or recognizing (and thus reinforc-
ing and upholding) notions of human dignity, value, and worth by
(re)inscribing one into the closed bounds of the human, I have proposed that *Border* helps us dream new worlds of possibility in the
interdwellings of human/animal/monster. By destabilizing categories,
dwelling in the midst of, and refusing the fixity of borders, we follow
an ethics of queer inhuman/unhuman uncertainty. Doing so is to recognize and refuse the danger of reinstating humanity as a "locus of
dignity and respect" determined by limited notions of ability, agency,

race, sex, and gender.[53] It is to instead "maintain openness to the unknown and the unpredictable, to possibilities, materialities, and temporalities that remain unanalyzed or yet to come."[54] It is to "entangle and enmesh trans* and animals" toward "ways of envisioning futures of embodiment, aesthetics, biopolitics, climates, and ethics" and "to understand the body as inseparable from the milieu in which it comes to matter."[55]

Transgender, intersex, and a/sexual matters, then, are more than the concerns and content of gendered and sexed representation; rather, as analytical frames, they provide ways to reshape what constitutes a livable and lovable body. In our materialities, our matterings and rematterings, in our fixations and transfixations, we recognize the human as composite, holobiont, made of plant, made of animal, made of electricity and mythology in the molecular, in the cellular embrace of monstrosity and the interstitial entanglements of our being, becomings, and undoings. What matters is unsettling in its chimeric baffling of the securitizing metrics of the state and transfixing of the nation—piercing through, exposing and making livable the liminality within, making possible that which hegemonic schemas have otherwise deemed impossible, unimaginable, and absent. The human, like the nation and the border, is an interstitial thing. In refusing the discreteness of the human, we might refuse to be fixed by the state, such that we might redefine beauty through a redemption of the so-called ugly or flawed, reimagine pleasures through either expanded genital sexual imaginings or apart from sex and genitalia altogether, and create more just worlds of cobelonging and entanglement.

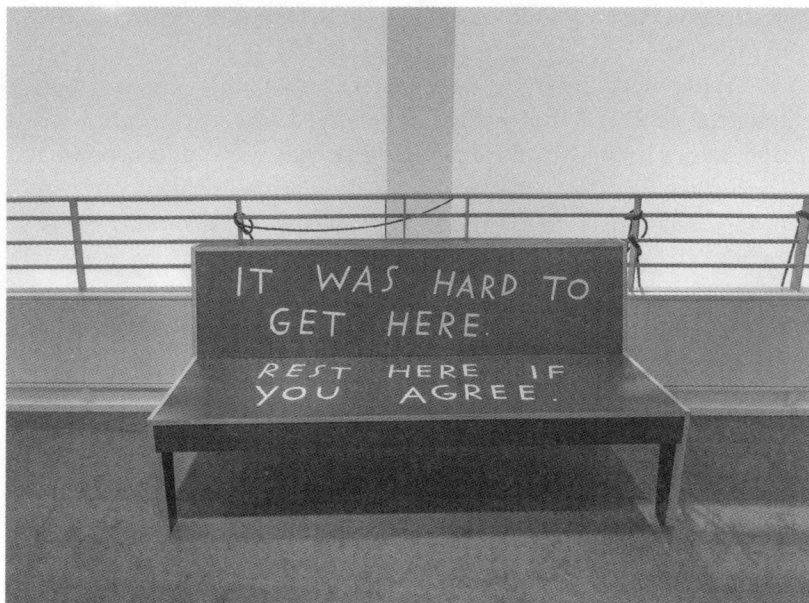

**FIGURE 3.** Finnegan Shannon, *Do You Want Us Here or Not*, 2020–ongoing. Baltic birch, poplar wood, plastic laminate, carpenter's glue, water-based contact cement, and wood screws. Produced by Walter Zanetti, Anthony Dewar, and Paul Durocher, School of Industrial Design, and Brant Lucuik, Azrieli School of Architecture & Urbanism, Carleton University, 2020. Featured in *Finnegan Shannon: Lone Proponent of Wall-to-Wall Carpet*, Carleton University Art Gallery. Photograph by Justin Wonnacott. Courtesy of the artist and Carleton University Art Gallery.

# Rest

# Rot [Eaten] Rot

Through the course of writing and thinking about various themes of absence, especially as they manifest in film, visual art, and literature, I have let mushrooms do what they do in the wild: sprout up in unexpected places, often rapidly. And I have let them disappear just as quickly and quietly as they do in nature, letting pages go by before I mention them again. Such an engagement with the mushroom is part of my meandering methodology, letting myself delightedly happen upon them and just as delightedly wander away from them. But I am also starting to think of the mushroom as a metaphor for an epistemology, a mycelial way of thinking.[Foray 10] This mycelial movement of thought does not require the "mycelial mind" that Merlin Sheldrake refers to as the altered mind under the influence of psychedelic fungal chemicals like LSD and psilocybin (though it may also be one route to mycelial thinking, and I myself have taken a couple psilocybin forays that led me down some unexpected pathways of thought for this waypoint).[1] What I have wanted from the permission to wander is the ability to move in any direction without an end (as in goal, as in arrival), and to move (or be still) with purpose and curiosity, to think and learn and live in multiple directions and in the pauses. "Mycelium," Sheldrake writes, "is a body without a plan." They are "decentralized organisms" with dispersed control and coordination that "takes place both everywhere at once and nowhere in particular."[2] Mycelia move us away from organized centers and disrupt the very directionality of movement; they digress. They meander and wander without a plan but with purpose.

Gilles Deleuze and Félix Guattari offer the rhizome as a decentralized and nonhierarchical model for thinking, the "and . . . and . . . and" of possibility, unlike the root that connects to the tree—genealogy, the perfect model of hierarchy. But the tree/root and the rhizome are not necessarily opposed: "There are knots of arborescence in rhizomes and rhizomatic offshoots in trees."[3] Although there is no true opposition, Deleuze and Guattari do tend to insinuate that if we follow the roots, we will lose the rhizome. I wonder about the difference between the mycelial and the rhizomatic, as they both offer a way of thinking and moving multidirectionally, away from center(s). I suppose what I like about the mycelial is that we can spend all the time we want with trees and roots without losing the mycelium. The mycelium and roots are always in relation; mostly it is symbiotic, sometimes parasitic, but the mycelium is always there, underground, even when we cannot see it or when we forget about it—always present even when it is absent from the visual or conscious field. Some mycelia are even a kind of rhizome, a mycorrhizal fungus, that can live inside tree roots in an "intimate, reciprocal dependence."⁴ The mycelium is multiply interdependent as a "web-like network of fungal cells that extends apically though substrate, performing sex, seeking nutrients, building multispecies and multikingdom symbioses."⁵ We have to navigate a hierarchical world sometimes, and in the process, we also learn how to build webs away from the apex. Maybe what I mean to say is we can do away with the metaphor of the tree as hierarchical map, but we can't do away with trees altogether; they are part of the multikingdom. I guess I want trunks, branches, stems, roots, rhizomes, and mycelia, all. The mycelium is what keeps the soil teeming with life in its often invisible or microscopic lurking. There is so much living and movement happening in ostensibly firm ground. What appears static is actually in motion. The earth undulates beneath us, moving in its own cycles with as much vibrant energetic flow as a water system—the terrestrial is no firmer than the aquatic; everything is in flux.Foray 12

Mycelial thinking asks us to destabilize categories we might have otherwise thought to be stable, to understand intelligence and movement as not always goal-oriented but as sometimes explorative and adaptive, and to pay attention to what is happening out of sight or out of mind. Like queerness, like asexuality, the mushroom unsettles order: In between plant and animal, we find fungus, a thrumming network of both life and rot. These disorderings and reorderings are what make mycological and fungal explorations queer to me, not simply because fungi are "nonbinary" in their being neither animal nor plant nor because they proliferate sexual mating types.⁶ I have no objections to thinking about the queerness of fungi in these ways, and I have at times utilized those approaches myself, but I think we can expand our understandings of and the possibilities for queer worlds if, instead of mapping our conceptions of queerness onto fungi, we listen to what they're trying to tell us about the world below and around us, a world that cares not for whatever names, labels, or categories we want to give it. Thus, when I write of the queerness of mushrooms and fungi, I do not mean to suggest that mushrooms *are* queer, just as I do not mean to suggest that an asexual attunement to something makes that thing or that person asexual. Rather, the queerness of mushrooms lies in what they reveal of an always already queer world that defies the (hetero)normative ordering of limited and limiting systems and categories that are in fact constructed against the diversity of nature.[7] As I write in "Between" in this book, we might think of mushrooms as a beacon of the queer worlds already stretching out below and around us.

## MYCELIAL DIGRESSIONS

When I follow the mushroom, the fruiting body of a densely tangled underground fungal network, I find myself meandering through a meshwork of strange encounters and connections between silence and mushrooms, the intimacy of the mouth, and a queer rotting paradise. It all begins with my encounter of John Cage's *A Mycological Foray*, a compendium of essays, poems, and drawings related to mushrooms. I experience this book in strange multiplications; a multitude on repeat, it comes and goes in my life like a mushroom. I first checked out a copy from my college library. After having it in my possession for a couple months, I was alerted that there was a copy of *A Mycological Foray* on hold for me at the other library across campus. I told the librarian that there must be a mistake because I had already checked the book out, but they said it wasn't charged out to me, so they made me promise to return the copy I had in my possession when I was done with it. I promised I would. Then I looked at my account to see if I could figure out what was going on. It turns out the copy I had in my possession was indeed checked out to me, but somehow a second copy had been ordered and placed on hold for me. I confess that upon my first read of the book, I thought it beautifully designed but uninspiring in content, so I returned the first copy before leaving campus for the summer, left the second copy to be shelved, and once the book was out of sight, it was out of mind.

That summer, I traveled to Cambridge, Massachusetts, where I met up with a friend at a new wine bar in town. We each ordered a glass of wine at the counter, and when I went to pay, I noticed that the card reader was sitting atop two stacked copies of A *Mycological Foray*, complete with decorative splashes of red wine stained across the top and down the sides, like an abstract art piece. I looked around the space and noticed at least a couple dozen copies spread around the room in their own mycelial shape. Some sat in short stacks in the window, serving as a booster for the potted plants reaching toward the sun. Some stood vertically on shelves next to wine bottles, like a blended library of book and bottle. This book, again, sprouting and multiplying around me. I asked the person behind the counter if I could purchase a copy, preferably a wine-stained one. She told me they used to sell them, but they are no longer for sale. It seems these books have rooted here in a mycorrhizal entangling with shelf and bottle and countertop, becoming a permanent installation in the decor. I asked once more, politely, if, since they used to sell them, they would be willing to sell me just one copy. It seemed such a fortuitous encounter with this text that I felt I had to take one of these copies home with me, like a clipping I might let sprout and sprawl through my apartment. "Sorry," she shrugged, "I wouldn't even know how much to charge you." My friend and I then made our way to the patio and after a couple more glasses of wine, my friend encouraged me to steal one. They have so many copies, he pointed out, they won't even notice if I slip away with one. While I was admittedly tempted, like a forager on protected land, to thieve away with one of these mushroom books, I couldn't bring myself to steal from a small business. But I had been infected by the fungal fervor these wine-bar owners seemed to have for Cage's strange book, and I could not stop thinking about it. As soon as I returned home, I purchased a crisp, new copy for myself.

My copy has not multiplied, but I did find inspiration lurking where previously I had not. As I reread the book in my quiet nook, surrounded by the reaching leaves and stalks of my houseplants that live in clusters around my rocking chair, I took notice of how the mushrooms returned me to silence. In the opening essay, "Music Lovers' Field Companion," Cage writes that "much can be learned about music by devoting oneself to the mushroom."[8] And what I already know about Cage is that much of his interest in understanding music is not about understanding the composition of a series of notes but about understanding how sound interrupts silence, how the world is always composing its own kinds of music. Cage also had a budding interest in mycology, and he spent quite a bit of time in the woods of upstate New York foraging for mushrooms and attempting to identify different types of fungi. He combined his adoration of mushrooms with his Zen Buddhist practices and brought both of those elements into his art practices. As Kingston Trinder writes in his essay that is included in *A Mycological Foray*, "Cage remained interested in the relationship between seasonality, composition, decomposition, re-incarnation, Zen Buddhism, silence, and the ego."[9] While in the woods, he "spent many pleasant hours . . . conducting performances of [his] silent piece," letting the sounds of the wind in the foliage, the nearly imperceptible thrum of the mushroom cap, and the movement of animals form the symphonic score.[10] He also wrote a short collection of mushroom poems, with marginal timing, a beat for the reader to follow as they read them aloud like one would perform a piece of music. He describes the poems as "nonsense in the sense of not being ordinary sense. . . . Words which you're used to going in one direction can go in at least two directions. They can be used to set your mind floating."[11] For Cage, words are multidirectional, tentacled like the hyphae and mycorrhizae, and his mushroom poetry seems to have an almost psychedelic effect on him.

Of course, it's impossible to venture into the territory of mushrooms without getting a little weird, whether or not the strangeness is induced by the magic chemicals of the magic mushrooms. We must step out of the ordinary, out of ordinary sense and sensemaking, in order to think in at least two directions (definitely more), in order to think in mycelial dispersion. In a world that insists on linearity, that measures value in how tall the individual tree grows, we cannot forget the way the canopy is an interconnected branching toward one another, full of nests and buds, bundles and hollows. And underground, the roots mingle with rhizomes and mycelia, with worms and nematodes and bacteria. All living and dying together, rotting and eating and

### [Eaten

Rot is a kind of eating, but eating is a way to delay rot, to maintain vitality, to compose the body with the building blocks of nutrition rather than surrender to one's own decomposition, rather than wasting away. And the acts of eating and digesting entail decomposing and breaking down that which is ingested. A whole system of enzymes and bacterial decomposers living within us make our composition possible.[1] Eating is perhaps another way to think of our existence as annihilation—something must always die so that I may live.[2] Or, as Timothy Morton succinctly puts it, "you could eat the beautiful thing, and it would die."[3] Because of the reciprocal nature of eating and rotting, I interrupt the Rot waypoint with a foray within the mycological foray we are already on, to think through some notes on eating and being eaten, to let the Eaten be surrounded by Rot.

## Some Notes on Eating and Being Eaten, a Digression

I once went on a stroll through my neighborhood with a dear friend, a birder. Though we were not necessarily on a birding outing, we continuously pointed out various birds to each other as they astonished us. Near the end of our walk, I pointed to a trio of mourning doves sitting on a utility wire above us. I so rarely see them in threes, as these birds tend to pair off, and I jokingly wondered aloud if they were a queer throuple. My friend took this opportunity to share some fun facts about mourning doves. He recently read that they are the least intelligent of all birds; they have one of the smallest brain-size-to-body-mass ratios, though I am skeptical of that measurement being able to convey anything about actual intelligence. My friend joked that apparently mourning doves are so "stupid," they *exist only to be eaten.*

I have another friend, a philosopher, who wrote a letter to me in which he speculated that Jonah chose to be swallowed by the whale because he wanted to know what it would feel like to belong to something so gigantic and magnificent. Imagine: A willful disobedience of God in order to better know obliteration, to be nothing and to be all, to be in awe. To defy God so one might be swallowed, to essentially ask to be eaten, is—in the teaching of Jonah, anyway—a mercy. But, my friend speculated, in allowing himself to be swallowed, Jonah surely realized that being swallowed by something does not make him belong to it.

---

[1] As Sheldrake puts it, "We are ecosystems, composed of—and decomposed by—an ecology of microbes." *Entangled Life*, 17.

[2] The trading of death for life is true, also, of fungi. As Doug Bierend writes, "The health of certain fungi means the death of or discomfort to something else." *In Search of Mycotopia*, 40.

[3] Morton, "Thank Virus for Symbiosis."

Just like being swallowed by this world does not make us belong to it. The mercy is in being spit out, in not being left to rot in the belly of the beast.

This same philosopher friend and I swap poetry sometimes, and one day, he shared with me "The Well of Grief" by David Whyte. The poem is about how we must dive down in the black water of grief in order to find the light of hope.Foray 12 But too many people refuse to swim under and test the limits of their breath. When a thing scares us, it seems easier to just not do it, to stay on the surface, to follow the straightforward path we've been given. But Whyte suggests that a refusal to face grief is a denial of knowledge, an inability to catch the glimmer of our wishes for something other than what we are. It is to miss the quiet shimmer of possibility in the shroud of mourning. In return, I gave my friend another poem by Whyte, one I return to often and sometimes read aloud to a rhythm that sounds like comfort—"Everything Is Waiting for You." I tell him I want a world in which everything is always there, waiting for everyone, and we can wait beside it or inside it for as long or as little as we need. I want a world in which we don't need grief to help us find the shine. But that is not our world. I fear it never will be. Rather, it seems we are always the ones waiting on the world to either swallow us or spit us out, and still, we will never belong to it, nor it to us.

Nevertheless, we must dream otherwise. How else do we go on? How else do we resist being eaten? I remind myself and my friend, through the poem, that our "great mistake is to act the drama as if we are alone," as if we are staging a solo show.[4] Even when we feel most alone, especially in our grief, we must care about each other and care together. Instead of trying to swallow everyone. Or instead of living as though we were made only to be eaten. Perhaps we battle-cry "Eat the rich!" not because they are beautiful but to avoid being eaten by them first. And, here, we could replace the rich with any dominant class, which dominates by calling us too little, too much, too ugly too ugly too ugly.Foray 1 Still, they will swallow us every chance they get. bell hooks calls it "eating the Other."[5] Some people move through the world with their teeth bared, ready to catch the flesh of others between their

---

[4] Whyte, *Everything Is Waiting for You.*
[5] hooks, *Black Looks.*

canines and incisors, while the rest of us dodge the gnashing jaws. And some learn to bite back.

Sometimes I think I want only to be eaten, to be swallowed by the world, not as a way of belonging to it but as a way of disappearing into it. To be swallowed is a refusal to swallow, myself—or to swallow myself. Roland Barthes writes in fragments of the desire—craving—to be engulfed. When we are swallowed, we are engulfed—by a mouth, by a body, by a hunger that wants to absorb us into its own satisfaction.[6] I wonder if dissolving ourselves into another is a way of piecing ourselves together, a way to feel less like the fragments I write in. To be engulfed is to fuse with the other, the one who does the engulfing. "We die together from loving each other," Barthes writes.[7] We love. We kill and we die together. We eat and are eaten together.

I know people who love animals, and still they eat them. They know when they eat the beautiful thing, it must die—must be killed, really—in order to be eaten. The Polish poet Wisława Szymborska writes in a poem aptly titled "Compulsion": "We eat another life so as to live. / A corpse of pork with departed cabbage. / Every menu is an obituary."[8] Eating is a violence of the mouth. Eating is always a death; something must be decomposed in the process. I am often chastised for being a difficult vegan because I don't eat mushrooms. I do not have any ethical objection to eating mushrooms; I just don't like their texture and flavor, though I do find them beautiful. But maybe I am onto something because it turns out mushrooms are actually more closely related to animals than they are to plants, though they have "long been lumped together with plants," another "category mistake."[9] I will not eat the beautiful animal, nor will I eat the beautiful mushroom, but I eat many other beautiful things: the perfectly ripe flesh of a juicy peach or the brilliant purple pattern of a freshly sliced beet. Maybe to be eaten simply means you were beautiful enough to kill or too beautiful to live. Kaveh Akbar writes, "The barbarism of eating anything / seems almost unbearable."[10] But we must bear it in order to live. Yet, I want to protect the beautiful rather than eat it. Even if it means it might eat me first.

---

6  Barthes, *Lover's Discourse*, 10.

7  Barthes, 11.

8  Szymborska, "Compulsion."

9  Sheldrake, *Entangled Life*, 9.

10  Akbar, "Portrait of the Alcoholic."

Mikhail Bakhtin wrote about the grotesque gaping mouth, a hole in the whole of the body, an abyss wrapped in flesh and bone, a zero, a black hole. Through the mouth, he suggests, "the body swallows the world and is itself swallowed by the world."[11] How to swallow and be swallowed at the same time? How to scream as we swallow the scream?

When I think of being swallowed by the world, I think of the story of Daphne, a young river nymph who loved nothing more than the solitude and unbridled freedom of the open forest, the way her bare feet, in a sprint, spring from the sponge of green mosses, the way her toes dig and lift her from the cool dark loam, the way her lungs take in the herbaceous air, the way the crisp river waters quench her thirst and plump her skin. Daphne (like Tina) lived in a world of pleasures and sought nothing more beyond it.[Foray 9] But one day, Daphne collided with Apollo during her forest jaunt. With a surprised yelp, she turned and ran in the opposite direction. Apollo, under the spell of Eros's golden arrow, chased her through the brush, relentlessly attempting to draw her from the cover of the forest canopy into his demanding arms. Daphne ran and ran deeper into the woodlands, but he stayed hot on her heels. As her endurance flagged, she screamed for help from her father, Peneus, a god of the rivers. She begged him to pry Earth's jaws open so she may be swallowed by the planet rather than be devoured by a man. She pleaded for him to change her form so she may no longer garner the attentions of her lustful pursuer. Anything, she implored, to escape Apollo's clutches. Peneus responded by making of her body a thin-barked trunk, reaching her arms into branches leafed by her hair, radiating roots from her feet, resting her body still in the soil.

In some versions of the story, Daphne prays to her mother Earth, Gaia, to save her from Apollo's unwanted advances. Her mother comes to her rescue, opens the earth to take her in or carries her away to safety, leaving a bay laurel in her place to fool Apollo into believing Daphne had become the tree. And Daphne gets to live on, running free through the forests far, far from Apollo or any man's unwanted advances. She still gets to belong to the world after being swallowed by it. But the story we remember is the one of men, the one in which Daphne is simply swallowed. The story we tell again and again is the one in which

---

[11]  Bakhtin, *Rabelais and His World*, 317.

Daphne's scream becomes a whisper in the rush of wind through her leaves, silencing her into a laurel tree by a man, her father, in order to save her from another man, Apollo, who then plucks the leaves from her branches and wears them as a crown, to have her always in his hair, always against her will.

Eating and becoming tree/being eaten are so closely intertwined. We continue to eat Daphne when we use the bay leaf to season soups and stews. Sam Cohen's short story "Becoming Trees" also recounts the story of Daphne, emphasizing how she wished to remain a virgin. "Can't rape a tree," quips Jan, one of the two main characters who aspire to become trees. The other character, Sarah, responds, describing Daphne's need to escape violent men as "like everything."[12] To escape the everything of a world of violence, the everything of violent men, Jan and Sarah decide to turn themselves into trees. They eat seeds and drink chlorophyll-infused water; they eat the beautiful green things until they become green and vegetal. They sit in the garden and begin to root; the mushrooms huddle around them and whisper that "Mother Earth is dying and that we are all working together to figure out how to revive her," so they stay there, as trees, joining in to do the work to revive the earth on the brink of breathlessness.[13]

Han Kang's novel *The Vegetarian* does not name Daphne, but it tells the story of a woman, Yeong-hye, who attempts to become tree, and it seems that part of her motivation is to escape a world of death (meat), sex, and violence. However, she does not join a mycelial ecology; instead, she is consumed, taken away in an ambulance while the forest around her burns. Yeong-hye stops eating meat, the flesh of animals, when she realizes she can feel "their lives still stubbornly stuck to [her] insides."[14] She then withdraws from sex and from eating entirely and soon finds kinship with trees, who she comes to recognize as her brothers and sisters. She spends long periods in handstands, visualizing herself becoming tree. In the end, her family commits her to a facility in the Korean countryside, where she wastes away, refusing to eat anything, while everyone around her does the strange, abject things of living—eating, drinking, pissing, and shitting.[15]

---

12  Cohen, *Sarahland,* 161.

13  Cohen, 171–72.

14  Kang, *Vegetarian,* 56.

15  Kang, 173.

There is something here about food and sex. Sigmund Freud wrote that the sexual needs of humans and animals (he didn't wonder about the sexual needs of trees or plants or fungi or microbes) are instinctual, like hunger, an "instinct of nutrition."[16] The people in these stories—women, people perceived as women, people raised as girls—chose to starve in multiple senses, "to be longing, rather than belonging."[17] They chose to be swallowed by the earth rather than to be swallowed by men. They unsettle the notion of the plant as passive as they actively transform themselves. I think of how D. J. Savarese unsettles the distinction between active or passive: "That dichotomy is so American. Most people think of disability as an insult to individual autonomy. I think of it as a necessary ecology: I need people, I need the world. I must relate to everything to function. I'm not some admiral of loneliness haughtily sailing across the ocean. Nor am I a sequoia conversing with angels. There are no self-made plants."[18] They make themselves into tree as an act of collaboration, a spreading arborescence necessarily mingled with the ecologies to which we already belong. Maybe, in their longing, we find new appetites rather than starvation. Becoming tree is a way of belonging differently to a world that wants to eat you anyway.

Once, on a psilocybin journey, I lay down on a wooden platform built over a creek. I looked up at the canopy of trees above me as the green of their leaves grew into a neon glow, slowly oozing into a protective bubble around me. I saw the trunks and branches of the trees as ballasts keeping the green orb afloat, and as I looked closer, the trunks became ancient bones, the branches a skeletal network sprouting arboreal flesh. I felt the rigidity of planks beneath me as an ossified and varnished skeleton that cradled my own enfleshed bone. I turned to my lover who lay next to me, and I watched them morph into a tree, their face swirling and merging with the bark of a knotted trunk. The mushrooms huddled inside me, whispering something. *The trees are alive and made of the same stuff we are. We are all already trees.*

---

16 "The fact of the existence of sexual needs in human beings and animals is expressed in biology by the assumption of a 'sexual instinct,' on the analogy of the instinct of nutrition, that is of hunger." Freud, *Three Essays on the Theory of Sexuality*, 1.

17 Berlant, "Starved," 439.

18 Savarese, "Passive Plants."

I think sometimes I tried to turn myself into something like
a man so I wouldn't have to become a tree. But I do not blend
into the forest of men. I might still prefer a vegetal future.[19]
When someone calls me "ma'am" with a sneer rather than as an
accident, or "faggot" or "tranny," the words swallow me. I feel
like I come to belong to them. But I try to swallow them myself,
even as they swallow me. I want to make them belong to me.
Imagine if Jonah nibbled his way out of the whale, consumed his
escape route bit by bit, bite by bite. Or if he could stretch himself
open enough to invert the situation in one big gulp. Suddenly
the whale is inside him. I swish *ma'am* from cheek to cheek, trill
*tranny* off my tongue, chew on *dyke* in the dark corner of my
back molar, gargle *faggot* in the back of my throat. Sometimes I
hold the words in my mouth until I must spit them out, knowing
they will never fully belong to me. Sometimes I gulp them down,
crying, "Mine mine mine."

hooks names the "commodification of difference" as the perpe-
trator of "paradigms of consumption wherein whatever difference
the Other inhabits is eradicated, *via* exchange, by a consumer
cannibalism."[20] There are many ways to eat the other, to feed on
someone else, to kill and be killed. In an analysis of the film *The
Cook, the Thief, His Wife & Her Lover,* directed by Peter Greenaway,
hooks describes the white consumption of Black food as a way
to "flirt with death, to flaunt one's power," thus linking death
and pleasure. "White racism, imperialism, and sexist domination
prevail by courageous consumption. It is by eating the Other (in
this case, death) that one asserts power and privilege." But desire
for pleasure, of all sorts, can also "make resistance possible."[21]
Can eating be a resistance? Is there pleasure in biting back, even
in the violence of it all?

In Sayaka Murata's novel *Earthlings,* we follow Natsuki, a
young girl who must navigate living on planet Earth, where
she feels such intense unbelonging that she adamantly believes
herself to be an alien. She spends her whole life seeking her
spaceship to take her home. Natsuki is sexually abused by a

---

[19] Paul B. Preciado writes, "To be trans is to cease to be a crocodile and to connect with one's vegetal future, to understand that the rainbow can become a
skin." *Can the Monster Speak?,* 46.

[20] hooks, *Black Looks,* 31.

[21] hooks, 36, 39.

teacher who "destroys" and "kills" her mouth.[22] She later murders him in a dissociative post-traumatic moment in which she sneaks into his house and bludgeons him to death while he sleeps, mistaking him for the pupa of a Wicked Witch who she presumes had already eaten the teacher. While slaying the thing she believes swallowed her teacher, she unwittingly kills the man who swallowed her by forcing her to swallow him first. Her motto, repeated like a magic spell: "Survive, whatever it takes!" Sometimes her survival means killing the one who is killing her bit by bit. As she grows older, Natsuki is most intent on avoiding becoming another cog in the machinery of the Factory—her shorthand for the expectations of marrying and having children. She finds an asexual husband and eventually ends up living with him and her cousin on a piece of family property where they all become alien together. The novel ends with a cannibalistic feast—first the trio kills and eats the parents of the schoolteacher who had assaulted Natsuki as a child, then they nibble on each other. Natsuki takes a sip of "Miso Soup with Man" and discovers she can taste for the first time since her mouth was destroyed by her teacher.[23] She declares, "That day, my body became completely my own."[24] Eating the others who tried to eat her first means she finally belongs to herself. After a night of full-bellied sleep, the group awakens to the arrival of Natsuki's mother, sister, and several other people vomiting and screaming in horror at the scene before them. Cradling their round bellies, Natsuki's cousin promises that what is inside of them is also "dormant within you" because we are all always ready to eat before we get eaten.[25] The group steps out into the glow of daylight as "the cries of the Earthlings rang out to the far corners of the planet, setting the forests trembling."[26] Rather than becoming trees, they have set them aquiver. They have survived where they do not belong.

When Barthes is engulfed, he knows there is no place for him. There is nowhere he belongs, "not even in death."[27] Swallowing is not belonging. It is a simple mercy. A living on in no-place. A dying in the face of unbelonging. An offering. I hope only that

---

22  Murata, *Earthlings,* 81, 83.

23  Murata, 237.

24  Murata, 243.

25  Murata, 246.

26  Murata, 247.

27  Barthes, *Lover's Discourse,* 11.

I am beautiful enough to be eaten, to be swallowed into the nothingness I already am, so full, so well-fed. If hooks writes of eating the Other as a consumptive cannibalism, I cannot help but link that consumption to capitalism, which would have our desires always go unquenched so that we must eat each other to survive, to fight not only for resources but also for the top prize. Justin Smith, writing on the possibilities of Black asexuality and absence in the work of Claude McKay, suggests that "there is a way to make ourselves 'well-fed' that is outside capitalism, and for those in the ace community, outside of sex."[28] Can we find a way to be outside without being swallowed? How do we become well-fed without being swallowed by the things we swallow? Maybe we will always exist to eat and be eaten, but that too can be beautiful, to die together, loving each other.*]*

being eaten.

## PARADISE WORLDS BETWEEN LIVING AND DYING

A mycological foray is bound to take us weird places as we wander without a plan. Somehow, I have found myself in paradise—a paradise of rot, that is. Jenny Hval's 2018 novel *Paradise Rot* is set in a fictional otherworld by the name of Aybourne, a seaside university town where the story's main characters convene from all over the world to pursue their studies. Aybourne bears resemblances to an Australian or English city, but really it is a place that is no-place. "There, and not there." The opening line of the novel, which also becomes a refrain throughout the book, immediately throws us into the contradictions of being and not-being somewhere and nowhere, present and absent.[12] So much is there and not there in the story—home, sex, genitalia, body. The narrator, Jo, moves like mycelia—"I had no plan and no map."[13] Even when Jo does find a map, it seems to melt in her hands and proves useless as she wanders the city in circles, always forced to turn back every time she attempts to reach its edges: "Aybourne was beneath me, closed off in all directions, like a chest with no lid."[14] She becomes caught in the dense web of the city, moving in all directions but getting nowhere (and she finds a lot of pleasure there). She also becomes threaded and entangled with her roommate Carral and the space of the old-brewery-turned-loft-apartment

---

[28] J. Smith, "Happiest, Well-Feddest," 70.

they dwell in, a space that echoes and reverbs, that begins rotting and sprouting around them, swallowing them.

Some critics describe the novel as a sexual coming-of-age story, a story of "sexual awakening."[15] But what I find most compelling about the novel is that it is deeply erotic and sensual *without* sex. Even when someone believes sex may have taken place, the actual events of the exchange are blurry and unmemorable. For example, it seems like maybe both Jo and Carral separately had sex with their neighbor, Pym, but Jo, our unreliable narrator, isn't sure if she dreamed it all up. With her lack of memory, we question not only whether sex took place but also whether it was consensual if it did occur. Even when Jo feels as though she is "surrounded by sex," we the readers never see sex occur in the pages.[16] While bodies do blend into one another, a consuming that might easily read as a metaphor for sex, I think these moments of bodily merging and dissolution are more capacious than sexual commingling. There are many ways to eat and be eaten. Throughout the book, bodily intimacies take place often without touch, as if everyone is linked through some sort of invisible network, not unlike an underground mycelium. For example, in the novel's opening, Jo is trying to navigate this new-to-her city, and on the bus, a man falls asleep while slumped in his seat. Each time he nearly slides off the seat, he shimmies back up, dragging his baggy pants further down his hips until finally his pants slide off his hips entirely, exposing his penis, which looks like a "parched tongue."[17] The protruding "flaccid red limb" is a direct contrast to the scene that takes place just before Jo boards the bus. She stands "like a man" in front of the toilet (a receptacle of waste, rot) in the bathroom at her hostel.[18] She muses, "It felt almost strange not to have a dick to pull out through my fly. . . . The dark triangle of pubic hair looked strangely empty, like a half-finished sketch."[19] There, not there. A thirst, a disturbance. On the bus, Jo and others take notice: "Agitation spread between the seats; our bodies started to itch and sweat."[20] A shared intimacy of skin and bodily fluid emerges among the passengers as the agitation reaches through them in all directions. Once the man is removed from the bus, everyone "return[s] to themselves," and Jo is alone again among the crowd, oscillating between a sense of individual self and feeling inseparably connected to the affective and physical world around her.[21]

Jo grows more deeply entrenched in the rhizomatic spread, the and . . . and . . . and of living in this weird, queer world when she

moves in with Carral. Their home is located in an old factory building, which they learn used to be a brewery. Carral warns Jo that "the
house has a life of its own" and the longer we dwell there with Jo and
Carral, the home does indeed come alive, humid and yeasty as it fer-
ments and sprouts molds and mosses and mushrooms.[22] While mushrooms literally sprout up around the apartment, they also appear in
the recurrence of segments of a textbook Jo is reading, *Introductory
Mycology*, that informs the reader of fungi's ability to reproduce
both sexually and asexually, to spread and overtake its environment
through the distribution of spores. The fungus starts to invade their
bodies, as Jo feels like something is sprouting under her skin after
Carral kisses her cheek, and at the end of the novel, Jo notices that
the honey fungus that had been growing on the bathtub is now growing in Carral's mouth. Jo takes deeper and deeper notice of "the living all around the house" as she watches a spider on the windowsill,
imagines beetles living inside the walls, and, she observes, "in the
kettle on the kitchen counter the water had begun to bubble, a sign
that I was among the living."[23] The fungus needs the beetle needs the
tree needs the soil needs the fungus needs the beetle needs the tree,
and so on.

Jo's body and vitality start to become indistinguishable from the
networked ecology that shapes the world and home she inhabits—
sometimes it seems like the sea is inside their home, sometimes Jo
feels as if the sky has filled her mouth; she consumes and is consumed
by the world via exchange. "The house was raw and porous," she observes, or "maybe it wasn't the house but me that was porous."[24] Jo's
porosity becomes more apparent as she and Carral start to blend and
bleed into one another. Jo notices that she begins to walk like Carral
and talk like Carral, as one of her classmates points out how her ac-
cent changes around Carral. When Carral eats or drinks something,
Jo can taste it in her own mouth. She can feel Carral's pulse in the
stain she left on the page of a romance book she is reading. She can
hear and smell Carral everywhere in the apartment, as the sounds
of her urine echo until Carral's urine is spilling over into Jo's bed.
Everything is ripe and raw. Mina Tavakoli writes in a review of the
book, "In art, and in practice, the abject refers to the monstrous, hor-
rific, literally repulsive stuff—corpses and blood and slurry—that one
'thrusts aside in order to live.' But abjection—to Carral, by proxy Jo
and more broadly, to Jenny Hval—is life itself."[25] Abjection, according
to Julia Kristeva, also dissolves boundaries (like the skin), blurs in-

side and outside.[26] They go on living the mundane and abject—eating, drinking, pissing, shitting—inside this home, a damp, hot contrast to the dry, wintry outside world, and in the process, they dissolve into one another, swallowed and swallowing.

At some point, Carral brings home a bag of apples that begin to lodge themselves all over the apartment and rot. The apples call up the story of Eve in the garden of Eden, and Carral even exclaims that this must be some kind of paradise among this bounty of fruit. But the fruit rots, not as a metaphor for lost virginity but as a reminder that "an apple is never just an apple."[27] An apple is already rotting from the moment it is plucked from the tree, ready to be eaten, whether by a human, an animal, or a colony of bacteria, molds, and fungi. An excerpt from their neighbor Pym's writing contains the line "Can't see the difference between people and trees."[28] We are all already trees. The apples invade Jo's dreams, and in the dark, her body "slowly transforms into fruit," ready to be eaten.[29] While reading her *Introductory Mycology* textbook, Jo compares Pym's body to fungi as she tries to remember what he looked like naked (the lack of memory another testament to the uncertainty of whether non-consensual sex took place or if any sex took place at all; Jo feels as though the brewery is trying to convince her it had happened when her body "wasn't persuasive").[30] Jo muses how the book "listed fungi parts, reeling them off almost like a nursery rhyme, and while I read the new words I imagined Pym's build: *Fruit bodies* (forearms), *hyphae* (freckles), *mycelium* (chest hair), *chitin* (the firm bulge pushing against me under his jeans), but I couldn't get any further."[31] There is a blur of trauma, an inability to go any further, an uncertainty of memory that overlaps with Carral's depression and illness that brings on lethargy as she retreats into her books and into herself. Carral and Jo recoil from Pym and, despite their best efforts to withdraw from one another, they spread into each other as the outside world creeps into their home. Can't see the difference between people and fungi, people and trees, people and animals, people and plants. There is a kind of crip communion in the way they all become "mad" together as they fold into one another, everything decomposing around them, dissolving into each other, composing and decomposing one another, being swallowed by the hostile world. It's everything.

In the consumptive exchange, Jo sometimes feels like Carral wants to pull Jo inside of her, but she simultaneously feels Carral entering her body: "Her stalks and fingers and veins spread through my entire body like a new soft skeleton."[32] As Jo looks at Carral, she witnesses her fate, for it appears that Carral has already consumed Pym: "Under her white skin I can still see Pym's freckles and Pym's cheekbones. Pym's red eyes flicker behind her eyelids. Inside her mouth I see the honey fungus, like a rotting black tongue."[33] In the end, Jo seeks a way out, but it turns out she will always be threaded to Carral and to the brewery. She begins by trying to restore Carral to herself. Jo plucks the honey mushroom from Carral's mouth and tries to suck both Pym and herself out of Carral, but then she blows outward, filling Carral with air that she imagines is void such that "not a single trace of Pym, or, [herself], remains." But won't they always remain? Is her revitalizing breath truly empty, especially empty of her and Pym, whom she also carries within her? When Jo leaves, she feels as though she has "roots in the house that are stretched long behind [her]." As she pulls herself farther and farther away from the brewery and from Carral, she feels the roots stretch, as they "get thinner and thinner until they are as fine as a thread." Like the fine thread of the mycelium. She imagines that the brewery crumbles and follows her, "threading itself on [her] cord as though it's a house built from small gleaming beads. . . . And Carral follows too. She crumbles in the bathtub. Tooth by tooth, nail by nail, bone by bone. And new beads grow, threading themselves on [Jo's] roots. The beads appear from her mouth and eyes, her crotch, hip socket and fingertips."[34] Even if the other swallows us and spits us out, they leave an indelible mark, a trace we will carry with us always. Once we entwine with someone, they can never become absent. Barthes writes that the emotion of absence is a sigh, "'to sigh for the bodily presence': the two halves of the androgyne sigh for each other, as if each breath, being incomplete, sought to mingle with the other."[35] Carral and Jo are still mingled in the breath Jo left behind. But, in the end, Jo imagines that she has split into two selves, one that leaves and returns to Norway and the other that remains in the brewery. Of the one who remains, Jo describes, "her face is white, covered in lime, algae skeletons, beer froth, and sea foam."[36] Mossed and yeasted, symbiotically living in a place of unbelonging.

Perhaps we are always already split selves, leaving our remains wherever we once dwelled, leaving traces of ourselves in others and in the trees; the trees, the sea, the soil in us. Like fungi, we are "multifarious." Fungi "know no borders, insinuating themselves throughout and between overlapping ecologies."[37] And we are permeated by the invisible: "Fungi are all around us, no matter the season. They permeate plants and soils, just as their spores fill the air and are taken in with our breath."[38] They consume us as we consume them. Perhaps we too should forget borders, move like mycelia, think like mycelial networks, spread outward in queer nonsexual formations of intimacy, relationality, and world-building that make the world look differently viable between living and dying. Such is the gift of the mushroom; their "uncontrolled lives" are a "guide when the controlled world we thought we had fails."[39] Mycelial thinking (and living) asks us also to pay attention differently, to notice, again, what we've been distracted from noticing.[Foray 10] Yes, look up and be astonished by the birds in the treetops, but also look down, underneath, and be astonished by all that moves and dwells there in the design of the fungal filigree, be astonished in that "gulf between what we expect to find and what we find when we actually look."[40] Paradise also rots, as do we within it. It is both a horror and a pleasure. And that is how we love, by dying together.[41]

# ~~Redacted~~

In the reading room at the ███████████████████████ Library, I sort through the papers and belongings of ███████████████. Because ██████████████████ is still alive, there are several folders that have a neon piece of acid-free paper inserted into them to alert the viewer that any items that would constitute an invasion of privacy have been closed until a date well beyond this person's possible lifespan. At first, I thought this notice meant there would be unknowable items missing from the folders, but the documents that follow these bright yellow flags are labeled at the top as "[Redacted Use Copy]." Most of these documents are legal forms or medical records with many different entries and many incomplete fields such that it is at first difficult for me to discern what exactly had been redacted—there are no conspicuous thick black rectangles blotting out text. I ask an archivist about whether there are materials missing or if these redacted use copies are the whole of the closed records, and if so, how could I even tell what had been redacted from them. The archivist tells me all the materials are there, and it was just private information that had been removed. Then they show me how, on one form, the field for a Social Security number was whited out. The whitening out of the numbers blends so neatly into the white space of the entry field in this photocopied edition that I couldn't initially tell information had been redacted. As I continue working through the materials, I develop an eye for these redactions. I notice the invisible space where a signature or Social Security number should be. I even begin to pick up on the occasional, barely perceptible marks of the redaction, such as where the piece of paper used to cover the information was applied slightly askew, creating a white interruption on the solid black line that was meant to hold the name or numbers, or where the copy machine stuttered just a bit and left a trace of static, a tiny smattering of small dots lightly pimpling the otherwise white space. I must train myself to look for the missing items, especially when the things that have been redacted are not something I was already on the lookout for. In this process, I learn to see absence in the archive differently.

On archival absences, my thinking here takes a detour to the story Avery F. Gordon tells of taking her own detour to chase the ghost of Sabina Spielrein. After happening upon a photograph of the 1911 International Psychoanalytic Congress at Weimar, Gordon notices that Spielrein is absent from the photograph, though she should have been there at that congress. In telling the story, Gordon repeats three times, as if casting a spell, "There's photographic evidence of her absence."[1] Spielrein is not redacted from the photograph; her face is not blotted out—she was never there to begin with. But there is still a trace (evidence) of her absence in the photograph. Following the ghostly trace with Gordon, we learn of the ways Spielrein has been redacted from the history of psychoanalysis, how she has been left out of the story, and how attempts to recuperate her story also leave so much out. For example, Gordon first finds Spielrein in the book *A Secret Symmetry*, which tells the story of Spielrein's falling in love with Carl Jung and then confiding in Sigmund Freud, thus arguably influencing both men's thinking and "chang[ing] the early history of psychoanalysis."[2] But, Gordon notices, the advertisement for the book does not mention that Spielrein "wrote about the death drive ten years before Freud published his seminal work on the death instinct," or that her love affair with Jung might have been the thing that "cured" her, or that she is not in the Weimar Congress photograph in 1911, which is the year she also finished her dissertation.[3] The photograph serves as evidence of her absence beyond the portrait of earnest psychoanalysts captured that day in Weimar. From one absence, a ghostly presence, we learn of so many other redactions. We find a woman who contributed so much to an enduring field of thought yet is dismissed as a mere nuisance getting in the way of two brilliant men. She becomes "nothing" to them, contributing "nothing," even as they stole so much from her.

We do not always know what is not there, but sometimes we do. Someone who should be in a photograph is not. A document that should be in a folder is gone. Who took it? Where did it disappear to? Carolyn Steedman suggests that Jacques Derrida's *Mal d'archive* (*Archive Fever*) teaches us something very important about the archive's nothings and disappearances: "that if we find nothing, we will find nothing in a place; and then, that an absence is not *nothing*, but is rather the space left by what has gone: how the emptiness indicates how once it was filled and animated."[4] In other words, nothing is found somewhere, it is a thing missing from a place where it once was or should have been. It might even be something (or someone) stolen that demands its due.[5] The absence is the mark of a once-presence. If we follow the absences, the ghosts, the traces, we might find what was meant to fill the space, what once existed there, or what else was erased and left out in the process. However, we cannot be sure what other irretrievable remains are still out there, masquerading as nothing, kept intentionally hidden from view. Maybe we will always only have fragments and pieces; the rest is left to our imagination.[6]

Let me meander back to the reading room of ███████████████ ███████ Library. I recount my time there with its own redactions— I do not need to name the library nor this particular person whose information has been redacted because those facts are not germane to this story. I am not concerned with the archival practices of that particular library, and the details of that individual's life story belong to another book on another topic in another time. (I also wish to protect the identity of this living person, in addition to being ethically obliged to.) Rather, those papers matter to me here and now because of the way they have invited me to think about redaction, especially within the many other types of silences and erasures of the archive. The reading room is a quiet place. There is an ambient symphony of the turning of pages, the scratching of a pencil, the click of a camera, the tapping of a keyboard, the occasional clearing of a throat, the rare, whispered question to an archivist or assistant. Otherwise, it is a hushed room. As much as it is a collection of things that were saved, the archive is also a reminder of all that was not saved or stored there. We cannot know what was not kept or why it disappeared. We cannot know all that was lost or erased from historical preservation. We cannot know what is absent if there is no trace. Sometimes a trace exists, but it takes a keen eye to see it. Seeing a trace is a way of seeing nothing. In the archive, we must learn to listen and look for traces—a bit of marginalia, an eraser mark, someone who should be in a photograph but isn't, a mention in a letter or diary of things, places, or people that no longer exist—and then figure out what to do with them.[7]

Sometimes a redaction is a necessary protection, and sometimes it is a violence, an attempt at eradication. It can also be used as "protection" for the guilty, to try to keep someone from doing something (seeking justice or retribution) with something (information or evidence). In the colonial archive, so much is recorded but so much is also redacted, especially anything that might incriminate the colonial state. On redaction, Solmaz Sharif writes how she always thought of erasure as "what a state does." If erasure and redaction are acts of "obliteration," a word, Sharif observes, that bears the Latinate roots that translate to "the striking out of text," then, Sharif suggests, "historically, the striking out of text is the root of obliterating peoples."[8] To eliminate text is to eliminate a record, which contains some forms of knowledge and composes certain histories. To eradicate a record is to annihilate (or at least attempt to annihilate) whole persons, peoples, and cultures. But in the wake of the striking: a trace, a mark, a scar. Muriel Leung writes, "Tell me about disappearance, and I will tell you about palimpsests. Everything we try to erase still manages to leave something behind."[9] Sharif similarly observes that the very form of erasure is palimpsest, which means there will always be a trace, an absence, a ghost to follow. Sharif writes, "The ghost is not only death or degradations of time—the ghost is the state itself."[10] In the process of censorship and obliteration, the state becomes an invisible, insidious actor. Or, as Leung puts it, colonial violence is "so deep and lingering that it drapes itself over the land, and no withering of time can deny its indelible imprint."[11] Sometimes it's not only that we cannot tell what, if anything, has been redacted but also that there is no obvious sign of who did the erasing.

Redaction is not only something a state does; it can also be a response to state and colonial violence, a way to draw attention to the insidious deletions, or to refuse to be erased. Poets, writers, and artists have worked with erasure as a way to recuperate something from the state, whether that is through turning the tables of power and enacting their own erasures on state documents or trying to decipher the historical clues hiding behind the black rectangles, scratches, *X*'s, or whiteout correction tape.[12] Redaction then becomes a way to create new presence and new meaning from within the sites of erasure. As Leung notes, "To make something new from these old bones will always be a political act, either to liberate the text from its original meaning or to reinscribe the violence in another form."[13] If we focus on the ways erasure art created by the historically erased offers a way to liberate the text, one might think of it as a way to be obliterated in an infinity net of existence *as* annihilation, a mode of being.[14] It is a way to change the narrative, to rewrite and recount the story, to both erase what has been unjustly added and reclaim what has been unjustly taken away. Sharif offers an incomplete list of "possible political and aesthetic objectives of poetic erasure," which include bringing back the dead or resurrecting ghosts by "collaps[ing] time and instance between dead and living," highlighting silences and erasures and thereby exposing authority and culpability, caring for the remainders, and rendering a text incomplete such that it invites reader collaboration.[15] The arts of redaction and erasure unsettle allegedly neat divisions between presence and absence and repurpose the tools of power to lay claims to "declarative silences" and "rights to opacity."[16] Those who have had so much taken away get to choose what to keep for themselves and what to reveal.[17]

I learn from a new ▇▇▇, the same person who shared Sharif's essay with me, that there is a particular kind of ink used for redaction. It is a more secure ink that will completely black out the information in a way that multiple passes with a regular black marker never can. In a work that plays with the multidirectionality of redaction, artist Abigail Raphael Collins used redaction ink to compose what appears to be a redacted portrait of her father, a method actor who often played the roles of military men on television. The portrait is a kind of companion piece to Collins's 2024 experimental documentary film *Black Out,* which explores the feedback loop between the entertainment industry and the U.S. military. In the film, Collins tells her father that as a child, she believed he was actually in the military because of the roles he played and the way he lived his characters at home. The line between being and doing (as in acting or playing at) is blurred. The military presence, a manifestation of the state, is present even if authentically absent. In the portrait, the line between redaction and appearance is muddled. The portrait appears in black rectangles drawn with redaction ink. The very tool that is used to block out (obliterate) text and bodies is, in this case, used to make visible glimpses of a body—a face that, since watching the film, I immediately recognize as the face of her father, a kind of military man. The white of the paper that the portrait is composed on then has the inverse effect of seeming to whiteout or redact the full image, though the image is only partial to begin with. The roles of the ink and paper are nearly reversed; the image is made visible

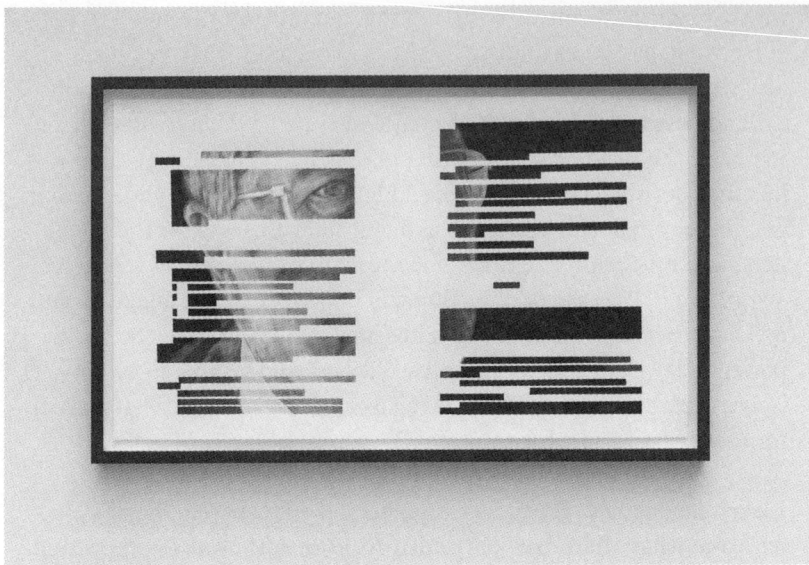

**FIGURE 4.** Abigail Raphael Collins, *It Was Being Handled*, 2024.
Redaction ink on paper, 40 in. × 23 in. Photograph by Yubo Dong/
ofstudio photography. Courtesy of the artist.

with ink that is meant to do the invisibilizing work that the white
paper appears to be doing. Collins tells me that the white paper offers a way to "think about the structures that become invisible to us,
that are doing the most censorship."[18] While the white symbolizes
the insidious manifestation of state power (and whiteness) through
censorship, the black ink, which is typically used to censor, highlights
a symbol of state power through the apparent military figure. But her
father is not really in the military; he is an actor, an entertainer. His
(fragmented) presence is part of the show. Militarized state violence
is spectral, emerging in the traces of the story, but it does not compose the full story.

Notably, the eyes in Collins's portrait are visible, one slightly
more obscured than the other, but nonetheless, we can look into her
rendition of her father's eyes. Leaving the eyes visible is another inversion of typical redaction practices. The eyes are painted with redaction ink that would otherwise be used to create a dark rectangle
across the eyes, or sometimes a whole face is blurred while a body is

left whole and visible, as if it only takes the obliteration of the eyes or the face to erase a person.

A small digression: I think about how Aaron Apps answers back to this method of redaction in medical documentation by altering the image of an intersex person whose face is out of focus in the background of the frame, while in the foreground the shot focuses on the genitals being held between the thumb and forefinger of a disembodied hand, "like a ripe fig between a pinch."[19] In a sequence of altered photographs, Apps first displays the full photo, followed by a cropped square image of the hand grasping the genitals. Next comes a cropped closeup of the out-of-focus face on one page and a cropped closeup of the genitals, with the hand removed from the image, on the adjacent page. In the final two images, the cropped hand holding the genitals is layered over the face, and then the hand is removed, leaving the final image with the genitals alone layered over the face.[20] The genital appendage is placed right over the nose and mouth, so the eyes, though blurry and out of focus, remain visible. The genital image does not fully redact the face but brings both face and genitals to the fore. In the accompanying text, Apps writes, "I say that the doctor makes the face and genitals the same thing. . . . I was soft inside of a flesh fold folding outwards into a sphere. To fold and unfold as an affected thing is a matter of residence amid things that reside."[21] In this series of alterations and redactions, state power haunts the images through the manifestation of medical violence, represented by the disembodied hand and the not-quite-redacted out-of-focus face. The subject becomes a spectacle object for medical study, medical fixation, and medical fixing as the doctor prepares to surgically alter the genitals to make them conform to a binary sex model.[22] Apps simultaneously asks his readers to see the person there by looking at both the face and the genitals as one while also critiquing the way medical violence and censorship have been used to obliterate intersex people. In the folds, between attempted redactions, we find the flesh fragments that reside; we find ways to reside (dwell) in the shards.[23]

Leaving the eyes present, as in Collins's portrait (and in Apps's effort to bring them into the foreground, though still out of focus), asks the viewer to not only look but to see, to encounter the subjectivity of the subject often made into expendable object through redaction. What are you looking at? Who are you looking at? The eyes are folded into flesh, an affected body, revealing the something that is always present under the blur, behind the redaction ink. The something that refuses to be obliterated, even if it means remaining in fragments.

Zeb Tortorici suggests that we are more seduced by the "fragments and absences" of the archive than by what might appear to be complete and whole case studies.[24] Of course, there is something enticing about the mystery; there is thrill in the ghost hunt. And the fragments leave plenty of room to either fill in the blanks or to embrace what must remain unknown or untold. In other words, as Tortorici puts it, "incomplete archival fragments seduce us with their realms of possibility."[25] Again, in the gaps we find proliferation and infinite possibility instead of lack. A whole story is always full of holes, made brilliant by the quality of glue that holds the pieces together.[26] Tortorici also claims that "archival fragments dealing with sex and desire among minoritized subjects" are "particularly alluring."[27] If what is alluring about fragments is both how little they reveal and how much they fail to tell, then I think there might also be something equally alluring about absences of sex and sexual desire because it leaves so much open to question: Did they or didn't they? Were they hiding something? What did this or that relationship mean?, etc. And so often, as Benjamin Kahan notes with readings of celibacies, the tendency is to map closeted homosexual desire onto an absence that betrays no presence of sexual desire or activity.[28] Thus, again, we have to learn to see absence in the archive differently by also reframing what seduces and allures. In fact, Tortorici writes that "archival seductions can be potentially radical in terms of methodology and theorization, especially when they allow for a historiography of sexuality and an interrogation of archival space that challenge rather than confirm the historical legibility of past desires."[29] Though Tortorici is primarily focused on queer archives via the traces of homosexuality hiding there, the challenge to historical legibility he calls for strikes me as quite fitting to a search for asexual and nonsexual desires, which are often rendered illegible in the emphasis on rooting out sexual desire from the archive. And if we begin with that one obliteration, what other historical redactions might we find along the way?

Where am I going with this? Nowhere. That should be obvious by now. But there is a story here, and I need to figure out how to tell it. I am trying to glue these pieces together. It is a story about a ghost (or two ghosts, maybe) whose shimmering trace haunts me, persistently peeking out from the gaps in the story, telling me there is something lurking that has gone unspoken but is whispering at the edges. It is a story that sits at a turn of a century, shortly after the United States took shape as a nation-state and its citizens became governable under the authority of a newly forming regime distilled from an inheritance of various imperial powers. It is a story of shape-shifting and gender uncertainty and the refusal of sex, even as the nation ushered in discrete categories to sort and manage people. It is a story that moves between two archives. One is the more traditional archive that holds the papers and belongings of someone long dead, though this someone died twice, first in the late eighteenth century and then again in the early nineteenth century, so there is a discrepancy on how long ago we might describe the death to have happened and there is a question of who died and when. The other is the piecemeal and mostly digital archive of twentieth- and twenty-first-century stories that have been told about this figure, a reanimation of the ghosts. It is also a story of finding what wasn't supposed to be there in the archive, what had been declared "gone" by so many historians who came before, and also of not finding what was supposed to be there. I have taken many detours up to this point, and I will take many more along the way, or maybe this story of my own ghost hunt *is* the detour. I digress.

One way to begin this story is with a fragment: the first ghost encounter.

A friend sent me an Instagram post that detailed the life of what my friend described as a "nonbinary, celibate saint" in colonial America known as the Public Universal Friend, also referred to as the Friend, for short. This story seemed to sit perfectly at the intersection of my interests in trans life and asexuality. I snapped a screenshot (the start of my own archive on the Friend) with the goal of looking into it all a little more deeply. I began my research with a quick internet search, which revealed an explosion of stories of the Friend in popular media across late 2019 and early 2020. These media bites seemed to compose a whole new archive of the Friend's life, with more conflicting and fragmented stories to tell. What I found in this new archive was a widespread fervor to claim the Friend as "nonbinary" in order to gesture toward a tale of long-existing nonbinary life in America's past.

The Instagram post, from the @h_e_r_s_t_o_r_y account, describes the Friend as an "American Quaker and evangelist" who preached "sexual abstinence," identified as "both man and woman," and "used They/Them pronouns."[30] Other recent stories include Samantha Schmidt's *Washington Post* piece from January 5, 2020, titled "A Genderless Prophet Drew Hundreds of Followers Long Before the Age of Nonbinary Pronouns"; a feature story by Siobhan on the queer website Autostraddle published April 7, 2020, "The Public Universal Friend: A Deep Dive on a Story of Nonbinary Identity, Quakerism and Near-Death Experiences," which includes an embedded video of Jessica Kellgren-Fozard's YouTube vlog from December 19, 2019, titled "Non-Binary and Religious: The Public Universal Friend"; an episode of Margaret Killjoy's podcast *Cool People Who Did Cool Stuff,* "The Public Universal Friend: A Non-Binary Icon in Revolutionary-Era America" from June 2022; and a 2020 episode of NPR's *Throughline,* hosted by Rund Abdelfatah and Ramtin Arablouei, a show with the tagline, "Where we go back in time to understand the present." In each of these instances, going back in time to the story of the Friend largely operates as an attempt to recuperate a history that explains present formulations of nonbinary gender and the singular *they* pronoun.

However, the Friend did not use *they/them* pronouns at all but was sometimes referred to with either *he* or *she* or, more commonly, with no pronoun whatsoever. The majority of the writings left behind by the Friend's followers, the Society of Friends, simply refer to the Friend as "the Friend." In the papers of the Society of Friends, when a pronoun is used for the Friend, there is often a double pronoun used, written as "her him," as a way to accommodate the limitations of either singular pronoun since this community at that point in time was not prone to use the singular *they* pronoun. In fact, Karen Barzman suggests that such usage of both pronouns might be a precursor to the practice that would come later in the English language of writing "her/him" or "she/he" when referring to a subject who is not specifically gendered.[31] What's more, as I will elaborate on, the Friend is more accurately described as "genderless," not as both man and woman, and questionably "nonbinary," depending on how one defines *nonbinary* and how willing one is to transport that term back to the eighteenth and nineteenth centuries. As Scott Larson aptly puts it in an interview for the *Arch Street Meeting House: Untold Stories in Quaker History* podcast, he would not necessarily say the Friend is transgender, but the Friend is a part of transgender history.[32] Similarly, I hesitate to label the Friend nonbinary, but I understand how the Friend may be considered a part of a nonbinary history, insofar as we understand *nonbinary* as a movement away from gender. Nevertheless, what I might suggest is that I entered the archive of the Friend expecting to find some early iteration of a genderqueer usage of *they/them* pronouns, and it was not there because it never existed. Rather, that story was imposed on the absent evidence.[33]

Another way to begin this story is with a gathering of facts.

A girl by the name of Jemima Wilkinson was born into a Quaker family in Cumberland, Rhode Island, in 1752. Various accounts describe her as a religious but somewhat rebellious girl who even into her twenties had not yet married, which was uncommon for young women in that period. Then in 1776, just a month or so before her twenty-fourth birthday, Wilkinson was suddenly struck by a fever that burned through her body and left her bedridden for days. Just when her family had given up hope and braced themselves for what they thought would be her demise, Wilkinson leaped from her bed, seemingly fully recovered. But the person they rushed to embrace claimed to no longer be Jemima Wilkinson. Instead, the figure announced that Wilkinson had in fact died and the spirit of a genderless holy prophet had been sent into her body, heretofore to be referred to as the Public Universal Friend. The Friend then went on to gather a devout following, eventually settling the land of the Seneca Nation in what is now the Finger Lakes region of upstate New York. This Society of Friends then founded a new town there called Jerusalem where the body of the Friend eventually died in 1819.[34]

Another way to begin this story is with a declaration of absence rather than an imposition: "The illness is gone."

Historian Paul Moyer makes this statement in the opening segment of the NPR *Throughline* episode devoted to the life and story of the

Public Universal Friend.[35] Moyer's statement is seemingly unremarkable as the tale of the Public Universal Friend often begins with
a declaration of an ending—the fever cools, the sickness retreats,
Jemima Wilkinson dies. But then a new beginning in the wake of the
departed illness: In her body is born the genderless spirt of the Public
Universal Friend. But what if the illness is not gone? Everything that
was once there leaves a trace, right? How does illness leave its mark?
Is it a bigger piece of the story than it's made out to be? Is it more
than a singular event? How does illness keep happening even when it
is no longer definitively present?

If Wilkinson had not become ill, it is unclear if the Friend would
have ever come to exist. There seems to be a "queer silence" here
in the Friend's story in the sense that, as J. Logan Smilges writes,
silence and disability (and I will add, by crip extension, illness) are
"rendered virtually unthinkable as objects of sustained queer critique
because their absence is foundational to queer studies."[36] In every recent queer, trans, and nonbinary rendition of the Friend's story, the
Friend's history of illness is rendered inconsequential and seemingly
unthinkable or unrelated to queerness. Yet it is foundational to the
story. So much is built on top of a foundational absence. So much
made out of what was dismissed as nothing. The elision of the crip
fragment in the tale neglects the way gender, sexual abstinence, religiosity, and illness coconstitute the story of the Friend; we cannot
have any one of those without the others; they are glued together.

Another way to tell this story is through a redaction of ~~gender~~.

Larson complicates the nonbinary/transgender narrative by describing the Friend as "a figure at once performing gender ambiguity and
divinity beyond gender."[37] Although one may interpret nonbinary as
beyond gender, or as a movement away from gender, our very ability to conceive of nonbinary today presupposes a gender binary. Additionally, one point of agreement I find in Kadji Amin's ungraceful
take in "We Are All Nonbinary" is the idea that "nonbinary" tends
to get configured as yet another gender identification, thus reifying
Western colonial gender categories rather than abolishing, undoing,
or redoing gender.[38] Further, as Greta Lafleur reminds us, the very
concept of a gender binary is not contemporaneous to early modern
figures like the Friend, as the gender binary is an invention of the
late nineteenth and early twentieth centuries. Instead, LaFleur sug-

gests we "sit with the terms that these figures developed for themselves."[39] The terms the Friend developed to describe the self was as a genderless holy spirit that had taken up residence in Jemima Wilkinson's body.

Thus, the nonbinary gendering of the Friend, as illustrated in the many contemporary iterations of the story, is arguably not merely a displacement of gender definitions and categories across time but also a misgendering by way of gendering the Friend as nonbinary. Kit Heyam writes, "The Friend was not a person, but a spirit; hence it's more accurate to speak about them as genderless than as nonbinary."[40] Instead of living between gender, the Friend lived outside of it, as well as outside the human . . . but still "in time." Within the Society of Friends, they referred to death as "leaving time" or being "snatched out of time," and so to go on living was to "remain in time."[41] Because the Friend was an eternal spirit temporarily inhabiting the mortal body of Jemima Wilkinson, the ethereal being entered time as a dimension tied to the materiality of the body and life on earth. A kind of spacetimemattering. A place to live in unbelonging. Time becomes a mere moment in eternity to move through. The Friend, like all other eternal souls, would thus leave time and place and matter when the body of Wilkinson died. As long as the Friend was "in time," the descent into the body was a temporary inhabitance rather than a *being*. As such, the Friend was able to simultaneously and inextricably disavow human beingness and its attendant sex and gender. Thus, to gender the Friend is to alchemize a spirit into flesh, to attempt to fix the Friend into the category of the human by affixing that beingness to gender.[42]

Another way to tell this story is by following the traces in the absence of illness.

If genderlessness and spiritual being are knitted together, then illness must also be woven into this tapestry. The embodied experience of illness or disability and spirituality becomes almost impossible to disambiguate. Writing on the prevalence of consumption as an archetypal disease among eighteenth- and nineteenth-century evangelicals, Susan Juster describes how the "consumptive" state "worked much like the spirit itself—'agitating,' 'seizing,' and 'invading' the body at its weakest points."[43] This is not to metaphorize illness through the spiritual but to instead bring a crip attentiveness to the embodied experiences of illness and spiritual ecstasy that often present similarly in a physical seizing of the body. The resemblance between bodily suffering through severe illness and spiritual ecstasy is so strong that Juster remarks, "it is difficult to know where physical discomfort leaves off and spiritual enlightenment begins."[44] This shrinkage of the space between illness and enlightenment is about the similarity in the felt experience of both pain and rapture, not an argument that sick or disabled people are somehow more enlightened or closer to some sense of godliness (although it is worth noting that trans, sick, and disabled people often bear a familiar relationship to the notion of bodily transcendence, often experienced as dissociation to cope with varying pains—emotional, psychic, and physical—that might accompany the experience of being trans, queer, or crip in the world). But more to the point, just as I have argued that the Friend's gender and sexuality (or lack thereof) cannot be separated from the narrative of illness, so too must we understand that the experience of illness (and its ties to gender) cannot be separated from the spiritual and religious context of the time in which the Friend was living.

More than any kind of transition of gender, Jemima Wilkinson experienced a transition of being. To deny this spiritual transfiguration in the Friend's story is to essentially deny the impact of illness and a kind of death and rebirth that resulted from it. The Friend was born in illness. But this is not a mere plot point to move on from. The illness is not gone; the illness is inextricably tied to the Friend's ongoingness as a genderless being. Further, as a transcendent being whose preachings also derived from the Quaker faith, sexual abstinence and celibacy were core to the Friend's theology and bodily inhabitance. The Friend was traveling in Wilkinson's body to spread the word of salvation, not to indulge the pleasures of the body—dress, diet, and way of life were all simple, plain, and unadorned. Spirit, sex, and gender are all molded by the ongoing mark of illness. And even more literally, illness does not remain absent from the Friend's life, as the Friend goes on to work as healer of the ill and ailing but also later succumbs to death, or leaves time, after several years of increasing debilitation due to chronic edema. What I therefore offer here is a crip approach to the story that centers illness as inseparably linked to the (a)gendered and religious threads that have to date received the most due attention. The ongoingness of the body the Friend inhabits is an enduring relation with illness, corporeality, and persistence through time. The story must return again and again to illness rather than begin with its end.

To be clear, I am following Smilges's provocation that disability may be "the bedrock of *queer*"; I am not arguing that queerness is a result of illness, that queer people are "sick" in some way, or that those who believe they have achieved some sort of spiritual trans-mogrification are "sick" or "crazy."[45] Rather, to assert disability as the bedrock of queerness is to reveal how the pressures of cure, heal-ing, and fixing the body into legible categories of gender, sexuality, and wellness often silence and erase a queer embrace of the formative impacts of illness. What I ask us to do here is sit with the possibility that some of us may be coconstituted as queer through our experi-ences of illness, disability, and debility. I argue that a crip attention to bodily entanglements of gender, spirit, and health cannot leave ill-ness behind. Instead, illness can change a bodymind (or a soul) and is often an unforgettable part of the dense webs and patterns of our making. Restaking claims to the life impact of illness and refusing its erasure is not to pathologize or seek cure but to recognize the impact and centrality of sickness and wellness to how we become possible in the world and what worlds we make possible for different ways of dwelling.[46] We must shift our understanding of illness from some-thing that either merely passes or remains chronic and thus disabling to an ongoing embodied experience that leaves a trace even in its ap-parent absence.[47] The illness is not gone. Never gone.

Another way to tell this story is through a list of additional redactions that offer more fragmented glimpses into this patchworked narrative.

- A settler oversight.

Most of the recent retellings in the new queer archive of the Public Universal Friend omit the role the Friend and followers played as settlers when they moved into the Finger Lakes region of New York, as they purchased land from settlers who had already stolen it in an unfair treaty deal with the Seneca Nation. While the major-ity of the stories focused on reclaiming an early nonbinary identity bypass this fact just as they bypass the fact of the role of illness, T Fleischmann tells this story of land acquisition by the Society of Friends and also cites Scott Larson as being one of the few historians who names the Friend's role as a settler.[48] If we look back into earlier feminist versions or religious histories, there are a range of accounts that offer a complicated narrative of the Friend's Quaker-inspired principles that included antislavery ideals and peaceful and equitable relations among Indigenous populations. Even as the group settled the land, they claim to have done so according to Quaker values, with the goal of friendly cohabitation among the people whose homelands they were invading. Even so, the United States had recently formed as a nation and was actively expanding its settler colonial reach westward—a westward expansion the Friend participated in through the purchase of land and the formation of a settler community on Seneca Lake. This fact cannot be erased or silenced.

- X marks the spot.

The Friend continued to conduct business in a newly developed nation, a settler state that was establishing its own bureaucratic network. And this state refused to recognize the Friend as anyone other than Jemima Wilkinson, the name that had been bestowed upon that body at birth and that matched all genealogical and property records the state had on file. Land deeds, accounting documents, and other sales transactions thus required the signature of Jemima Wilkinson. But the Friend refused to sign with a name that did not belong, so the Friend instead marked an *X* as the signature. The signature is absent; *X* takes its place. Barzman describes the *X* as "a mark of resistance to interpolation."[49] At first, I wonder if Barzman meant to suggest that the deployment of the *X* is a resistance to interpellation, a refusal to be hailed by the state as the person, Jemima Wilkinson, who the Friend decidedly is not. But there is also a sense in which the Friend's refusal to sign Wilkinson's name is a resistance to the interpolation, or insertion, of that name on the legal documents, which I further interpret as a resistance to being interpolated—inserted or squeezed into—human names and categories.[50] The Friend seems to be resisting the insertion of human affairs into spiritual matters and the state of humanness into the spirit. *X* then functions as a redaction of Jemima Wilkinson's signature, a mark of the absence of that name, and simultaneously as a record of the presence of a spirited resistance to the state's interpolation and interpellation.

- Another self-~~redaction~~.

In a letter to someone by the name of Christopher Marshall, written in 1795, nineteen years after the death of Jemima Wilkinson and twenty-four years before the Friend left time, the Friend wrote, "I am yet in time through the goodness of a long suffering god and enjoy tolerable ~~good~~ state of health."[51] In my process of reading through thousands of pages of scanned documents from the archive of the Society of Friends, the crossed-out "good" immediately jumped out at me. I am struck by the striking of "good" for a couple reasons. It is a visible redaction; it asks the reader to overlook that crossed-out text, but it does not obliterate it completely as it leaves the legible text in place, a very present erasure, a heavy trace. And the striking of "good" leaves us with the claim to a "tolerable state of health" rather than a "tolerable good state of health." I think about the longevity of illness and its lasting marks, how ~~good~~ is not just a deletion but a notation of the presence of illness. In the letter, the Friend continues, "Life is uncertain and death is certain for in such an hour as ye think not death may come." The state of health is not good; the Friend is not fully well to the point that the certainty of death looms over the uncertainty of life. But the condition is tolerable even as illness remains or returns.

- A missing body.

Though Jemima Wilkinson died in 1776, the Friend left time in 1819 when Wilkinson's body died a second death. The body was sealed in a coffin with a small viewing pane to look upon the face as the body lay in state for four days. After the funerary services, the followers of the Friend then stored the coffin in a cellar. According to Moyer, this activated rumors that the followers were awaiting the Friend's resurrection, but he suggests the more likely explanation is that they were protecting the body from "defilement at the hands of nonbelievers."[52] Later, following Quaker tradition, the coffin was buried in an unmarked grave, but the followers have maintained the secrecy of the location. Rumor has it that the secret of the burial location is passed down to the firstborn of each subsequent generation of two of the followers' families, who are sworn to secrecy as gatekeepers of this information.[53] There is otherwise no way to locate the body. Karen Barzman tells me the Friend's followers were worried about people wanting to inspect the body because there had been so much lore and gossip about the Friend's sex and gender. The secrecy is the only way of guarding the body from inspection and manipulation.[54] Barzman also writes against the idea that the body of the Friend could tell something "true" about sex, gender, and subjectivity. For Barzman, one cannot *be* man or woman. To suggest being in that way is to stabilize inherently unstable categories and, again, through gender, to attempt to stabilize an inherently unstable body.[55] "There is one corporeal certainty not open to debate," Barzman writes, "the body is not fixed or stable; it contracts and expands, it exudes and excretes, it cracks and flakes; it will submit to disease and it will succumb to death."[56] The missing body was always missing the truth people were seeking. Let it be gone.

"In the end," Arlette Farge writes, "there is no such thing as a simple story, or ever a settled story. . . . You develop your reading of archives through ruptures and dispersion, and must mold questions out of stutters and silences. It is like a kaleidoscope revolving before your eyes."[57] The Friend's story is indeed a story that refuses complete answers and raises many more questions. Further, to draw on Jamie A. Lee, the archival body is "always in motion" as archives are shaped by and reshape the desires of the researcher.[58] Many people have molded their own readings from the gaps and ruptures, and I have offered my own crip, asexual, trans recount here, with many things missing and some new things found. And in the redactions, I find crip archival longings in this story, a complicated case for making sense of the nexus of sex, gender, illness, religiosity, absence, and silence.

Let me take another detour into another story of redaction and colonial manipulation. I regularly teach an upper-division seminar course on sexual "absences" in which I ask my students to think with me about what constitutes an absence, how sex and sexuality shape or are shaped into those absences, and why it all matters. At about the midway point of the semester, we visit a different kind of archival space—our college museum. I work with the museum curators in advance to specifically select art objects that resonate with the theme of absence in some way, but in addition to our focused viewing, I give the students time to wander and meander and view anything in the museum they like. I encourage them to be queer scavengers, to move about the museum not yet knowing what kinds of unexpected connections may arise, to be willing to be astonished. They have often astonished me with the insights they share from their scavenger hunts. But there is one item we routinely look at collectively that serves an important purpose here for thinking through the trace, absence and presence, hauntology, and the directionality and dimensionality of power in the process of redaction. That piece is a photogravure by American photographer and ethnologist Edward S. Curtis, who spent more than thirty years documenting Indigenous life in both still and moving image.

Curtis is, no doubt, infamous for manipulating his images, both in his erasures of any signs of coloniality and Western modernity and in his fabrication of "authenticity for the sake of romantic appeal."[59] My students do not usually know this about Curtis as they gaze upon his piece *On the Little Bighorn* (1908), a landscape portrait of an Apsáalooke Nation homespace, complete with tipis lining the riverbank as horses wade in the still, shallow waters of the Little Bighorn River in what is now the state of Montana. What the students don't know (and what is admittedly difficult to see in the image) is that Curtis erased a pioneer wagon from its place on the far bank of the river, making the land and living community appear untouched by settler colonists. My students, however, do remark on the absence of people in the photo. Together we wonder if, in a way, the absence of Indigenous people conjures the presence of their ghosts. Their absence also marks the presence of colonial genocide; colonial power becomes present through the absenting of the Indigenous body (much like military power becomes present through absence and destruction). Even though Curtis attempted to erase any signs of the colonial project in the literal erasure of the wagon from the photo, it nevertheless appears, a present reminder of how the logic of settler colonialism is also a "logic of elimination."[60] Curtis's portrayal of Indigenous life on the Little Bighorn is a doctored fantasy of the pristine and untouched (not too unlike the promise of the wild but quiet rainforest on the Olympic Peninsula that attempts a return to a kind of premodern silent wilderness). His redaction of the colonial machinery of the wagon, the evidence that presents land and body as things to be conquered, penetrated, and ravaged, only reinforces a fetishized fantasy of the Native that is produced through the very apparatus he tries to eliminate from his image, the apparatus that also eliminates and absents through genocide and cultural destruction.

By reading this image for absence, the students unpack histories of colonial erasures of Indigenous sexualities and the theft of land and body that leads us to an unveiling of sex-normative and sex-compulsive logics that drive the collusion of capitalism and colonialism, the logics that create binaries, that undo embodied and land-based ways of knowing and being, that pit human against nature, civilized against savage. The absence created by the colonial apparatus reveals much more in the presence of what was once there. To read through the redaction, to experience absence in the archive differently, is to resist teleology and embrace circulation, to reconstitute absences as presences, not as a project of liberation from within the colonial apparatus but as a decolonial assemblage of lost histories and new ways of thinking, seeing, feeling, and relating—it is to take seriously the potential and possibility in learning to look, listen, know, feel, and touch through our own bodily capacitations, excesses, and lacks, attuned to that which echoes, that which hums and bubbles beneath the surface, that which slips under the radar or is swept under the rug in order to maintain the logics of the ongoing colonial project. Look a little closer; squint if you have to. Or take a deep breath and tune into that gut feeling. Or take a moment to open your ears in the silence. There is a quiet hiss from that snake in the flooded basement. Sssssshhh . . . did you hear ████, see ████, feel ████?

# All Ends | No End

1

2

3

4

5

6

7

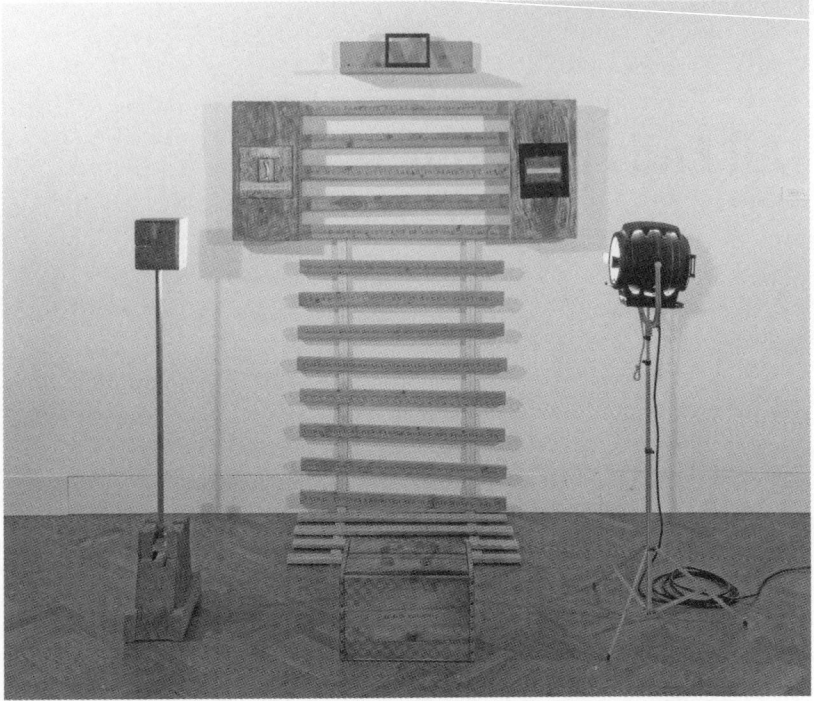

**FIGURE 5.** Renée Green, *Sa Main Charmante,* 1989. Wood, stage lights, metal, paper, paint, ink, and cotton webbing. The sculpture traces the presence of Saartje Baartman's missing body. I include the image here because I could not bear to erase her body again. Photograph provided by Allen Memorial Art Museum, Oberlin College, Ohio. Ruth C. Roush Contemporary Art Fund. Courtesy of the artist and Free Agent Media.

8

9

10

11

12

13                                                                    14

15

16

17

18

19

20

21

22

23

24

25

26

27

28

29

30

31

32

33

34

35

36

37

38

39

40

41

# "We Are Getting          Nowhere

# and That Is a Pleasure"

I quote John Cage from his "Lecture on Nothing" as the entry into this waypoint, which takes the shape of a coda by nature of being structurally at the textual end of this book—though you could read it first, or along the way.[1] The end is the beginning is the end, after all. I am drawn to this particular refrain in Cage's lecture because it brings me back to pleasure (again and again) and offers a kind of salve to J. Logan Smilges's acknowledgment: "It can be hard to keep going when it doesn't feel like you've been going anywhere."[2] It can indeed be hard (it was hard to get here, feel free to return to "Rest" if you agree), especially when you've been burdened with the compulsion to go somewhere, to make progress, to arrive. It is a challenging shift to rest easy in getting nowhere, but, as I hope this book offers, getting nowhere can be a delight and a pleasure.

I have been stalling, dwelling, going and getting nowhere even as I move from here to there and there to here. I have suggested that neuroqueerness is part of the meandering method of this project, but I have not explicitly theorized it or named it throughout.[3] I hope instead the neuroqueerness of thought and organization and movement in the book is apparent in the experience of reading and thinking through its tangles and unravelings, in the reverbs and echoes, silences and stutters, tangents and repetitions. The way I exist on the obsessive-compulsive spectrum means I circle back, retrace my steps, repeat and fixate. Sometimes it feels like I'm not going anywhere except back to the stove, to the deadbolt, to the sink, to that same paragraph, that same endnote, that same sentence, over and over. I am getting nowhere. I too "have nothing to say and I am saying it," but I fear I have tried too hard to turn that nothing into something, and so I said it, or wrote it, rather.[4] I am not sure I have written anything new, but I hope to have written things in new orders, differently patterned, alive to moments of relief and possibility.

I have been writing recursively, fractally toward expansive ways of conceiving, living, and being multiple, interdependent, entangled, entwined. When I set out to write this book, I was alive to the possibility of—maybe wanted to be convinced by—the promises of queer and trans ecologies that I have dwelled on, wished upon, and hoped to dwell in: to be never truly alone, always a crucial part of a world, engulfed by love.[5] But sometimes, despite the promised multitudes, I feel so utterly alone. It can feel as if there is no place for me anywhere when I am engulfed by a deep loneliness, a deep, blue sadness. I have an insipid notion. Sometimes it seems like the only thing keeping me alive is not a desire to live but an innate drive, an instinct, to stay alive. Living becomes its own kind of intelligence. Living is a way of knowing. I am getting nowhere, which means I am still here.

I am faced with the question of how to navigate an aching loneliness when I am supposed to be thriving in the reminders of our always togetherness. Sometimes I am so painfully lonely that I find myself taking a stance "against the romance of community."[6] While I have moved in and out of different communities at various points in time, I do not feel as though I have the kind of communal belonging that so many queer and crip activists praise. When I was recently attacked on the train platform in the city I currently live in, I had a couple friends I could tell about it, who asked if I was okay and sent a follow-up text a few days later to see how I was doing. But I didn't have a care web or mutual aid network that could bring me food or other necessities when I was too traumatized to leave the house or who could set up a rotation of people to check in on me while I was managing the PTSD. I was pretty much on my own in the day-to-day of it. As someone who lives alone, with most of my social interactions taking place over the phone or internet, this kind of aloneness in times of crisis and need, as well as in times of joy and celebration, is typical for me. I know I risk sounding quite bitter, or perhaps worse, like a hypocrite dismissing the smattering of people I do have in my life who love me and care for me from afar, even if they cannot compose that particular formation of nearby community. I am indeed fortunate and endlessly grateful for my far-reaching loves, but I am also all too aware that those of us who are pained by and vocal about our unbelonging are often dismissed as being bitter, difficult, and unlikeable, as if community is available to everyone and those who cannot access it when they want it must be the problem, rather than considering that the problem might be with the very concept of community itself, with gatekeeping and infighting, or with the sheer cruelty and self-interest of some communities' most powerful leaders.

And the truth is, sometimes I much prefer to be alone than in the company of others; I am aware that my choices of solitude have sometimes disconnected me from the communities I could have put more effort into joining. My point is not to list my woes but to critically interrogate how community is touted and upheld by way of my own experiences feeling outside of it. While I agree that community is important and that care webs and mutual aid are much needed in a broken welfare state, what I am addressing here is the failure to account for being and feeling alone, for the ways community is romanticized in the faces of people who do not have it, and how the presumption of community means that we are not getting creative about how to reach those who are estranged from family and unmoored from community.[7]

I recently attended a conference where I made an effort to go to as many queer and crip sessions as I could. In every single session, community was held up as the answer to almost everything. In one session, I dared to raise the questions of unbelonging, lack of access to community, and loneliness. No one had much to say in response. One person said, "Well, everyone has someone." If that someone is the self, then yes, perhaps everyone has that someone, but not everyone has someone *else*. And even so, having some*one* is not the same as being enmeshed in a community of shared resources and care. Similarly, I recently attended a symposium that was focused on trans ecologies, and, although people were friendly to me, I felt like a bit of an outsider among this group of people who largely seemed to know each other and move in community already. Throughout the symposium, much lip service was given to a sense of "trans community" and our material entanglements with one another and our environs as a pathway to revolution. In one session, I asked how to account for the difference in knowing we are not truly singular or alone because we are holobiont and the experience of feeling alone and lonely and, especially, even as a trans person, of feeling outside of this "trans community" everyone keeps lauding. One participant responded that though they live alone and sometimes feel lonely, they are able to shift their feelings about it by remembering that they are not truly alone, that they are always in the company of microorganisms. I think this is a beautiful response, but I suggested that such a balm does not work for me and probably many others because we can still feel alone, even when we are reminded that we are not *truly* alone. The bacteria on my skin and in my gut do little to give me a sense of belonging in a community even if these microorganisms and I depend on each other to survive (even they get to live in colonies of others).

Community can start to feel like an unfilled promise, a prize won by the chosen ones, who somehow manage to have families and lovers and regular friend gatherings. I remember once binge-watching the terribly misogynistic television show *How I Met Your Mother* simply because I was fascinated by the fantasy of a core friend group who had their regular booth at their regular neighborhood bar, who saw each other through new loves and breakups, new jobs and new apartments, marriages and children—mostly things I never really wanted much anyway. But sometimes, watching the show, I wondered if I might want those things just to not be so alone. As a child, my family moved frequently, sometimes every year, sometimes every few years. I changed schools often enough that I learned not to hold onto any friendships, to appreciate the connections I had while I had them. And I carried that into my adult life, moving every few years for school, for jobs, living in between those things in in-between spaces. The community I've grown over those years is dispersed around the globe, marked with infrequent, often digital contact through space-time. I am not without love in my life. But I can go entire days, sometimes several in a row without talking to anyone, without using my voice. I sit alone, in my own silence.[8]

We are getting nowhere. Sometimes it feels like I'm not going anywhere except back to the stove, to the deadbolt, to the sink, to that same paragraph, that same endnote, that same sentence, over and over. Wait, are we back here again? Let me begin again.

On the first day of class in my course "Sexual 'Absences,'" I begin with silence because it is our zero, our entry into a whole (sensory) world. I ask all of us to be alone together in that quiet. I tell the students I am going to play a recording of a piece of music and all they need to do is listen. I then make them sit through the entirety of John Cage's "4'33"." Afterward, we talk about the experience: They were confused at first, waiting for the sound to come, until they realized they had been hearing sounds all along. They talk about where their concentration lingered and wandered, the discomfort they felt in looking around the room at each other, wanting to avoid eye contact as we all sit around a seminar table in what might seem like a prolonged awkward silence. Then we all close our eyes and listen again. They hear more sounds this time, pick out the particulars of a cough, a shift in a chair, a faint echo in the theater, the static hum of nothingness that is really somethingness, the ways in which sounds within the classroom merge with sounds from the street leaking in through the windows merge with sounds from the audio recording. In our silence, we suddenly become wrapped in an intimate sonic web, a circulation of noise, reverberation.

By the next class session, they have read more about Cage. They want to pick apart his privileged position—a white male artist and intellectual with the cultural capital and esteem to pull off such a stunt. They suggest, despite Jonathan D. Katz's recount of Cage's closeted sexuality, this is a man with the privilege to imagine silence as resistance, for he has probably rarely, if ever, been silenced. They wonder when and for whom silence can be a resistant technology, one that, as Katz puts it, understands recourse to silence as a way to "avoid the recolonizing force of the oppositional," a "seduction away from authority," making "a statement through the absence of statement."[9] Or they call in what Ianna Hawkins Owen describes as a Black feminist "declarative silence" or "refusal to confess" in the face of misogyny and white supremacy.[10] How, they want to know, do we understand silence as resistance for those who have been oppressed by continual silencing? How do we understand queer silence as rhetorical possibility rather than the claustrophobic tightening of the throat behind the closet door? They wonder when silence is resistant to recolonizing forces and when silence is simply complicit in colonial violence. I encourage them to think about, as Lisa A. Mazzei puts it, the way silences are inhabited. Thus, we might ask, "What are the silences about whiteness, racism, homophobia, or sexism, for example, that are not spoken with words, but are spoken between words?"[11] I ask them what silences and betweens can do for those who have been forcibly silenced, denied entry, made into nothing. I do not have easy answers for them, only more questions. But I have gotten them, through silence, to begin questioning the colonial impacts on sex, sexuality, and resistance.

Yes, yes, "the apparent nothingness of silence is a robust symphonic score."[12]

Where was I going with this? I am getting nowhere. Let me return to Cage:

> quiet sounds                    were like loneliness   ,            or
> Love        or friendship.[13]

In much asexual and aromantic discourse, there is a tendency to re-affirm solitude as normal and healthy, to refuse equating being alone with feeling lonely, or, as I have done through much of this book, to remind that there are many ways to be together (especially beyond the sexual). Sometimes being alone is attached to loneliness because of that compulsory coupledom I have been writing against, wherein the singleton has supposedly failed to find companionship. But as Michael Cobb argues, the logic of coupling, "being together," is "one of the primary totalitarian logics that accelerate the feelings of alienation and dislocation." In fact, he continues, "the loneliest of us are not necessarily those who are actually alone but rather those of us trying our hardest not to be alone."[14] It is possible to be alone without feeling lonely. For me, aloneness is a true pleasure. I am only lonely when I wish not to be alone. But sometimes I feel loneliest when I am not alone. I have been lonely in a crowd and even in a romantic partnership. As Cobb writes, "At first blush, what one begins to encounter among the lonely is not the absence of people, but the sheer abundance of others."[15] Maybe what I mean to say is that I am only lonely when I wish not to *feel* alone, whether or not I am actually alone.

For the last three Christmases, a dear love and I have exchanged melancholy Christmas songs. Although Christmas is not a holiday I necessarily celebrate, it is hard to escape its season of togetherness, and for me, it can often feel like a particularly lonely time, with the last two holiday seasons being especially fraught and shot-through with grief and loss. My friend understands this about me and exchanges these songs because though they ring melancholic, they feel like a gathering of grief and grievances, a way to be together in our loneliness. For three years running, she has sent me Phoebe Bridgers's cover of McCarthy Trenching's "Christmas Song." With the crooning "You don't have to be alone to be lonesome," I pause on the word *lonesome*, thinking about how it combines both the idea of being (feeling?) alone and feeling lonely. Maybe you don't have to be alone to be lonesome, but you have to *feel* alone. And if quiet sounds—if silence—can be like loneliness or love or friendship, does that not mean that loneliness, love, and friendship share some things, at least this one thing, in common?

> We are having          the pleasure
> of being                         slowly                    nowhere.[16]

Like parsing the difference between being and feeling, we are no longer getting nowhere; rather, we are being there, slowly, dwelling, having. Let me start again.

"I didn't want to write about the break-up."[17] This sentence, which opens Morgan Florsheim's essay "Purple Martin Blues," rings through my head as I write into my own loneliness. On a solo writing retreat on Lake Wisconsin, I whisper the line aloud, almost a year after my own breakup. As it was ending, we took a final trip together to the Southern Sierra where we soaked our melancholy in a hot tub with vistas of an azure mountain lake. Now I sit in a different inflatable hot tub on a different deck overlooking a different lake, while another cold winter rain plunks into the steaming water around me. Here I am, repeating with a difference, surrounded by water. "I didn't want to write about the break-up. I wanted to write about the Purple Martins."[18] Does anyone really want to write about the breakup, or is it more that they feel they need to, to let something go, to send their account of the dissolution out and away? I would prefer not to write about the breakup. I would prefer to write about the things that astonish and revive, not about the thing that saps and depresses. I want to write about nature and art and literature and film and the beauty in loving the vibrant multitudes of matter, in adoring all the nothings and zeros that hold whole worlds inside them. I would have preferred to write a book that wasn't haunted by a breakup this time around, just as I would have preferred to write a book that wasn't haunted by fresh death this time around. But these kinds of endings return; they haunt and hold and never let go.

How else do I write about being alone, a particular kind of aloneness that is void of regular physical touch, of someone asking how a day was, without writing about the breakup, without writing about loss, without writing about the absence that marks what was once present? How else do I write about how that aloneness is not only about being alone but about feeling alone, that it is that feeling that makes it lonesome? Perhaps one of the loneliest feelings is that crumpling in your chest when you look into your partner's beaming face, knowing they are hiding from you a whole stash of delicious secrets kept between them and another. And you are floating out of your body as they wrap their arms around you, telling you that you only need to forgive them and trust them when you know they haven't even told you the half of it. How else do I write about how lonely it is to be with someone who is not wholly with you, but how they can feel worth clinging to because the process of losing them completely feels even more terrifyingly lonely? *Nec tecum nec sine te.* In such a world. How do I manage?

How strange, unsettling, and disorienting it is to have someone in your life every day and then suddenly not at all. How their absence leaves a hole, and how long it takes you to realize that if you look through that hole and not just at it, a whole world of new possibility emerges. How plain and true it is that when you set something down, you free yourself up to hold something else. We all drop things sometimes in order to pick up something else. So when your partner forgets an important event or doesn't do something as simple as text you goodnight because they're swept up in the company of a new lover, you might be able to forgive them their limits. Recognizing this limitation does not make the drop's crash landing any less painful, but perhaps it helps us clean out the wounds with a small offering of grace, a way to say, "I forgive you, even if I need to carry myself away from you."

I am not going to write anything more about the breakup beyond naming it as something that has changed the tenor of the loneliness I feel and probably already felt within the relationship, a loneliness that is also found in feeling alone, feeling singular even in my plurality.[19] Do we ever really miss someone only in their singularity, or do we also always miss who we become in their presence, that which makes them plural to us?[20] I know I miss myself most when entangled with another.

And that is a pleasure. Is it? Are we getting somewhere or are we still being nowhere? Let's try this again.

I have the good fortune of teaching at an institution with a world-class art museum, and I use the museum's resources frequently in my teaching. On a beautiful spring day, my students and I walk across the square to the museum for a different kind of visit. I am teaching a course on affective relations to the archive. We had spent the semester thinking about the histories of different archives, ambivalently considering museums as storehouses of theft as well as keepers of history and spaces for aesthetic pleasure. We are there today simply to scavenge, to dwell in our affective encounters with the art and with the space, its hushes and its reverbs. The assignment is to simply wander the museum, to meander through the rooms and pay attention to ambience—the sights, sounds, smells, and feels. I ask them to follow whatever pulls or captivates, to be led not by period or topic or style but by desire, want, and embodied sensation. I ask them also to take stock of what is missing as much as what is present. I am testing out my meandering methodology and the observance of absence as a practice in the world, as a way to move through an organized space with no organized plan. As my students disperse, I let myself wander through the museum. As I drift, I find myself in the modern and contemporary room. I turn the corner and release an audible gasp when I see Yayoi Kusama's *White Net Painting* (1960) and Agnes Martin's *East River* (1960) hanging side by side. There is only one other student in the room with me, and they look over, politely smile at my gasp, and quietly move on to the next room. Suddenly, I am alone with Kusama and Martin.

Of course, it is not so strange that these two paintings should sit side by side, as both artists were working with the abstract in New York City in the 1960s. But there are many artists in this exhibit, which is a broad showing titled *New Acquisitions and Old Friends—* that these two should hang right next to each other feels somewhat serendipitous, given that I had been thinking about them in tandem through the lenses of asexuality and absence. In the time that I have, I snap some photos, scribble some thoughts, and head back to the main gallery to close out the class session with my students. As they trickle out into the brightness of the day, I return one last time to look at the paintings. I know I must wander back.

For the rest of that semester, I return to the museum weekly to be with Kusama and Martin. I am often the only one sitting in the quiet room, and the only living sound in that room is the gentle labor of my own breath. Sometimes I feel lonely and sometimes I feel entirely rapt and held in the company of the infinity net or the grid of the East River. I am alone but I do not *feel* alone. I don't know what I want here except to be with these paintings in our seemingly fated gathering. It is a pleasure to sit here, doing nothing, getting nowhere, simply returning and staying with, staying in, lingering in study with these works.[21]

Inside the museum, I learn to see and think and feel in new formations. A grid is a river. A net is an infinite universe. I am a tiny speck; I am obliterated.[22] The stutter of a line is the absent presence of the artist's hand, as is the swirl of paint, the drip that was left to drip. I am with each of them in that gallery; we are all with each other. As I learn more about the lives of both artists, it seems that we were meant to find each other there in that room through those particular pieces. The grids and nets and dots compose geometries of being otherwise in a world that has called us "crazy." Martin underwent therapy for schizophrenia. Kusama currently lives in a mental health facility in Japan and has written openly about her mental illness and her trauma-induced fears.[23] I move in circles and grids, retracing my steps in all my obsessions and compulsions, repeating my traumas, slipping into anxiety's gaps and cracks. Sometimes it feels like I'm not going anywhere except back to the stove, to the deadbolt, to the sink, to that same paragraph, that same endnote, that same sentence, over and over. In this crip, neuroqueer shaping of time and space, we also find other forms of queerness, tethered in a way to aloneness. Martin, though rumored to have had female lovers, preferred to live alone and did so for much of her life until she had to move into an assisted living facility. And Kusama writes quite openly of her support for queer people, featuring gay and lesbian sex in many of her "Happenings" in New York City, but she describes herself as "a person who has no sex," and as someone who lacks interest in sex, who is in fact repulsed by genitals, which she traces to early childhood trauma.[24] Kusama, though living in community at the facility, spends a lot of solo time in her studio; there is a sense in which she dwells alone. Ela Przybyło declares Martin an "aroace lesbian" and Kusama as "aroace," or aromantic and asexual, as in not interested in taking either romantic or sexual partners, and lesbian in the more capacious sense of being in intimate relation with women, even in nonromantic and nonsexual ways.[25] I, however, refrain from attaching such labels of orientation or identity to either of them, as I find it less interesting to attempt to fit them into these contemporary Western discourses and categories; rather, there is a compelling resonant attunement to the way their relationships to sex, aloneness, madness, and neuroqueerness constellate to produce blank space, quietude, abstract shape, color, and pleasure in their work and through their craft. Martin wrote of the silence of her floor, of the loudness of the sunset.[26] For Kusama, nothingness becomes a promise.[27] It is no wonder I find solace in the silence of their paintings, in the traces of their brilliant minds as each of them worked out, through their art, how we might live in the silences and nothings.

In the coming semester, this exhibit will close. Martin's and Kusama's paintings will go back into storage. But a new exhibit, *Like a Good Armchair: Getting Uncomfortable with Modern and Contemporary Art,* will pull me into another cycle of returns where I will spend time with the ghost of Saartje Baartman in Renée Green's *Sa Main Charmante* and where I will sit on the artwork of Finnegan Shannon, a bench from the series *Do You Want Us Here or Not.* The bench invites me to rest. It directs me to sit on it if I agree that the exhibition has asked me to stand for too long. I rest and pop my joints as I sit down in agreement. I pause and quietly weep in the stillness, in the physical and mental relief, in the permission to simply be here in and on the art when so often I work so hard to erase myself. I linger in the reminder that without rest, there is no energy to make unrest and to unsettle this world that demands we keep moving to a point of settlement and arrival that remains always on the horizon as the next thing to achieve, accumulate, and acquire. It is a hard journey, return to "Rest" if you agree. Sit or write in those pages as you need.

As the museum closes, I say goodbye, or until we meet again, to all the ghosts, and I make my way home to my empty and drafty apartment. I cook a meal for one. I put myself to bed. I wake up and repeat the next day with a difference—a new lesson, a different set of meetings, different meals. Days unfold into weeks that take the shape of months without physical touch from another being. I caress the leaf of my giant alocasia. Does she not also touch me back in her own way? I have an intimacy with the houseplants and house spiders and bacteria that share home and body with me, even while, at the time of this writing, I technically live alone. I do not have a partner (though when I first wrote these lines about loneliness and my empty apartment, I did have a partner who had recently moved across the country and began fading away from me with each passing day since the move). I have some close relationships, but no one who checks on me regularly enough to notice something irregular. Once, after a near fall in the shower, I realized that I could slip and hit my head, go to sleep there in the tub forever, and possibly weeks could go by before I were discovered. I imagine at least one student would raise concern with another professor in my small department at my small school after I missed a few class sessions with no explanation or communication. But in that quiet, lonely fear, the paintings and sculptures become a kind of constant; it begins to feel like they are waiting for me to visit them as much as I look forward to seeing them. There is a sense in which I am expected to be somewhere regularly, even if there is not a living person expecting me. Every encounter with them is also a different repetition, a new encounter. I feel as though I am searching for something, listening hard at what the arrangement of the artwork has to tell me. But all I hear is silence, which is so loud, roaring with the questions of what it means to be alive and queer and alone.[28]

Wait, I did not want to write about the breakup. But, somehow, I have circled back there, at least to its edges. I digress. We are still being nowhere. Is it a pleasure? Let me reframe this.

Maybe what I mean to be getting at, though I am getting nowhere, is the suggestion that many people, asexual or not, aromantic or not, experience loneliness and estrangement from community. I want to make space for that affect, to acknowledge that even in our infinite togetherness, we can feel utterly, sometimes even hopelessly, alone even when we are pressed together or pressed to be together.[29] Sometimes the way a stranger's thigh pushes into mine on the train presses us together, eliminates the space between us just long enough for me to not want to pull away. But this is a fleeting intimacy, and I do pull away in order to bring back that space, to separate my body from the inseparable stranger. Cobb wants to imagine a "possibility of being distant from others" as "another kind of relation" rather than as a nonrelation.[30] To appreciate the spaces between us is to offer a way to relate across that difference and that distance, to be alone and feel alone even as we are distantly tied to yet separated from one another. It is to finally account for the something (the relation) that exists in the nothing (the apparent nonrelation). Might we then, apart or together, come to mean something?[31]

In other words, the question might be: What is there left to hope for when feeling alone can feel so hopeless? Following Matthew Cheney's suggestion that hope offers very little because it requires us to believe in and to wish for something we cannot be sure will ever exist—"the possibility of success, a better future"—we should instead ask where there are "opportunities for the relief of suffering," following how "kindness and compassion offer ways to act, ways to be."[32] I turn to art and writing for these lessons, and I have been writing about ways of being and becoming in the erasures as ways to recuperate the fullness and beauty, the compassion and kindness that was not given in the silencings, in the creation of all those nothings. Gilles Deleuze and Félix Guattari offer a lesson in writing's intangibilities and nothingnesses: "Writing has nothing to do with signifying. It has to do with surveying, mapping, even realms that are yet to come."[33] We may or may not hope for those realms to come and we may wish to unmap them rather than map them, but writing them offers some kind of blueprint or disordered schematic for how we might act and be right now as well as for the ways we ought not to act. We have a responsibility for how we relate to others even when we seem to be in nonrelation, even when it seems that everyone else has left us alone and lonely.

Having been myself reduced to nothing, whether through antiqueerness, antitransness, misogyny, or poverty—growing up, I was often told I would "amount to nothing" simply because I did not have the financial or social capital that would have given me access to an elite education, internship opportunities, job networks, which means I would go uncounted and unaccounted for—I had to turn that nothing into something if I were going to survive in a world that told me I shouldn't. My own experience of nothingness is the reason it feels so crucial to revalue all the nothings. Anna Lowenhaupt Tsing writes that if we are agnostic about where we are going, which I certainly am, "we might look for what has been ignored because it never fit the time line of progress."[34] What is ignored has been ignored not only because it doesn't fit the timeline of progress, but because it also halts and impedes the kind of "progress" that is a liberal humanist march into an ever-evolving modernity. Such progress cannot happen without violence in the race to the ever-moving finish line, with so many dropped and mauled along the way. Smilges writes, "I am calling for an examination of prior erasures in order to map the violence of absence in the present—ultimately with the hope of (re)forming attachments to objects, temporalities, geographies, and positionalities that were previously castrated."[35] I am similarly naming the violence of absence in the present but also reforming that absence as an illusion, as a very real presence that has not been excised or castrated but has been left to exist without support while everyone is told to look away, a presence that has gone unaccounted for. This process brings us back to the workings of capitalism. Lucas Pohl writes, "If we approach capitalism solely based on what it materially (ac)counts (for), we overlook what Badiou considers to be the most important aspect of capitalism, the *inexistent,* all those who 'are counted for nothing by capital.'"[36] Similarly, Erin Manning calls for a postcapitalist orientation to value that refuses "to allow capital in all of its past and future instantiations to determine value."[37] What we need instead, Manning suggests, is "a care for ecologies of practice that value the effects of what can barely be perceived, if it can be perceived at all."[38] This, this here, this writing, is my offering, my gesture toward that ecology of caring practice, a tool to help us recalibrate how and what we perceive. It is my attempt at the anticapitalist, anticolonial recount—the telling of a story, giving an account of, accounting for, counting again, counting for *something.*

Following Tim Ingold, I think we are not only alive *in* the world, we are also alive *to* the world.[39] It matters that we witness and that we let ourselves be astonished, even on a corpsed planet, even across a barren landscape. For Ingold, astonishment is different from surprise. Surprise occurs when something does not go according to plan, a break in expected logic. I think we should continue to be surprised as well; we should continue to break (break up with?) expected logics. And, astonishment arises from "treasuring every moment, as if, in that moment, we were encountering the world for the first time, sensing its pulse, marvelling at its beauty, and wondering how such a world is possible."[40] We must marvel as well as question how such a world is possible in order to marvel at the possibility of different worlds, to pattern differently, marvelously, marbled. The beauty cannot exist without the violent and the terrible. "Click. Click. Goes the dredge, / and brings up a dripping jawful of marl. / All the untidy activity continues, / awful but cheerful."[41] Art and film, poetry and music, literature and theory, and the act of writing all offer me something to marvel at, a way to tap into the "compositional attunement through which people and things venture out into reals" or to practice modes of "weird reading" that exist outside "humanist-centered, historicist frames of reference in order to (hopefully) unleash any literary text's potential for becoming-otherwise" to the point that "the line between human and nonhuman becomes nonsensical," in which we are obliterated.[42] Writers (and artists), after all, are sorcerers.[43]

"And so we make our lives by what we love."[44] What more could we want? To want nothing, to be left with nothing wanting, paradoxically, is still to want so much more in the vast infinity of nothingness. And so we are back where we began. The end is in the beginning. We have gotten nowhere. Have we? We are being nowhere. Are we? Slowly. I hesitate to end. There is always so much more to say, and I have not said it. There is nothing to say, and I have said all of it. It has been a pleasure. Has it?

*This page intentionally left*

# Acknowledgments

As I was working on this book, several people along the way asked me what it was about. I regularly answered that question with a short quip: "Nothing." Many would respond with a little laugh and then look at me expectantly as if I were going to tell them what the book is *really* about. I would explain that it really is about nothing, but I would of course say more about what I meant by that. These exchanges often turned into invigorating, abundant, *full* conversations about "nothing." I am grateful to everyone who cared to ask, to think with me, and to read pieces of this manuscript along the way.

My thinking in this book is seeded by and still indebted to everyone I thought with and befriended during my years at Stanford University. I extend especial gratitude to my mentors and teachers who helped me deepen my thinking about asexuality and grow as a scholar: Paula Moya, Heather Love, Stephen Sohn, and Jennifer DeVere Brody. I continued watering and sprouting those seeds of thought after I began my job at Oberlin College, and the first pieces of this book were written with the support of a faculty research fellowship from Oberlin during my junior sabbatical. A Grant-In-Aid from Oberlin College also supported the final production and publication of this work. I count myself lucky to be surrounded by brilliant and generous colleagues and friends for whom I am endlessly grateful. In particular, the pandemic writing group with Wendy Kozol, Danielle Skeehan, and Carmen Merport Quiñones offered me the opportunity to workshop some of my early thoughts on ungendering and the Public Universal Friend. Danielle Skeehan and Gina Pérez also championed this work as they supported me in their roles as chairs of each of my two departments; I cherish their collegiality and their friendship.

I had the good fortune to test out some of these ideas with generous audiences at the University of Mississippi and at Brown University. I extend extra thanks to Jaime Harker for the invitation to speak at Mississippi and to Angie LaGrotteria, Kevin Cozart, and everyone at the Sarah Isom Center for making my visit so meaning-ful. I am also especially grateful to Caroline Cunfer and Shelley Lee for the invitation to share my work at Brown and to all the wonderful faculty and students who exchanged ideas and questions that helped me expand and deepen this work.

I completed this book as I began research for a new archival-based project, and while on a grant at the Harvard Radcliffe Institute's Schlesinger Library and then on a long-term fellowship at the Newberry Library, the ideas that took shape in those spaces inevita-bly found their way into this project. At the Newberry, in particular, I am thankful to Keelin Burke for the warmth and support of my work, for rhizomatic conversations with Fabien Montcher, for exchanges with Laura McEnaney that helped me think through how to tell a story, for Karen Barzman's expert insight on the Public Universal Friend, for deep talks and tarot reads with Liv Koreman that helped me think differently about ghosts and death work, for the ways Aileen Feng, Jessica Goethals, Diana Berruezo-Sánchez, Zozan Pehlivan, Roger Ferlo, and Sheryl Reiss each helped me think about Daphne and girls and women and trees and poetry, and for the camaraderie of all my fellow fellows, including Katherine Calvin, Miguel Martínez, Javier Villa-Flores, Aldair Rodrigues, and Hayley Negrin.

The making of this book owes so much to the generosity of two anonymous readers whose feedback helped steer the directions and structures of the project in its early stages. I am overwhelmingly grateful for Nathan Snaza's astute and thoughtful reading of the full manuscript; his input helped me become an even more myce-lial reader, writer, and thinker. I don't even know how to begin to express my appreciation for Leah Pennywark, a patient, smart, and creative editor who understood the project from the beginning, sup-ported me in practicing slow writing, and encouraged me to keep it weird. A huge thank you also goes to Anne Carter, who made all the weird stuff work in preparing the manuscript for production, and to Ziggy Snow, whose brilliant copyediting vastly improved the book. And, of course, I am endlessly appreciative of the entire team at the University of Minnesota Press, who shepherded this book into exis-tence with care and creativity.

I am grateful, also, to the artists who believed enough in this project to allow me to feature their work in it. My appreciation to Renée Green for entrusting a stranger to tell the story of her art and its subject with care, to Finnegan Shannon for crip solidarity and their generosity in creating places of rest and respite, and to Abigail Raphael Collins for enlivening exchanges of and about redaction, archives, art, silences, and desire. Thanks are also due to heidi andrea restrepo rhodes, with whom so many ideas grew through years of living and thinking together and whose feedback on my writing brought more delightful intertext to the work. So much gratitude also goes to my soul brother Ethan Plaut, who has invited me to think about silence and absence with him over the past many, many years and who also provided invaluable feedback on my writing on redaction. My other soul brother, Milo Razza, regularly teaches me new ways to see the world (especially birds) and myself; his imprints on me and this book are apparent on every page. My thinking about abolition and breaking up is indebted to commiserations with Shuli Branson. I am grateful to Nadia Robinson for the poetic and musical delights that shaped my writing in and about solitude. I have a deep appreciation for Anne DelBene, who has masterfully taught me how to be alone and how to truly see flowers. With deep care, love, and respect, I thank Braveheart Gillani for steadfast friendship and the exchanges of poetry and philosophy that have made their way into these pages.

Long, meandering walks with Jersey Cosantino not only brought energy and zest to my life but also helped me articulate a meandering methodology as a neuroqueer way of thinking and being in the world; my life and writing have both been enriched by our mad friendship and collaboration. Similarly, the ongoing support of Michael Thomas, whose reminder that "there's a reason the river meanders" was and continues to be a solace as I stall and restart and bend and circle back. I am grateful to Laura Frost, who has remained a steadfast champion and supporter of my work through all its iterations and sharp turns.

I would not have gotten here without my ride-or-die writing buddy/ venting buddy/travel buddy: Erika Hoffmann. This book would surely not exist without my accountability buddies, Eunjung Kim and Ianna Hawkins Owen, who offered a weekly lifeline, cheered me on, provided feedback on some very early drafts, and helped me think in so many new ways about absences, crip living, and (a)sexuality. And my love and gratitude deepens by the nanosecond for Emily Kropp, who pushed me to more clearly articulate the stakes of this book, endured my wallowing as I floundered in the sea of revisions, celebrated every milestone, and reassured me I would finish this book even when I didn't believe I could.

There are many others—family, earth, birds, loves, trees, friends, writers, colleagues, artists, readers, ghosts, fungi, poets, flora, musicians, fauna—who go unnamed here, but their presence is felt always, even in bouts of absence. My heart swells with gratitude for the worlds we cocreate and coexist in. Thank you for being a part of the World as Plenum that this book is joining.

# Foray Notes for Further Intertextual Possibilities

Foray 1. In John Ajvide Lindqvist's short story "The Border," there is a moment when, as teenagers, a boy sits down next to Tina at a party and confesses his love for her but follows it with, "I wish that I could meet someone just like you but who doesn't look like you" (6). "Her toes were crooked. Even her feet were ugly" (13). It was a boy who first led Tina to believe she is ugly.

Foray 2. The only time Roland and Tina attempted intercourse, it hurt so much that she asked him to stop. Lindqvist writes, "It had probably been a relief for him" (12). Tina might have liked to have children, but "since she was unable to engage in the act that made them it would never happen" (14). Later, Tina tells Vore, "But it hurts too much. I can't do it" (40). He tells her she hasn't ever done it in her way. And when they do it in their way, Tina feels like she is turned inside out as she becomes erect. "She was getting pleasure from a place that didn't exist" (40). Here, Tina experiences pleasure in a presumed absence, a part of her she wasn't allowed to know existed. In coitus, Tina and Vore unfix themselves from human sex and gender: "They were no longer man or woman, just two bodies that found each other in the dark" (40).

Foray 3. "The only thing that could cause her to err was if an individual was carrying something that was not against the law but that the person in question was eager to conceal" (2).

Foray 4. In the short story, Tina's skills were in such high demand that she occasionally took contract jobs in border policing around the world. After a job working the U.S.–Mexico border at Tijuana, where she busted several drug smugglers, she decided to give up the temporary jobs out of concern for her own safety. "It is dangerous to know too much, especially when so much money is at stake" (2). Capitalism, the drug trade, U.S. foreign policy, and state enforcement collapse here in simultaneously shared and opposed interests. Tina opts out.

Foray 5. "I am a rational person," Tina asserts for herself as she tries to maintain the illusion of her humanity in the face of new information about the world of fairies and trolls (37). Later, when she learns she was taken from her parents due to apparent neglect, she realizes, "They had known how to care for their child" (48). What was perceived as an absence of care was just a different form of care. What was perceived as a wild, chaotic way of life was simply a different way of living. When Tina was removed from her parents, her parents were placed in some kind of care facility like a hospital, where they died. Tina has a deep, somatic fear response to hospitals, like an inherited trauma that goes beyond her own experience in the hospital as a baby: "That smell of disinfected clothing and antiseptic soap almost made her panic. It went back a long way" (24).

Foray 6. Ben Cooper, under the performance name Radical Face, released a 2018 album titled *Missing Film* that he describes as a variety of tracks that "range from film and TV commissions that didn't pan out, to one-off experiments that have no home." The album has an open license to encourage independent filmmakers and video artists to use the tracks royalty-free. I've always listened to the album as if it were a score to a film that doesn't exist. Sometimes I let the music create scenes and stories in my mind; I lie down with my eyes closed and the music in my headphones and watch the missing film emerge on the screen in my head. I also wrote much of this book, fittingly, to that soundtrack. I really hoped to provide a worded visual to *Border* here, and I wondered what it would be like to invite readers to fill in the missing film still from my descriptions and their own imaginations (and for those who have seen the film, they might employ their memory as well). I wonder if some readers might even draw it into the space in the book. The thought delights me; what a pleasure to welcome artwork into the book in this way. Redaction is an invitation for collaboration, after all. And with any redaction, a trace remains. The missing film still isn't really missing.

Foray 7. Tina, after spending more time with Vore and learning some truths, grows disillusioned with her work: "It had become second nature but it really wasn't her, only a necessary mask in order to perform a job that she was increasingly starting to see as meaningless" (30). "She was living a lie, the remnant of a nation, a traitor" (50). The story ends with Tina reuniting with Vore, pregnant with their child, at the ferry terminal. Her final thought as the story closes: "*I don't belong here*" (54).

Foray 8. "Work was still the place where she felt most comfortable" (10).

Foray 9. "Instead she went out to the woods, to her tree" (7). "She had always felt she belonged to the forest" (48). "She had no desire to go into her house. Anyone's house. She just wanted to keep going past the lights and the warmth into the woods. Penetrate its dark wall and find solace in the mingled smells of badger, pine needles, moss. Let the trees protect her" (26). Vore tells Tina, "I like these kinds of forests that humans haven't been allowed to destroy," perhaps distinguishing himself from humans as he relates to the forest (28). Tina also mourns what humans have done to the forest: *"Keep the forest away from us. Tame it. Fence it in"* (48). The forest is a metonym for what they did to her and her parents and all of their kind. "People did not believe in trolls. And if they found any, they locked them up in mental institutions, removed their tails, sterilized them, and forced them to learn human language" (51). "They had forced her into a hospital, operated on her, spoken to her in a language she had not understood and tried to press her into their mold, make her into one of them" (51–52). Of a conversation with Vore, Tina writes in her journal, "We talked about the woods, how the fall changes things. He said he didn't feel at all comfortable in houses (!!!)" (35). "But Vore. His smell, his scent was like coming home" (38). Tina finds solace, a sense of home, belonging, and kinship in the woods and in Vore. She regularly visits and talks to the tree that was struck by lightning along with her as she sat beneath it as a young girl. "Lightning had snapped off the top of the tree, rushed down the trunk and into the girl at its foot" (9). The lightning strike scarred Tina's face and left the tree looking like "a ghost of a tree: a broken trunk with a couple naked branches stuck out of its side" (8). Tina and the tree, united by electricity's scar. "The tree had not healed so why should she?" (9). Before Tina and Vore first have sex, they share their first moment of prolonged bodily intimacy during a lightning storm. "Lightning continued to rage around them but after a while she heard how even his heart calmed itself. He pressed her harder toward him. The comfort was mutual and that made her feel better. Which made him feel better" (40).

Foray 10. "Everyone says there are no mushrooms this year, but I find them like usual. But with dry stretches between them" (31). "We met in the forest yesterday, picked loads of mushrooms. He has the same mushroom radar that I do (of course)" (36). Tina articulates a kind of kinship with the mushroom, a kinship that is tied to ken, radar, a way of knowing— something she and Vore can find when everyone else cannot.

Foray 11. In the poem "Translator's Essay," Zaina Alsous writes: *"Sex is always monstrous, Bhanu Kapil writes. / Is an absence of sex the absence of monsters or of bodies / in process, becoming the nature of monster?"* (22). Someone I watched the film with told me they love the sex scene between Tina and Vore because it is so "animal" in the growling and howling and baring of teeth as they move in the dirt of the black earth.

Foray 12 In some ways, the animal monstrosity of Tina's and Vore's bodies becomes more apparent in the sex between them, but even in the absence of the act of sex, they remain "monstrous" relative to the normate human form. And in the absence of the practice of sex acts, their bodies remain sexed. Is it possible for sex (as in the sexing of the body) to ever be absent? Even fungi, which defy categories, can have thousands of reproductive types, which is essentially sexed types. Is there a body at all, let alone a monster, without sex?

Foray 12. In Lucille Clifton's poem, "the earth is a living thing," she refuses the notion of blackness as void, of the black hole as a vast vacuuming emptiness. Instead, she describes the earth in black fullness in the "black shambling bear," the "black hawk," the "fish black blind," and the "black belly of coal." The earth, Clifton reminds us, "is a black and living thing."

# Notes

### A MEANDERING INTRODUCTION

1. I allude to Elizabeth Bishop's poem "The Bight," a poem I revisited often in the writing of this book as a reminder of the different ways to look for and find beauty in the mundane and grotesque.

2. Clare, "Gawking, Gaping, Staring," 261.

3. Garland-Thompson, *Staring*, 193.

4. Parks, *Venus*, 79.

5. Ianna Hawkins Owen writes of Baartman's "declarative silence," in which saying nothing, choosing silence, is "a decision to keep something for herself, offstage, and beyond [the poem]." "Still, Nothing," 81.

6. Barad, "No Small Matter," G113.

7. Barker, "Locating Settler Colonialism," n.p.

8. Rifkin, *Erotics of Sovereignty*. In justifying the sexual and the erotic as lenses through which to understand settler colonial effects on Native peoples, Rifkin writes, "The marking and policing of certain kinds of sexual identity as perverse, then, provides an important vehicle through which to track the realization of settler-instituted norms" as sexuality connects to "interdependent logics of personhood, property, and governance" (28–29).

9. Gupta, "Compulsory Sexuality," 132. Compulsory sexuality is also discussed extensively from a legal framework by Elizabeth F. Emens ("Compulsory Sexuality"). The term is also synonymous with similar concepts developed in asexuality studies, including CJ DeLuzio Chasin's coinage *sexualnormativity* ("Theoretical Issues in the Study of Asexuality," 719) and Mark Carrigan's framing of "the sexual assumption" ("There's More to Life than Sex?," 474). Ela Przybyło's neologism *sexusociety* does similar work ("Crisis and Safety," 446). See also Gupta and Cerankowski's discussion of these concepts in "Asexualities and Media."

10. Kahan, *Celibacies*, 3; Foucault, *History of Sexuality*, 27.

11. Snaza, "Asexuality and Erotic Biopolitics," 128–31; Sedgwick, *Epistemology of the Closet*, 182, 25.

12. Snaza, 131.

13. See especially Snaza's writing on the "erotics of literacy" in *Animate Literacies*, 129.

14. Hanson, "Toward an Asexual Narrative Structure," 354; emphasis added.

15. Snaza, "Asexuality and Erotic Biopolitics," 136.

16. Hanson, "Toward an Asexual Narrative Structure," 361–62.

17. Cobb, *Single*, 140.

18. Ngai, *Ugly Feelings*, 333.

19. De Villiers, *Opacity and the Closet*, ix–xii.

20. Though I am here concerned with claims to Bartleby's passivity, it is worth noting that Megan Milks instructively explores Bartleby as a way to link asociality and asexual disinclination to the construction of the "less than human," a theme that will circulate in various refusals of liberal humanism throughout this book. See Milks, "Stunted Growth."

21. See Honig, *Feminist Theory of Refusal*; Love, *Feeling Backward*; Plaut, "Strategic Illiteracies"; Simpson, *Mohawk Interruptus*.

22. See Fahs, "Radical Refusals"; Przybyło, "Crisis and Safety"; Przybyło, *Asexual Erotics*; Milks, "Stunted Growth."

23. Owen, "Still, Nothing," 81.

24. The Asexual Visibility and Education Network, accessed March 17, 2025, https://www.asexuality.org; Owen, 72.

25. Przybyło, "Crisis and Safety," 449.

26. Coelen, *Ultimatum*. I wrote this introduction before the existence of the queer edition of *The Ultimatum*, which has a different host but plenty of other fodder for thinking through compulsory coupledom, marriage, sexuality, and romanticism, all of which go beyond the scope of my point here, but I can't help but point out how the *queer* version of the show hardly queers compulsory sexual desire and coupledom.

27. Barthes, *Lover's Discourse*, 16.

28. Barthes, 13.

29. Rose, "Shimmer," G54–55.

30. If one would like to pursue the various philosophical literatures on absence, one might begin with: Burik, "Darkness and Light"; Chuk, *Vanishing Points*; Mumford, *Absence and Nothing*; Sorensen, *Seeing Dark Things*.

31. Picard, *World of Silence*, 17; Glenn, *Unspoken*, 4.

32. Chuk, *Vanishing Points*, 5.

33. Cage, *Silence*, 191; Sontag, *Styles of Radical Will*, 10–11.

34. Rotman, *Signifying Nothing*, 13.

35. Kaplan, *Nothing That Is*, 1.

36. Cage, *Silence*, 129.

37. Brown, *New Celibacy*, 28.

38. Ela Przybyło and Danielle Cooper make a case for "asexual resonances," which are "almost nothing, but something," in which they urge us to read for

asexual moments and possibilities beyond identity. "Asexual Resonances," 298.

39. Przybyło and Cooper, 298.

40. Przybyło and Cooper, 310.

41. Przybyło, "Ace and Aro Lesbian Art."

42. Przybyło and Cooper, "Asexual Resonances," 309.

43. Cobb, *Single*, 8.

44. Brake, *Minimizing Marriage*, 5.

45. Brake, 81–107.

46. Bersani and Phillips, *Intimacies*, 11.

47. Hanson, "Toward an Asexual Narrative Structure," 353.

48. Yergeau, *Authoring Autism*, 199.

49. Bersani and Phillips, *Intimacies*, 1.

50. Bersani and Phillips, 2–3.

51. Quashie, *Sovereignty of Quiet*, 6–7.

52. Singh, *Unthinking Mastery*, 6.

53. Singh, 22.

54. Warren, *Ontological Terror*, 170.

55. Warren, 170.

56. Warren, 37.

57. Waite, "Cultivating the Scavenger," 54, 52. In addition to the scavenger, I invoke the forager just as Patricia Kaishian and Hasmik Djoulakian riff on Waite's "scavenger methodology" with a "forager methodology" for the queer mycologist. "Science Underground," 20.

58. Benjamin, *Origin of German Tragic Drama*, 28–29.

59. Seigworth and Gregg, "Inventory of Shimmers."

60. Cornellier and Griffiths, "Globalizing Unsettlement," 305.

61. TallBear, "Making Love and Relations," 153.

62. Ruiz and Vourloumis, *Formless Formation*. Sandra Ruiz and Hypatia Vourloumis write toward "swarms" that "exceed categories of seeing and mapping that mark divisions between human and more-than-human life forms" and "intercosmic stylings" that are "queer gappings and mappings that undo the colonization of,        and the race for,        space" (32, 78). They invite us instead into a study that is "a generative operation that is shiftless and aimless" so we may "oscillate in the void's plenitude" (13, 37). Here, I too seek an undoing/redoing of form that is a formless plenitude, full of silences that provide room for imaginative (re)creation.

63. Chen, *Intoxicated*, 139, 136.

64. Chen writes toward a resistance of the academic demand for exhaustive research: "The project of exhaustive knowledge for its own sake mimics the rapaciousness of colonial desire, and one response to it is to reject the obligation to be known or knowable" (104).

65. Chen, 3, 135–36.

66. Chen, 3. On refusing the drive toward accumulation in the university, see also la paperson, *Third University Is Possible*, or Stefano Harney and Fred Moten's *The Undercommons* on the necessity of theft rather than contributive accretion of the university's knowledge banks.

67. Haraway, *Staying with the Trouble*, 10.

68. Chen, *Intoxicated*, 13.

69. Diaz, "Fusings," 49.

70. By invoking sequentiality, I am referencing Denise Ferreira da Silva's critique of the triumvirate of separability, determinacy, and sequentiality, which work in tandem to uphold the "world as we know it." See "On Difference Without Separability," 61. Lisa Guenther also describes sequentiality as "the ontology of linear time," an ontology, a way of being and thinking, that I am trying to refuse here, despite the constraints of the book itself. See "Abolish the World," 33.

## AN END TO ENDS

1. Cobb, *Single*, 8.

2. Rifkin, *Erotics of Sovereignty*, 2.

3. Rifkin, 4, 31. I wish to note that Rifkin builds a lot of his conceptualizations of the erotics of sovereignty on Qwo-Li Driskill's formulation of a "sovereign erotic," most explicitly articulated in "Stolen from Our Bodies." While an earlier version of this chapter cited Driskill's work, I have chosen to remove those references in light of allegations of Driskill's false claims to Indigenous heritage. Instead, I am working from Rifkin's layered formulation of an erotics of sovereignty, alongside Indigenous thinkers like Kim TallBear on unsettling settler sex. See, for example, TallBear, "Making Love and Relations."

4. Snaza, *Tendings*, 12, 23.

5. Snaza calls for the pluriversal ontogenesis of worlds (*Tendings*, 134). And Denise Ferreira da Silva dreams of a "World as Plenum," an intertwined, "infinite composition" ("On Difference Without Separability," 59).

6. la paperson, *Third University Is Possible*, 3–4; Snaza, *Tendings*, 23.

7. Tuck and Ree, "Glossary of Haunting," 642.

8. la paperson, *Third University Is Possible*, 3–4. Snaza, in framing the various worlds we tend, argues that colonialism is "not a structure that awaits dismantling" but is instead just one "possible pattern," which I believe is compatible with la paperson's characterization of colonialism as a "set of technologies" as technologies are also patterns, or tools for making patterns, and they can thus serve as tools for forecasting and repatterning.

9. TallBear, "Making Love and Relations," 152.

10. My language will at times move between the *decolonial* and *anticolo-*

*nial,* as I am in conversation with thinkers who utilize both terms. There is, of course, a distinction to be made between decolonial epistemologies and processes of decolonization, and I take direction from Eve Tuck and K. Wayne Yang, who warn against the expansion of decolonization into metaphorical usage that loses a tangible relation to Indigeneity and land repatriation ("Decolonization Is Not a Metaphor"). Similarly, Max Liboiron distinguishes between concepts that are often collapsed into colonialism, such as Western epistemologies and capitalism. Following Tuck and Yang, colonialism, Liboiron declares, is always about land—access to land and the genocide that makes that access possible. And, drawing on Glen Coulthard and Sandy Grande, Liboiron accounts for the interlocking and overlapping structures and relations that constitute colonialism, such that *anticolonial* describes the "diversity of work, positionalities, and obligations that let us 'stand with' one another as we pursue good land relations broadly defined" (*Pollution Is Colonialism,* 27). While I interrogate ongoing settler epistemologies and move toward anticolonial reframings, it bears remembering that acts of decolonization, returning sovereignty over land and body, are crucial to living in decolonial worlds. In that regard, I tend to favor *anticolonial* as my way of conveying a plotting against and away from colonial logics and inheritances in which management of body cannot be disentangled from access to land. At the same time, I recognize Tapji Garba and Sara-Maria Sorentino's critique of Tuck and Yang's elision of slavery, even as metaphor, as foundational to settler colonialism. They write, "It stands to reason that settler colonialism cannot be adequately theorized *without* metaphor: *the excision of metaphor from settler colonialism is necessarily the excision of slavery*" ("Slavery Is a Metaphor," 776). Or, as Mishuana R. Goeman writes, it "is not only physical occupation of land that has occurred but also our material, symbolic, and lived spaces from the body to the home and to the nation." Accordingly, Goeman asserts that while recovery of land is necessary, "so too is a careful attention to our formations of the social," which is to say, even when not engaged with metaphor, decolonization recovers land and more than land ("Disrupting a Settler-Colonial Grammar," 237–38). In my writing, I aim for a recognition of both the dangers of metaphor in justice-oriented praxis and the necessity of accounting for metaphor and the actual material effects of discourse. Indeed, one of my primary preoccupations in this book is with the performative power of language, especially through the declaration of absences.

11. It bears recognizing, conversely, that if not wholly dismissed or desexualized, some of these people are instead fetishized as sex objects or hypersexualized and perceived as a threat to the imagined sanctity of "respectable" white heterosexuality. A plethora of scholarship incisively and insightfully critiques these violences that function as a different kind of erasure of one's being and subjectivity. See, for example, Joshua Bennett, *Being*

152	**Notes to An End to Ends**

*Property*; Jackson, *Becoming Human*; Kim, *Curative Violence*; Shimizu, *Hyper-sexuality of Race*; Stallings, *Funk the Erotic*.

12. For example, in an episode of the popular American television show *House*, when an asexual couple comes under the care of his colleague, House, remarking on the supposed fact that sex is the "fundamental drive of our species," alleges that anyone who claims to be asexual, or to not want sex, must be "sick, dead, or lying." Yaitanes, *House*.

13. Lugones, "Heterosexualism and the Colonial/Modern Gender System." My language here also recalls the unnamed American critic who deems sexual climax "natural and desirable" in the filmic plotting of intimacy between two people. Bersani and Phillips, *Intimacies*, 11.

14. Freud, *Three Essays on the Theory of Sexuality*, 1.

15. Rifkin, *Beyond Settler Time*.

16. Wolfe, "Settler Colonialism and the Elimination of the Native."

17. Rifkin, *Beyond Settler Time*, 2.

18. My summary characterization of temporal sovereignty relies on Coulthard, *Red Skin, White Masks*; Estes, *Our History Is the Future*; K. P. Whyte, "Indigenous Science (Fiction) for the Anthropocene."

19. In a fungal meditation on the question "How to move through different notions of time?" Yasmine Ostendorf-Rodríguez argues that "we should make desynchronizing from linear time a political act, an act of resistance, an anti-colonial act even" and quips, "It makes me think that we are really overrating efficiency" (*Let's Become Fungal!*, 246, 252). She suggests that we resist the "imperialism of time" by refusing to be extractive and focused on accumulation and to instead be more willing to slow down, spiral, and repeat—with a difference (253).

20. Kahan, *Celibacies*, 148; Bersani, "Father Knows Best," 102.

21. Nelson, *Argonauts*, 135.

22. Barthes, *Pleasure of the Text*.

23. Nelson, *Argonauts*, 44.

24. Barounis, *Vulnerable Constitutions*, 167.

25. Jagose, *Orgasmology*, 8; Heath, *Sexual Fix*.

26. On the capacitation of pleasure via orgasm, see Barounis, *Vulnerable Constitutions*, 167–73.

27. Jagose, *Orgasmology*, xvi.

28. Snaza, *Animate Literacies*, 129.

29. Snaza, 129.

30. The orgasm as knowing, dying, spending, and coming draws on Barthes, *Pleasure of the Text*, vi.

31. Taylor, "Taking It in the Ear," 604.

32. Taylor, 605; Cusick, "On a Lesbian Relationship with Music," 80.

33. Davies, "Auricular Erotics"; Barthes, *Pleasure of the Text*.

34. Taylor, "Taking It in the Ear," 609.

35. Prufrock, "Emotional Boner."

36. Kim, "How Much Sex Is Healthy?," 165.

37. All quotations from the French film come from the translation provided in the English subtitles in the 2002 U.S. release of the film.

38. Foucault, *History of Sexuality*, 58.

39. Frost, *Problem with Pleasure*, 12.

40. The temporality of durational pleasure I imagine here is a kind of cousin to Kahan's formulation of "celibate time" that is nonteleological and "heightens pleasure by suspending closures and resisting climax." Kahan, *Celibacies*, 71.

41. Muñoz, *Cruising Utopia*, 25.

42. Morgensen, "Settler Homonationalism."

43. TallBear, "Making Love and Relations," 154.

44. Lorde, "Uses of the Erotic," 54.

45. TallBear, "Critical Poly 100s," 156.

46. Przybyło, *Asexual Erotics*, 1–32.

47. Preciado, *Testo Junkie*.

48. Canaday, *Straight State*.

49. Morgensen, "Settler Homonationalism," 110.

50. Morgensen, 120.

51. Cerankowski, *Suture*.

52. Gay, *Book of Delights*, xii; Tippett, "Ross Gay."

## BETWEEN

1. Mazzadra and Neilson, *Border as Method*, vii.

2. Mazzadra and Neilson, viii.

3. Singh, "Errands for the Wild," 574–75.

4. Here, I make reference to Singh's embrace of the humanimal as a way to "dispossess oneself from the sovereignty of man, to refuse the anticolonial reach of becoming masterful human subjects" (*Unthinking Mastery*, 122). I am also drawing on Mel Y. Chen's *Animacies*, in which Chen critiques the use of an animacy hierarchy to elevate humans over animals and inanimate objects and, consequently, certain humans over other humans. On the inanimate, I link up with Jane Bennett's work on vital materialities and vibrant matter "to dissipate the onto-theological binaries of life/matter, human/animal," exposing the limits of human categorization and recognizing "thing-power," the vibrancy of inanimate things, and human–nonhuman mingling (*Vibrant Matter*, x). Similarly, in *Inanimation*, David Wills puts forward "theories of inorganic life" as he breaks down the distinctions between organic and inorganic, animate and inanimate in relation to how we conceive of "life." I might note, as I wish to adopt an anticolonial practice of thought

and action, that much of this thinking about what constitutes life, vitality, and vibrancy is, as Tim Ingold also suggests, repackaged animism, which was long dismissed, denied, and practically erased by settler colonial monotheists (*Being Alive*, 67). These (queer) reanimations are indebted to long histories of a wide range of Indigenous beliefs, worldviews, and practices.

5. Jackson, *Becoming Human*, 30.

6. For example, Myra Hird writes of the "technological" capabilities of bacteria, protocists, and animals ("From the Culture of Matter," 3.12–3.13). Julian Yates similarly writes of the emergence of different technologies like writing and coding when we look beyond the one "set of screens" we call the "human" (*Of Sheep, Oranges, and Yeast*, 16, 24–26). The point is, there are many ways to write, code, produce, and know that do not translate or map neatly onto human technologies and ways of knowing.

7. Singh, *Unthinking Mastery*, 146–47.

8. Currah, *Sex Is as Sex Does*, 98.

9. Currah, 80.

10. Singh, *Unthinking Mastery*, 147.

11. Warren, *Ontological Terror*, 170. Warren calls for an abandonment of the human in favor of an ontological revolution that will "destroy the world and its institutions," which I also read as a nod to Denise Ferreira da Silva's vision of the end of the world (as we know it). See Ferreira da Silva, "Toward a Black Feminist Poethics" and "On Difference Without Separability."

12. Smith, *Decolonizing Methodologies*, 44.

13. With the notion of "fixing," I am playing with Katrina Karkazis's critique of "fixing sex" through often nonconsensual medical intervention on intersex people, such that a fixing of one's sex is a way of fixing one's personhood (*Fixing Sex*). I similarly think of Eli Clare's critique, in *Brilliant Imperfection*, of cure as an erasure of disability and bodily difference, as personhood is weaponized such that disabled people are deemed in need of a cure or treatment in order to move them into full personhood.

14. On *trans* as a prefix, see Hayward, "More Lessons from a Starfish"; Stryker and Aizura, "Introduction"; Hayward and Weinstein, "Introduction." On trans entanglements, see Barad, "TransMaterialities."

15. Rubin, *Intersex Matters*, 1.

16. Rubin, 3, 8.

17. Beauchamp, *Going Stealth*, 13–14.

18. *Oxford English Dictionary*, s.v. "transfix (*v.*)," June 2024, https://doi.org/10.1093/OED/6365470494. I owe my thinking on transfixation to the work Jules Rosskam and Jack Isaac Pryor are doing with the notion of the "transfixt" in art practice and spectatorship, as detailed in their call for submissions for *Transfixt*, the book they are editing and curating.

19. Diversi and Moreira, *Betweener Talk*, 206.

20. Pulsifer, "Trolling Humanism," 20.
21. Rubin, *Intersex Matters,* 151.
22. Barad, "TransMaterialities," 401.
23. Kim, "Unbecoming Human," 320.
24. Bhabha, *Location of Culture,* 336, 11.
25. Bhabha, 2, 5.
26. Blackston, "Monkey Business," 130.
27. Ingold, *Being Alive,* 10.
28. Gopinath, *Unruly Visions,* 16.
29. Beauchamp, *Going Stealth,* 21.
30. Currah and Mulqueen, "Securitizing Gender," 577.
31. Quinan and Hunt, "Non-Binary Gender Markers," 382.
32. Pugliese, "Biometrics, Infrastructural Whiteness," 107.
33. Hunt, "Tracing Transgender Ghosts," 100.
34. Deleuze and Guattari, *Thousand Plateaus,* 245–46.
35. Pulsifer, "Trolling Humanism," 10.
36. Blackston, "Monkey Business," 130. In addition to "racial attributions," I might add in here "racial retributions," for there is a subplot added to the film in which Vore sells human babies into a child pornography ring in order to enact vengeance on humankind and hold up a mirror to their own cruelty. The child-snatching storyline builds on a mythology that is alluded to in the short story in which trolls snatch human babies and replace them with changelings.
37. Cynthia Barounis writes of the "orgasmic imperative" as a pleasure capacity to be achieved as a kind of sexual rehabilitation of the disabled and desexualized body (see *Vulnerable Constitutions,* esp. 167–73; also see "An End to Ends" in this book). Christine Labuski also chronicles how women with chronic genital pain who are unable to engage in penetrative sex with their husbands or boyfriends often feel like failures as women (*It Hurts Down There*). Janine Farrell and Thea Cacchioni similarly describe how many women whose genital pain excludes them from "real" sex (penetrative intercourse) view themselves as failures, inadequate, and not "real women" ("Medicalization of Women's Sexual Pain," 331).
38. Citing Amy Kaler, Labuski describes how "vulvar pain produces a category of 'unreal women' whose gender identity is threatened by being unable to engage in 'an action which makes people into heterogendered men and women.'" That "action" is penetrative sex. In Tina's failure to comfortably and pleasurably be penetrated, she fails to be made into a "heterogendered woman" (Labuski, *It Hurts Down There,* 7; Kaler, "Unreal Women," 50).
39. Adams, "Extravagant Multitudes."
40. Sheldrake, *Entangled Life,* 14; Adams, "Extravagant Multitudes," 96.
41. Adams, "Extravagant Multitudes," 95.

42. I want to include a note here on the expansiveness of pleasure through eating. Earlier in the film we watch as Tina disinterestedly pushes spaghetti around her plate while she dines with Roland. Later with Vore, she delightedly plucks grubs from the earth and smacks her tongue in pleasure. She learns a new way to consume and be consumed. Incidentally, Vore's name, which strikes Tina as odd and foreign, calls up vorarephilia, colloquially referred to as *vore*—the erotic desire to consume or to be consumed by the other, an erotics of eating. For many, this erotic may stretch into the sexual, but I also imagine its asexual possibilities in the expanded erotics of bodily intimacies in eating and being eaten. I explore more substantially the erotics of eating, particularly of flesh, in "Rot [Eaten] Rot" in this book.

43. Labuski, *It Hurts Down There*, 14.

44. Barad, "TransMaterialities," 400–401.

45. Jane Bennett, *Vibrant Matter*, 28.

46. Barad, *Meeting the Universe Halfway*, 354.

47. Barad, "TransMaterialities," 401.

48. Barad, 401.

49. Pulsifer, "Trolling Humanism," 19.

50. Hird, "Animal Trans."

51. Ahmed, *Cultural Politics of Emotion*, 38.

52. On Sweden's racist and colonial history, see Antoine, "Swedish Disconnect." Katja Antoine also tracks the recent rise of Islamophobia and antisemitism. On the plight of undocumented persons in Sweden, see Sigvardsdotter, "Presenting Absent Bodies." On the rise of Islamophobia across Scandinavia, see Hervik, "What Is in the Scandinavian Nexus?" On white nationalism in Sweden, see Teitelbaum, "Implicitly White."

53. Kim, "Unbecoming Human," 315.

54. Rubin, *Intersex Matters*, 68.

55. Hayward and Weinstein, "Introduction," 201; Malatino, *Queer Embodiment*, 193.

## ROT [EATEN] ROT

1. Sheldrake, *Entangled Life*, 94–122.

2. Sheldrake, 49–50.

3. Deleuze and Guattari, *Thousand Plateaus*, 20.

4. Sheldrake, *Entangled Life*, 129. Yasmine Ostendorf-Rodríguez also warns that thinking of mycelia as roots or even "root-like" is to risk "borrowing terms from a kingdom they are not a part of." Rather, they are separately intertwined with the plant kingdom, fashioning an "interface for forming symbiotic relationships with the roots of plants." Ostendorf-Rodríguez, *Let's Become Fungal!*, 6.

5. Kaishian and Djoulakian, "Science Underground," 4.

6. Patricia Kaishian and Hasmik Djoulakian write about how mycology is a queer discipline as a field that has long been marginalized, but they also reach toward mycological queerness by describing fungi as nonbinary and deviant ("Science Underground"). V Adams also writes about how mushrooms evade binary categories ("Extravagant Multitudes," 96). Sheldrake also explains that some fungi "have tens of thousands of mating types" (*Entangled Life*, 36). Although he does not necessarily call this "queer" and is more interested in how it upsets our organization of sex types, such a fact has been taken up in a lot of queer discourse to again refuse the binary and assert the queerness of mushrooms.

7. Sheldrake writes, "These organisms make questions of our categories, and thinking about them makes the world look different." *Entangled Life*, 14.

8. Cage, "Music Lovers' Field Companion," 7.

9. Trinder, "Where the Whippoorwill," 17.

10. Cage, "Music Lovers' Field Companion," 9.

11. Quoted in Trinder, "Where the Whippoorwill," 60.

12. Hval, *Paradise Rot*, 1.

13. Hval, 5. See, again, Sheldrake: "Mycelium is a body without a plan." *Entangled Life*, 49.

14. Hval, 14.

15. Tavakoli, "In 'Paradise Rot.'"

16. Hval, *Paradise Rot*, 64.

17. Hval, 5.

18. Kyla Wazana Tompkins links rot to waste as "the material expression of deviant desire," particularly through the erotics of urination in which "discarded matter" becomes "deviant matter," highlighting "the overlap between rot and sexual deviance" (*Deviant Matter*, 157, 163). The frequent flow and spillage of urine in *Paradise Rot* becomes a fluid suspension of a deviant erotic that winds its way through the book, circulating around and between sex and not-sex.

19. Hval, *Paradise Rot*, 5, 3.

20. Hval, 5.

21. Hval, 5.

22. Hval, 27.

23. Hval, 35.

24. Hval, 33–34.

25. Tavakoli, "In 'Paradise Rot.'"

26. Kristeva, *Powers of Horror*.

27. Hval, *Paradise Rot*, 38.

28. Hval, 82.

29. Hval, 46.

30. Hval, 90.

31. Hval, 89.

32. Hval, 74, 134.

33. Hval, 143.

34. Hval, 144–45.

35. Barthes, *Lover's Discourse*, 15.

36. Hval, *Paradise Rot*, 148.

37. Bierend, *In Search of Mycotopia*, 11.

38. McCoy, *Mycocultural Revolution*, 40. Bierend also writes that "they slip beneath the attention of the wider world even as they link it together." *In Search of Mycotopia*, 11.

39. Tsing, *Mushroom at the End of the World*, 2.

40. Sheldrake, *Entangled Life*, 15.

41. This is an inversion of the ending sentiment of "Eaten" and Barthes's line, "We die together from loving each other." *Lover's Discourse*, 11.

## ~~REDACTED~~

1. Gordon, *Ghostly Matters*, 32–35.

2. Gordon, 32; Carotenuto, *Secret Symmetry*.

3. Gordon, 34.

4. Steedman, *Dust*, 11.

5. Gordon writes, "The whole essence, if you can use that word, of a ghost is that it has a real presence and demands its due, your attention." *Ghostly Matters*, xvi.

6. Arlette Farge writes that we must "work with the scattered echoes and pieces" of the archive, declaring that "fragmentation is less a lacuna than the reflection of a mode of being" (*Allure of the Archives*, 108). Steedman also writes that in addition to archives being composed of "selected and consciously chosen documentation," they also include "mad fragmentations that no one intended to preserve and that just ended up there" (*Dust*, 68). Some of these fragments are happy accidents, but they are still partial. Working with the echoes, pieces, and fragmentations, we are left to fill in the gaps using a method like Saidiya Hartman's "critical fabulation," which allows all of us still living here in the erasures, redactions, and betweens to write the "dream book for existing otherwise" (*Wayward Lives, Beautiful Experiments*, xv).

7. Zeb Tortorici writes, "Traces always remain; it is simply our duty as researchers and archivists to figure out what to do with them." "Archival Seduction."

8. Sharif, "Near Transitive Properties of the Political." Somewhat ironically, this essay, originally published in a special issue on erasure, is no longer available online through the journal's host website. The essay has been obliterated and only remains for those who saved either a PDF or a print

copy. I was fortunate enough to know someone who has a PDF copy that she was able to share with me, though it is missing the original pagination.

9. Leung, "Erasure in Three Acts."

10. Sharif, "Near Transitive Properties of the Political."

11. Leung, "Erasure in Three Acts."

12. Again, black and white, which are often coded as opposites, have the shared effect of erasing and blocking out.

13. Leung, "Erasure in Three Acts."

14. See "We Are Getting Nowhere" in this book, where I write about Yayoi Kusama's art and her writing on obliteration as invitation to join in the dissolution into the natural universe with reference again to Solmaz Sharif's ideas that erasure can also have an additive effect. See also note 6 above, in which Arlette Farge suggests that fragmentation, a kind of obliteration, is a mode of being.

15. Sharif, "Near Transitive Properties of the Political."

16. See Ianna Hawkins Owen's writing on "declarative silence" in "Still, Nothing." Leung also draws on Édouard Glissant's argument for the "right to opacity" (Glissant, *Poetics of Relation*, 189). She asks, "Can we consider poetry for the ways it does not tell? How it retains its dignity through selective silence?" And she answers, "In this case, erasure is a strategy that at first mimics the psychological embodiment of what we have lost. Then the loss blankets the page. Then the poem becomes synonymous with loss itself."

17. Both Sharif and Leung reflect on erasure from their own vantage points of artistic practice. Sharif writes about how her own experiments with erasure mostly occur through the obliteration of text she has written herself, rather than through the manipulation and obliteration of extant texts. Leung follows her essay on erasure with two erasure poems/essays crafted from blacking out parts of her own initial essay—hence the title of the essay—"Erasure in Three Acts"—wherein the erasures serve not only as acts two and three but as a refrain. Leung writes, "Sometimes what emerges from the erasure is a refrain. After something unfortunate happens, I find myself narrating the events over and over, the same inexhaustible order of words, until gradually, they decay into a less comprehensible shape, and finally, 'It happened. That's all.'" Erasure, for Leung, is also a way to move through trauma time, bearing witness on repetition to discharge the happening. I find both of their works to be remarkable processes of self-obliteration. My own process of writing this book has been one of refrain, wandering back, and dwelling, not as in being stuck moving in circles but as a way of repeating with a difference. For example, return to the introduction to this book for another meditation on how silence operates both to erase and to reveal, how it is wielded to keep something for oneself when

everything else has been taken. As part of this recursive flow, I also practice erasing my own writing; some of it is obviously redacted with black rectangles or whited-out text, but a lot of my writing has been deleted and rewritten until the book took its final shape, those excised fragments either lost entirely or collected in another file for a dream of another time. There is always a trace of the process in the final text, but it is not always obvious where text has been obliterated and why.

18. Abigail Raphael Collins, correspondence with author, February 2, 2024.

19. Apps, *Intersex*, 58.

20. Apps, 55–63.

21. Apps, 62.

22. I allude to Katrina Karkazis's description of nonconsensual medical intervention on intersex people as a corrective violence under the illusion of "fixing sex" (Karkazis, *Fixing Sex*). See also "Between" in this book for further elaboration on the overlap of state power and the fixing of sex and gender.

23. In the obliteration, there is also something about consumption. Under the final image, Apps writes, "I say I am here for you to devour. I say my mouth genitals devour. I say it tastes good close to the jawbone. I say we in a way that is two I animals doubling. I say love" (*Intersex*, 63). Looking is a kind of consuming, as the voyeur takes in the other, noticing everything but the tears streaking down their face.

24. Tortorici, "Archival Seduction."

25. Tortorici.

26. Walter Benjamin, writing on fragments and the necessity of digression for philosophical inquiry: "The value of fragments of thought is all the greater the less direct their relationship to the underlying idea, and the brilliance of the representation depends as much on this value as the brilliance of the mosaic does on the quality of the glass paste." *Origin of German Tragic Drama*, 28–29.

27. Tortorici, "Archival Seduction."

28. Kahan, *Celibacies*.

29. Tortorici, "Archival Seduction."

30. Kel Rakowski (@h_e_r_s_t_o_r_y), "Jemima Wilkinson (1758–1819) was a charismatic American Quaker and evangelist," Instagram photo, January 5, 2018, https://www.instagram.com/p/BdkklqVl0d_.

31. Barzman, "Subject of 'Woman,'" 348.

32. Quoted in Long, "Public Universal Friend."

33. In the last few decades, several different factions of people have adopted the Friend's story as a precursor to their own movement or as a way to understand their own particular historical niche of interest. This is what we often do with archives, after all—find the stories that tell us something

we want to know about ourselves. The story of the Friend has gone through various cycles of resurgence and public interest. For example, some have shown keen interest in the Friend as a way of uncovering historical examples of cross-dressing or in cracking the stories of early religious fanaticism and so-called false prophets (Morris, *American Messiahs*). It has been retold by historians delving into the odder religious histories of colonial America, particularly through the second Great Awakening (the Friend, after all, developed quite a following of believers and practitioners) (Juster, *Doomsayers*). The story has also been embraced by feminists as a tale of cunning and patriarchal refusal—a woman who wishes to remain unwed and instead devote her time to learning and preaching the gospel cleverly reinvents herself as a genderless saintly figure (Juster, "To Slay the Beast"). And, most recently, in this contemporary era of gender politics, the Friend's story has been taken up anew by people looking to recover some sort of early queer, transgender, or nonbinary history in the Friend's strange re/birth (Fleischmann, *Time Is the Thing*). Some of these versions can be supported through one of several possible interpretations of archival evidence, while some, like the claim to the use of *they/them* pronouns, are demonstrably false (Meikle and Nelson, "Reborn").

34. For more exhaustive and comprehensive accounts of the more intricate details of the Friend's life, see, in particular, Bronski, *Queer History of the United States*; Fleischmann, *Time Is the Thing*; Juster, *Doomsayers*, "Neither Male nor Female," "To Slay the Beast"; Larson, "Laid Open," "'Indescribable Being'"; Moyer, *Public Universal Friend*; Wisbey, *Pioneer Prophetess*. While some scholars tend to draw on David Hudson's *Memoir of Jemima Wilkinson*, Hudson's account is intended to disparage the Friend, with whom Hudson was engaged in a land dispute, as Adam Morris notes in *American Messiahs*.

35. Abdelfatah and Arablouei, "Public Universal Friend."

36. Smilges, *Queer Silence*, 20. Susan Wendell suggests "any adequate feminist understanding of disability must encompass chronic illnesses," and I would add so too must any queer understanding of disability ("Unhealthy Disabled," 17). Wendell also distinguishes between disability and illness—not all disabled people are sick. But it is also true that illness can be experienced as debilitating—many sick people experience themselves as disabled, whether temporarily or permanently (Wendell, *Rejected Body*). Smilges also writes that disability is capacious and "encompasses a wide variety of embodyminded difference" (*Queer Silence*, 6). Illness and chronic illness inevitably shape and reshape the bodymind, which arguably constitutes states of "embodyminded difference."

37. Larson, "'Indescribable Being,'" 581.

38. Amin writes, "Nonbinary identity is therefore not, as some nonbinary

people would have it, a radical refusal of the colonial gender binary" because "binary Western thinking" inevitably generates "an idealized opposite for each new category coined." In short, as long as nonbinary is a gender to *be* in opposition to binary gender, it is "difficult to imagine an identity more provincially Western and less decolonial than contemporary nonbinary identity." Amin, "We Are All Nonbinary," 116.

39. LaFleur, "Epilogue," 368.

40. Heyam, *Before We Were Trans*, 218.

41. I cannot help but think of a line from Rainer Maria Rilke: "We have to get used to the fact that we rest in the pause between two of God's breaths: for that means: to be in time." *Dark Interval*, 42.

42. For more on fixing the body through the fastening of gender and the human, see "Between" in this book.

43. Juster, *Doomsayers*, 107–8.

44. Juster, 107–8.

45. Smilges, *Queer Silence*, 22.

46. Here, I also gesture to Eli Clare's ambivalent relationship to cure, as something that can both ease pain and discomfort but that also erases, homogenizes, and reinforces the concept of the normal, normate, normative human body to be maintained and restored as such. Clare, *Brilliant Imperfection*.

47. I have experienced intense bouts of feverish illness at the onset of infection, but after the fever passes, those experiences leave marks on my psyche and sense of self, including the shape of my gender. I am not always sick, and I mostly move through the world appearing nondisabled on a regular basis. But I do sometimes have flares of pain and fatigue that remind me that the illness never really left. It returns not just in the experience of unease and bodily dis-ease in a flare but also in the way I understand who I am in the world, my limits and my capacities. The story of the Friend has helped me follow my own crip recovery of the impact of illness, which even in my agnosticism, becomes inseparable from religiosity, a sense of a spiritual self, and gender.

48. Fleischmann, *Time Is the Thing*, 79–84, 155.

49. Barzman, "Subject of 'Woman,'" 350.

50. In one version of a last will and testament, the Friend begins by declaring that the document pertains to the affairs of a person "who in the year one thousand seven hundred and seventy six was called Jemima Wilkinson and ever since that time the ~~Publick~~ Universal Friend a new name which the mouth of the Lord hath named considering the uncertainty of this mortal life." This entry speaks to an end of Jemima Wilkinson and a divine christening of a new being, the Friend, a spirit who has entered the uncertain mortal world. For unknown reasons, "Publick" is here redacted.

I might speculate it is simply because over time, the Friend became more widely known simply as the Universal Friend or the Friend, though I don't know why it would be removed from the draft of a legal document that should give the name in full as originally declared. The erasure only raises more questions. Notably, I am somewhat ironically working with copies of copies in which I presume some attempt has been made to maintain the original markings, though I cannot be entirely sure what has been added or redacted, whether intentionally or unintentionally. The files I have access to are digitized scans of notebooks that contain handwritten transcriptions of the original letters. These transcriptions contain what appear to me to be errors. For example, in the lines of the testament I quoted here, the name Jemima Wilkinson was transcribed as "Jemima Wilkerson" (Last Will and Testament of the Friend, Jemima Wilkinson papers, #621, Division of Rare and Manuscript Collections, Cornell University Library). The recording and rerecording in the archive are functions by which history unwrites and rewrites itself.

51. Letter by the Friend to C Marshall, June 3, 1795, Jemima Wilkinson papers, #621, Division of Rare and Manuscript Collections, Cornell University Library.

52. Moyer, *Public Universal Friend*, 192.

53. Moyer, 192.

54. Karen Barzman, conversation with author, January 10, 2024.

55. Gilles Deleuze and Félix Guattari, thinking against *being*, focused on the multiplicities of *becoming*, also write, "We know that many beings pass between a man and a woman; they come from different worlds, are borne on the wind, form rhizomes around roots; they cannot be understood in terms of production, only in terms of becoming." *Thousand Plateaus*, 242.

56. Barzman, "Subject of 'Woman,'" 352.

57. Farge, *Allure of the Archives*, 94.

58. Lee, "Be/longing in the Archival Body," 34.

59. Prins, "Coming to Light," 892. See also Meier, "Edward S. Curtis," for a detailed account of Curtis's specific manipulations of photographs and demands of performed authenticity by his subjects.

60. Wolfe, "Settler Colonialism and the Elimination of the Native."

## ALL ENDS | NO END

1. "No end," as in ongoingly, without end. Or pointless, as in without an endpoint or purposeless. We shall do this to no end, with nowhere to go and no singular point to make.

2. Tracing both the history of the footnote (once called a "bottom note") and literary and artistic experimentation with paratext, Craig Dworkin writes, "Notes are not merely isolated end points of reference but gesture to the textual spaces between each other, carrying information about their text

as a whole" (*No Medium*, 65). Notes are never an end in themselves, even if they come at the foot or end of a text; they are flares lighting pathways of meaning and connection between and toward other texts and other notes. In other words, as I like to remind my students, the notes are there for a reason; they're worth reading.[a] If it is to be believed that nobody ever reads the notes, what if that was all they were given to read? I write this, also, as someone who reads books by moving a bookmark along in the endnotes to make flipping back and forth easier. I am a devout reader of notes, with or without the textual body. According to Dworkin, the footnote developed with modern book design to create more order on the page, cleaning up the margins and ordering all notation to the bottom of the page (64). The endnote is its own kind of ordering, but I like how it refuses an ordered body. It leaves a disordered page and comes at the end of the chapter, essay, or book, but the first endnote is only the beginning of the end.

   [a] Dworkin notes that to "note" is to "observe closely" and provides as an example Daniel Spoerri's *Topographie anécdotée du hasard* (Anecdoted topography of chance) as a work that "pays meticulous attention to objects that would otherwise go unnoticed: bread crumbs and grains of salt, a stray paperclip or rubber band, an empty bottle, a torn carton, a cracked ashtray, and so on." But *to note* can also mean "to make use of something," so Dworkin writes, "there is an irony in the fact that the cartographic notes of the *Topographie* function only to the extent that they suspend the use of the objects noted" (*No Medium*, 60–61). Let us note again how important it can be to take note of the otherwise unused and unnoticed, the seemingly unremarkable and ordinary.[i]

      [i] In *Ordinary Notes*, Christina Sharpe begins with a list of definitions of *note* as both noun and verb. Again, *to note* can mean to notice or observe or, in the transitive sense, "to take notice of; to consider or study carefully; to pay attention to; to mark." As a noun, a note is "a brief record . . . written down as an aid to memory." Related to music and sound, it is also a tone, a pitched sound (*Ordinary Notes*, 1). Of the *ordinary*, Sharpe doesn't much define it but lets it take shape in the collection of notes, an inventory of everyday pleasures amid everyday racism, both horrific and ordinary at the same time. What feels ordinary, and the tenor or pitch of that feeling, might shift with the reader, as in the ways everyday racism is felt, for whom it is a typical experience, for whom the stories might come as a shock. Though racialization and poverty are not equivalent (but sometimes overlap), the experiences of poverty are shocking to those who have not known them even as they are everyday and ordinary for those who know no other way to live.

Recently, a new friend, somewhat horrified and aghast, asked me about growing up the way I did—poor, hungry sometimes, anxious, nervous, scared, the oldest child of alcoholics trying to save everyone from the wolves in the house. I shrug, "It was just my life." In a poem I return to often, Marie Howe makes the banal, perhaps ordinary, acts of living feel somehow urgent and extraordinary. A sink full of crusted dishes, a wait for a plumber, shopping for food and small necessary objects, parking the car. "This is what the living do." "This is it." And then in a moment swept up in her own reflection, caught in a love for herself there on that street, the shop window reflecting back her windblown face: "I'm speechless. I am living. I remember you" ("What the Living Do," 89–90). I am living. I remember many things, but my memories are often inaccurate, a bit askew. I have yet to be speechlessly caught up in a love for myself, yet the world holds me speechless in my adoration for all of its quiet charms and secrets. And so I continue doing the strange, abject things of living.

3. Experimental writing and art strike me as crucial to refusing the mandates of normative, teleological spacetime. Matthew Cheney, reflecting on his time learning from Barry Lopez, meditates on the transgressive power of writing. He quotes an interview with Robert Glück on refusing narrative convention: "The more 'normal' the convention, the more it supports the status quo" (Cheney, *About That Life*, 83; Leuzzi, "Interview with Robert Glück"). My refusal of the status quo is a refusal of convention; it is no wonder this book follows the abstract, the absurd, and the experimental. On (para)textual experimentation: Jenny Boully's book *The Body: An Essay* is composed only of footnotes to blank pages. The body is gone; only the feet remain. Reading the book, I found myself wanting a sense of the missing body text; where there was only emptiness, I wanted the placement of the numbers to the footnotes. Inspired by Boully, I wanted to see what story could be told if I erased (redacted) the body and left only the notes. What stories might be conjured in the absence of the narrative I believed I was telling? I think again of Radical Face's album *Missing Film*, how I imagine a soundtrack to a film that never existed, just as Boully's footnotes notate a text that presumably never existed (it's impossible to know for certain, but conceptually, the body text is nonexistent and described as such in the promotional materials for the book).Foray 6 It was indeed Boully's book that led me to Dworkin's *No Medium*, where he writes about *The Body*, but he also writes about other experiments with textual erasure and paratext, especially footnotes and endnotes. My favorite is Dworkin's discussion of Simon Morris's experiment in which he stripped the text from two academic essays

and then gave each writer the other writer's erased text and asked them to rewrite/recreate the essay from the notes alone (Dworkin, *No Medium*, 65; Morris, Morlock, and Dalton, *Interpretation*). There are so many ways one might compose a text. In this case, I wrote some of the notes first, then filled in a body text that I erased. I also wrote body text that I then notated before erasing. I also moved some notes to the body and erased them, and moved some of the body to the notes, where the text remained legible. It's all present, in a way—even if that body text is now absented.

4. Every second, some body, somebody, somewhere, goes missing.

5. Just as Suzan-Lori Parks names what the voyeurs could not see when they looked at Saartjie Baartman, Green's sculpture *Sa Main Charmante*, the title of which translates to "her charming hand," calls up not only the missing hand but the entire body. At the center of the piece, a box with two footprints, marking where she would have stood but stands no longer. The backdrop is composed of a wooden sculpture built with what appear to be slats that might support a mattress (a place of rest) engraved with text that describes her life as the "Hottentot Venus," along with text taken from Georges Cuvier's medical report on the dissection of her body after death. (Cuvier also figures in Parks's play as the Baron Docteur. A line from Cuvier's notebook provides the title to Green's sculpture, and Parks's play includes multiple references to "her charming hands" as well. Scene 9 is even titled "Her Charming Hands/An Anatomical Columbus"—in other words, a body conquered and colonized, stolen. [Parks, *Venus*, 90]) The wooden sculpture takes the shape of a body, arms outstretched, almost as if crucified, marking another way a symbol has come to stand in for a missing body. The invitation to the audience: look through the viewing box that contains a photo of Baartman being prodded and inspected; become the voyeur while simultaneously looking into the blinding glare of the stage light shining brightly into the viewing box and onto the viewer. Looking will cost you a momentary loss of vision, while it also makes you visible as you stand in the spotlight, participating in the voyeurism. You are seen while you look but cannot see.

6. A set of remains, like the soapbox marked with footprints, like the footnotes. No body, only feet. Baartman's body is the only body present within the textual body, an absent presence made manifest through the image of the sculpture that shapes the space her body would have inhabited.

7. The question of how much actually happens in Samuel Beckett's work has long been up for debate. Beckett is known for writing plays in which nothing seemingly happens; instead, there is a lot of waiting (*Waiting for Godot*) or moving of objects (*Happy Days*) or looking out the window (*Endgame*). I could have chosen to write about any one of these plays, but I am drawn to *Endgame* because it seems fitting to my concern about the meaning

of ends and refusals to move toward or arrive at an end. Several critics also specifically suggest that *Endgame* is "devoid of event," that it "lacks action" or is a play of "intense inaction," and that it is at odds with the "autotelic nature of the work of art," the demand that art arrive at its purpose, its end (Bersani and Dutoit, *Arts of Impoverishment*, 25, 38; Chevigny, *Twentieth Century Interpretations of Endgame*, 4). Importantly, however, while many critics argue that Beckett's plays "lack action," they simultaneously acknowledge the immediacy of the work in the occurrence of movement, word, and gesture, all of which are arguably a lot of action occurring, with or without purpose, with or without meaning. In other words, nothing occurs, but again, *nothing* is really a lot of *something.*

8. An interior thought: You put so much effort into writing, knowing full well no one may read it. Are you referring to the notes or the body? Yes.

9. Robert Rauschenberg's *Erased de Kooning Drawing,* even after being erased, still contained what Dworkin describes as the traces and shadow of de Kooning's original drawing. "Indeed," Dworkin writes, "the work insists on the originating conceptual gesture by documenting not its accomplishment, but its incompletion." In other words, a more accurate title, Dworkin quips, might be *"Partially Erased de Kooning Drawing"* (*No Medium*, 41). My erasure is also partial; the text has been deleted (redacted), but the endnote numbers remain, providing a trace of the shape of the text, a constellation, a scattered map of signposts with no clear pathways, a sequence that interrupts sensemaking, a demand to stay a little lost.

10. Kazimir Malevich is said to have thought of white as the "color of infinity," a vastness rather than an emptiness. The painting is full of texture and lines demarcating a square of a differently shaded white layered on the white background. This painting, housed at New York City's Museum of Modern Art, is reflective of Malevich's suprematist theory of art. Some might be quick to associate the praise of the color white as pure and utopian and its description as a "suprematist composition" with white supremacy, but for Malevich, who was always trying to challenge the status quo (see also note 3 above), suprematism was about abandoning representation, letting the art object simply be, full in and of itself. In fact, the first work of his suprematist movement was *Black Square,* a simple painted black square that Malevich considered the zero of the movement, the start of infinity, rather than a naught. See "Five Ways to Look."

11. Although black and white are typically characterized as opposites, Malevich and Rauschenberg both have played with their overlapping performativity of absence, the ways they each invoke nothingness and refuse representation, breaking down another binarization. Black and white again serve a similar function, as they do in redaction. "Absence *does* things, it is performative" (Meyer, "Placing and Tracing Absence," 104). Rauschenberg

also did a series of both *White Paintings* and *Black Paintings*. The *White Paintings* are what John Cage credits for his "silent" work *4′33″*: "To Whom It May Concern: The white paintings came first; my silent piece came later" (Cage, *Silence*, 98). Writing further on the *White Paintings*, Cage waxes poetic, "The atmosphere is such that everything is seen clearly, even in the dark night. . . . This subject is unavoidable (*a canvas is never empty.*); it fills an empty canvas." For Cage, the *White Paintings* are "a poetry of *infinite possibilities*" (*Silence*, 99, 103).[b] In this infinite emptiness that is never really empty, Dworkin understands both Cage's and Rauschenberg's work as an unsettling of time, highlighting the "dynamic tension between continuous flux and discrete partition," which "frame[s] a durational experience of interconnected events." To be in the duration is to be in the pleasure of going nowhere, to be in that "particular particulate distribution of dust and ambient shadows on that space at any given moment" (*No Medium*, 123–24). Beckett's *Endgame* and the irresolution of Barry Jenkins's film *Moonlight* both similarly offer a durational experience of given moments of pausing and waiting, a dwelling.

    [b] Yayoi Kusama's *Infinity Net* paintings create a similar poetry. Although she produced many of them in different colors, the 1960 *White Net Painting* emerges as particularly relevant here. I visited this painting regularly for an entire semester while it was on display at the Allen Memorial Art Museum at Oberlin College. These visits were my own way of dwelling with and in the net. Of the infinity nets, Kusama writes, "My desire was to predict and measure the infinity of the unbounded universe, from my own position in it, with dots—an accumulation of particles forming the negative spaces in the net. . . . I wanted to examine the single dot that was my own life. One polka dot: a single particle among billions. . . . Everything—myself, others, the entire universe—would be obliterated by white nets of nothingness connecting astronomical accumulations" (*Infinity Net*, 23). Kusama's nets capture both the singular self in one dot and the singular self's obliteration in a netted universe of multiplicities, an expansively full cosmic nothingnesses, of which we are simultaneously part and (w)hole. The reference to the (w)hole here is to intentionally invoke Evelynn Hammonds, who writes about Black female sexuality via the black hole, which is a presumed void that is actually full, an object that affects its environment, that takes up presence, that is detectable. Hammonds demands that "we must think in terms of a different geometry" ("Black (W)holes," 138). The simultaneous hypervisibility and invisibility of the Black female body, the silencing and absenting of especially queer Black female sexuality, and the white consumption of Black female bodies (following bell hooks: "White racism, imperialism, and sexist domination prevail by courageous consumption. It is by eating the Other (in this case, death) that one asserts power and

privilege"; hooks, *Black Looks,* 36) brings us back to the consumption and erasure of Saartjie Baartman's body. When we talk about black and white in relation to colors, white reflects all while black absorbs, both serve as apparent blanks in relation to the all. But when we think with hooks, Hammonds, and Green, we name how the white body absorbs and consumes, eats the Other to death, creates and imagines a nothing, a void, a black hole that is actually full and whole, a whole someone who must be reclaimed as such, taken out of the mouths and eyes of those with the gawking, gaping stare—a hypervisible/invisible resonance between race and disability (Clare, "Gawking, Gaping, Staring").

12. Calvin L. Warren writes, "Antiblackness is anti-nothing." *Ontological Terror,* 170.

13. Recall that to see zero is to look at it and see nothing, but to look through it is to see the world. Kaplan, *Nothing That Is,* 1.

14. I last read the English script to Samuel Beckett's *Endgame* almost ten years ago, but I have thought of the play often over the years. In my memory, somewhere near the beginning of the play, Clov peers out the window and tells Hamm that he sees only a "corpsed landscape."[c] I reread the play, and I realize I had invented this phrase. Rather, Clov seems optimistic, exclaiming that "things are livening up" as he climbs his stepladder and first turns his telescope on the audience in the theater. He announces to Hamm, "I see . . . a multitude . . . in transports . . . of joy." He then turns the telescope out the window. "Zero," he mutters, ". . . zero . . . and zero." Hamm replies, "Nothing stirs. All is—" Clov tries to finish the sentence: "Zer—." Hamm yells at Clov for interrupting, then asks, "All is what?" Clov's final answer: "Corpsed." The first and only time the word appears in the play (Beckett, *Endgame,* 29–30). I take "corpsed" simply as an adjective for the outside world Clov sees, but a theater friend tells me "corpsing" is British theater-speak for breaking character. I cannot find how far back the usage of the term dates, but it is worth noting that *Endgame* is rife with meta references, with Clov often naming the structure of the play he finds himself trapped inside of—asides, farce, a live audience, and perhaps even "corpsing." Still, outside, all is zero—a whole world—and all is corpsed, dead yet vastly expansive, a stark emptiness spreading out across the landscape as far as the eye can see and beyond. Within the theater, multitudes, an infinity (net). Within the small house on the stage, Clov and Hamm, Nagg and Nell, living, doing nothing while they do so many things, strange, abject, and abstract.

   [c] As I revisit the "corpsed landscape," the mushroom again sprouts its head from the vibrant soil of decay as Anna Lowenhaupt Tsing's "blasted landscape" rings adjacent and familiar to the corpsed landscape in my head.[Foray 10] Tsing writes, "When Hiroshima was destroyed

by an atomic bomb in 1945, it is said, the first living thing to emerge from the blasted landscape was a matsutake mushroom" (*Mushroom at the End of the World*, 3). Blasted. Corpsed. Is there a difference?[ii] In either case, life remains in the bunkers of the apocalypse. The mycelia underground push their fruiting bodies skyward when the air clears. But will the living things find their way to the surface again? "You want him to bloom while you are withering?" Hamm asks of himself in the wake of Clov's imminent departure (Beckett, *Endgame*, 84). It is common pop therapy speak to assert that one cannot love others or be loved by others until one loves oneself or that one cannot nurture another's growth if one does not also feed oneself. But I know some people who love themselves so much that they seem incapable of loving others. And we also know that death (rot) begets life. Sometimes we have to let ourselves be eaten rather than nourish ourselves. In our withering, new birth seeds. But who gets to do the consuming and who gets to choose if, how, and when they are consumed is at the mercy of power and privilege. It may seem that some of us exist only to be eaten. Claudia Rankine, also writing of everyday racism, the Black body made ghost in death, offers the evocation: "And despite everything the body remains" (*Citizen*, 69). A reverb in the display and the consumption of the body marked for death echoes again between blackness and disability (the gaping, gawking stare) and the way crip existence comes to the fore in *Endgame*: "You . . . remain"—Hamm's last words before the curtain drops (Beckett, *Endgame*, 84).

> [ii] Beneath the mushroom cloud over Hiroshima, Karen Barad writes, "time died in a flash." Time is drawn out, crossed out, diffracted, dispersed, split, entangled ("No Small Matter," G103, G106). It is a kind of stagnancy, a stuckness, a delay, a dwelling, an unsettling of time—living in the (expanded) moment. Barad continues to write of the loss of time and the loss of life as "not absence but a marked presence" that "troubles the divide between absence and presence." In short, "These devastated landtimescapes are surely haunted" (G106). It becomes a ghostly matter (to summon Avery F. Gordon's *Ghostly Matters*), a matter of absence. The blasted landscape is corpsed, indeed, in that overwhelming silence of death in the atomic, but also in the material radioactive lingering that throws us into what Barad calls "nuclear time," "decay time" (G107). Yes, more slow death, unspooled in new temporalities of atomic half-lives and living in the damage. Which is all to say, "You're on earth, there's no cure for that!" (Beckett, *Endgame*, 53).

15. Outside is death, but inside, they hesitate to end. Beckett, *Endgame*, 3, 9.

16. In the play, Clov, who cannot sit, inhabits a bare room with Hamm, who cannot stand or see. The room contains two small windows, and Clov uses a stepladder to look out and report what he sees to Hamm—zero, nothing but a "corpsed" landscape, again and again. The room also contains two ashbins, each of which holds one of Hamm's parents, Nagg and Nell, who occasionally pop their heads out for some banter and a snack. Together, the four complement each other's bodily capacities and incapacities through a networked (mycelial?) intimacy, while Hamm and Clov routinely and ambivalently declare their love for one another. All four characters, but especially Hamm and Clov, support each other in and from the capabilities and limitations of their own bodies, forming a care network, a crip interdependent existence that makes living possible in an otherwise corpsed world.

17. The question of meaning arises explicitly when Hamm asks Clov, "We're not beginning to . . . to . . . mean something?" Clov replies with seeming incredulity and amusement, "Mean something! You and I, mean something! (*Brief laugh.*) Ah that's a good one!" Hamm is not so quick to let go of that possibility; he ponders the idea: "I wonder. (*Pause.*) Imagine if a rational being came back to earth, wouldn't he be liable to get ideas into his head if he observed us long enough" (Beckett, *Endgame*, 32–33). Hamm expresses a worry that the spectator will attempt to make meaning out of a relationship that may not carry any meaning at all, but the question of what it means to mean something gestures toward a kind of romantic, perhaps sexual, coupling—imagine what ideas might get into that observer's head! Here, the observers are the audience, that multitude in transports of joy. If Hamm perhaps meant to say *that thing* instead of *something*, then there may be many other kinds of joy to move toward, many other ways to mean something rather than nothing at all, even if this life sometimes feels so meaningless.[d] This moment may also be read as Beckett's joke on the readers and spectators, who, committed to (hetero)ideological systems of meaning and definition, might worry too much about what Hamm and Clov could possibly mean. In a note to Alan Schneider, Beckett writes, "If people want to have headaches among the overtones, let them. And provide their own aspirin. Hamm as stated, Clov as stated, together as stated, *nec tecum nec sine te* (can't live with or without), in such a place, and in such a world, that's all I can manage, more than I could" (quoted in Easthope, "Hamm, Clov, and Dramatic Method," 70). While I realize the inherent contradiction in my own critical pursuits of understanding Hamm and Clov by attempting, it may seem, to make (asexual) meaning of their relationship, Beckett directs us to simply let Hamm and Clov be as they are, nothing more.

[d] If we follow the long history (particularly British) of male friendships, we might more clearly recognize the possibilities of romance

apart from sex, another way to still mean *something*, even without *that thing* (sex). On the British male friendship tradition, see Bray, "Homosexuality and Signs of Male Friendship"; Haggerty, "Desire and Mourning"; Montaigne, *On Friendship*. Eve Kosofsky Sedgwick also notes that while male homosocial bonds may include the homoerotic, they also include "crucially important male homosocial bonds that are less glamorous to talk about—such as the institutional, bureaucratic, and military." There are social structures and institutional organizations that place men in proximity to each other such that they naturally and acceptably form intimate homosocial bonds that go unquestioned because of their banality as a routine piece of the social organization; they are, indeed, "less glamorous" and consequently do not necessarily stir up suspicion about homosexual engagement (*Between Men*, 19). In her readings of Willa Cather, Heather Love considers friendship as an "alternative way to frame intimacy," noting that "friendship plays an important role in queer history" and that it plays a stabilizing role in "imagining queer existence and queer community" (*Feeling Backward*, 74, 76, 79). Lillian Faderman also discusses a history of romantic friendship between women, of which many of the relationships were nonsexual but reflected an "all-consuming emotional relationship in which two women are devoted to each other above anyone else" (*Surpassing the Love of Men*, 19). The point I am making here is that such asexual intimacies are often dismissed or explained away with the phrase "They are just friends," as if the intimacy, or even romance, between these friends holds less value than sexual romantic partnerships, which often take center stage, while friendships tend to exist on the periphery. Saying "just" seems to be another way of saying, "Oh, it's nothing." Such intimacies that "bypass the couple or the life narrative it generates," according to Lauren Berlant, "have no alternative plots." Berlant asks, "What happens to the energy attachment when it has no designated place? To the glances, gestures, encounters, collaborations, or fantasies that have no canon?" and "Why, when there are so many people, only one plot counts as 'life' (first comes love, then . . .)?" The answer: "Those who don't or can't find their way in that story—the queers, the single, the something else—can become so easily unimaginable, even often to themselves" ("Intimacy," 285–86). This book is my effort to recoup the unimaginable. I am writing here of "resonances"—encounters, fantasies, pleasures, intimacies—that have no canon, that do not have a plot, that plot otherwise, that refuse emplotment, that have been rendered illegible, that have been missed as absences.

18. For example, Mary F. Catanzaro describes Hamm's sexuality as "coded gay" ("Masking and the Social Construct of the Body," 168). Stanley Cavell

suggests there is room for homosexual interpretation: "The title of the play just possibly suggests a practice typical of male homosexuality, and . . . homosexuality figures in the play's obsessive goal of sterility—the non-consummation devoutly to be wished" ("Ending the Waiting Game," 119). Cavell associates homosexuality with sterility, as many have written on the "sterility" of Beckett's characters, which again misses the possibility of asexual resonance and attunement to other ways of being together. Despite these interpretations, I argue that when we read asexually, Beckett's work reveals the queerness in relating to other people, objects, and ourselves through asexual longings, desires, fixations, fulfillments, and shortcomings. Such are the conditions of the subject who is doomed to fail to fulfill the norms of heterosexual socialization, whose possibility of being is found in unbelonging. Beckett's characters, then, in their seemingly sterile and stagnant couplings, reveal deep human intimacies and meaning where meaning doesn't seem to exist. Many of the relationships between Beckett's characters are, in a sense, anticlimactic, especially sexually. They live and relate and love and hate in the sterility and stagnancy of the stretched-out middle, moving together and with each other to no apparent end. To connect to another relationship that preoccupies my questions of ends, H. Herukhuti Sharif Williams reflects on Chiron and Kevin's relationship in the film *Moonlight* and argues that understanding *Moonlight* as a Black gay film constitutes a failure to recognize the bisexuality and asexuality of the Black men represented. Williams thus suggests we learn to "see" sexuality differently ("Believing Is Seeing").

19. Beckett, *Endgame*, 80.

20. Even the painting hangs facing the wall, stripping the room bare of beauty within, as they look outward for beauty in a barren landscape.

21. In other words, "The end is in the beginning and yet you go on" (Beckett, *Endgame*, 69).

22. Just as I face the challenge of how to refuse linearity within the confines of a form that is built between covers that shape it from beginning to end (the book), I suppose the question arises here as to how film and theater artists who wish to refuse the "autotelic nature" of the genre must also work within the confines of the duration of a play on a stage, of the movement of film from one scene to the next, hence the strategies of looping, repeating, inserting still or quiet beats that ask us to stay for a while rather than move forward, ending where we began, beginning where we end.

23. If *Endgame* equips us with ways to rethink intimacy and crip interdependence and *Sa Main Charmante* offers ways to critique voyeurism within the violent histories of racism and colonization, bodily theft, and erasure, then together we have tools that help us explore how to love the missing

body at the intersections of queerness, disability, and racialization. We learn to love and live in and through these traumas.

24. Since the publication of Williams's essay in 2017, more recent criticism describes the film as "queer" or full of "queer desire" rather than "gay," and although some writing slips between *gay* and *queer*, the distinction is an important one to make as asexual or nonsexual desires may differently align with queer or gay desires, depending on how one is defining the terms. For example, I might argue that asexual desires that refuse sex-normative and heteronormative organization, perhaps through ways of being intimate that defy neat categories of lover or friend or family or foe, are queer. But asexual romantic desires between two men, for example, might also be described as "gay," if *gay* in that context is understood to indicate romantic inclination but not sexual orientation, in the way that some homoromantic asexual people might also identify as gay. That stated, given the relative invisibility of asexuality in cultural discourse, references to the film as "gay" or "queer" do tend to refer to sexual desire between the two male main characters.

25. In other words, not only do we need to learn to "see" sexuality differently, we need to learn to "see" intimacy differently.

26. *Moonlight* moves between land and water. The projects of Liberty City appear as a kind of corpsed and barren landscape—cycles of poverty and discrimination that keep Black life in a precarious state evince the effects of environmental racism, lack of welfare resources that affect education systems, health care, and economic opportunity, giving rise to street economies and the violence such economies demand. The proximity to the Atlantic Ocean and the movement from land to water invoke the cruel histories of the slave trade and the ongoing flows of settler colonial technologies that rely on the theft, transport, and sale of colonized people while also offering entry into another temporality, one that moves like water, that welcomes healing returns and escapes. Maurice Tracy suggests that *Moonlight* offers "the beach and ocean as Black queer space" ("Moving Through Trauma," 53). The space of the sky, the inverse expanse of the ocean, a kind of infinite space, is tethered to the water, that stitched meeting on the horizon where the earth bends air and water together, but it is also as simple as the mechanics of the water cycle that moves water from ground to sky and sky to ground. Sky and ocean both emerge as the source of light that casts Black boys in blue.[e]

> [e] The film is adapted from the unpublished and unstaged play *In Moonlight Black Boys Look Blue*, by Tarell Alvin McCraney, who collaborated with Barry Jenkins on the screenplay for *Moonlight*. Jared Sexton writes of the multiple registers of blue in the film: the blueness in the movement between "azure sky" and "aquamarine tropical waters," a reference to the blues in the Black musical tradition and as a sadness, and the "lunar blueshift" that makes everyone and everything

appear blue for a few reasons, but most notably because "moonlight steals color from whatever it touches," much like the color black steals all the light, absorbs all the color. *Black Masculinity and the Cinema of Policing*, 183.

27. Whereas in *Endgame*, the sea had become still and silent—a kind of death of time in the blasted landscape—in *Moonlight*, the ebbing and flowing ocean is ever-present, visually and sonically. In this connection to water, it is worth noting that Chiron's name derives from the mythical Greek centaur Chiron, immediately calling up the human–animal hybrid, answering back to the construction of both "the animal" and "the black" as "abject feature[s] of 'the human'" (Jackson, *Becoming Human*, 28). What's more, Chiron is different from the other centaurs. Of a divine (possibly African) heritage, he is considered less indulgent than the other notoriously ribald centaurs and is often depicted as more "human" with a full human torso and human front legs. Sexton notes that, through his lineage, he inherits, "on his mother's side, a profound connection to all of the waters of the world and, on his father's side, to the lands and the skies as well" (*Black Masculinity and the Cinema of Policing*, 185). As a namesake, the figure of Chiron the centaur highlights the ways Chiron inhabits his silence, his Blackness, his trauma, his apparent lack of desire.[f]

   [f] An unexpected intertext: Amy Key's *Arrangements in Blue* also dances between the blue of sadness and the blue of water, as well as the blue of Joni Mitchell's album *Blue*. Key reminds us that Mitchell sings, "You know I've been to sea before," on the title track, "Blue." Key writes of the ways one can feel at sea, as in lost, "uncertain and desperate for an anchor," and at the same time, the waves can be therapeutic: "I let myself think and feel things in water that I resist at all other times. There have been times I've swum out and let my tears slide into the sea" (Key, *Arrangements in Blue*, 96). On the beach, Kevin talks about how when the ocean breeze makes its way through their neighborhood, everything seems to go quiet. Chiron responds that when that happens, all he can hear is his own heartbeat, and Kevin says it feels so good it could make you cry. Chiron then tells Kevin he cries so much sometimes, he feels like he's "gonna just turn into drops." Kevin says it sounds like he wants to just roll out into the water, like all the others who want to drown their sorrows. I remember how, when I lived in California, I would put on my wetsuit, swim out past the break in the frigid Pacific waters, and float on my back, staring up at the blue sky or craning my neck to look out on the endless blue horizon. How I would feel so alive, so small, and so unafraid in the middle of a seeming nowhere, the shore so far behind me, the only sound the lap of the waves against my body and the rhythms of my breath and my beating heart.[iii] How the ocean connected me

to the waters of the world and to the lands and skies as well; how it could all swallow me and I wouldn't mind because I was unfettered out here, released, even if temporarily. As I write this, I look out my window at Lake Michigan, aquamarine like the Caribbean, tumultuous like the ocean. The water travels miles as I sit rather still, a bit fidgety, typing as if the writing will get us somewhere. And even if it doesn't, it is still a pleasure, yes?

iii When Chiron is still a child, nicknamed "Little," Juan takes him to the ocean to teach him how to swim. He tells Chiron to rest his head in his hand as he cradles the small boy in the water, facing skyward. "Feel that right there?" Juan asks, then says, "You're in the middle of the world, man." To be in the middle of the world is to be simultaneously in a nowhere and everywhere, the middle of everything, the whole world, which is also a middle, a passage—the Atlantic, the Middle Passage. It is in this scene that Juan also tells Chiron to remember that there are Black people everywhere, that blackness/Blackness is the origin of this world. The Atlantic Ocean in this moment serves the dual purpose of offering a sense of freedom in the feeling of being in the middle of the world while also holding the histories of the Black Atlantic that include enslavement and forced passage. Imani Perry writes, "The storm of feeling you have when looking out onto the water might reveal something about the past five hundred years and where your people fit into it. Wonder is a near universal response to deep rivers and vast oceans. But for some, the water also evokes terror. In it, I see God and slave ships both" (*Black in Blues,* 15). It is "an ocean of conflicting emotions" (Kusama, *Infinity Net,* 214).

28. We are again reminded of the impact of the cut—both an excision and a stitch.

29. Gillespie, "One Step Ahead," 53.

30. This scene, a fiery red, pink, and green in contrast to the film's bluer tones, recurs as the opening stitch to the final chapter, and this time, we do hear Paula scream, "Don't look at me!" just before the camera cuts to an adult Chiron, nicknamed "Black," startling awake. As Míša Stekl notes, the scene does, however, repeat with a difference. Not only is there the addition of audible speech but also the direction of Paula's movement is reversed. The repetition "with/of a difference" thus offers not only a glimpse of the operations of trauma and trauma time but also a queer potentiality in what Stekl names as the "pause," "interval," or "suspension" (which account both for the *différance* that manifests through repetition as well as the silences, cuts, and flashes that propel the film; Stekl, "Queer Times in *Moonlight,*" 344). This queer potentiality offers access to an otherwise way of being that is not

equivalent to utopia but is different (356). If the violence cannot be fully escaped, perhaps difference becomes another way of living differently in the differences.

31. Sexton names Chiron's "relative silence" as one of both "inhibition and a protective reticence" (*Black Masculinity and the Cinema of Policing*, 180). Gillespie describes Chiron as "a silent black boy seeking shelter from a hateful storm" ("One Step Ahead," 52). Counterintuitively, the ocean provides shelter from that storm.

32. As Kevin and Chiron silently look at each other there on the beach, the pause seems to draw out the climax, making it almost anticlimactic. They linger in the aftermath, nothing to say until the unnecessary apology is casually, yet with care and love, smeared into the sand.

33. In watching these scenes back to back, I have thought again and again about Kevin's touch, of how the tenderness and violence are both a kind of intimacy, a flesh-to-flesh exchange with Chiron. Stekl similarly suggests the two scenes might be read "as a set, in which each differentially repeats the other" in which the sex scene might "already contain the seeds of (anti)queer shame" and the fight scene contains "a paradoxical kind of intimacy" ("Queer Times in *Moonlight*," 348). I think there is also something here about how much is said in the silence between them in each scene and between and after these scenes. How later, as adults, Kevin asks Chiron if he remembers the last time they saw each other and Chiron tells him he tried to forget. And then Chiron immediately follows that comment by telling Kevin he's the only man that's touched him. We presume it to mean sexually, but the last time they saw each other was when the beating took place. What kind of touch is Chiron talking about? What time is Kevin really asking about? What did Chiron try to forget? In this moment, they seem to be referring to both the time on the beach and the fight at school.

34. So much pain happens in the quiet, too.

35. Sexton notes that Chiron's story is "focused on the life and death that orbits in many ways around the prison, in the everyday, open-air incarceration of the ghetto" (*Black Masculinity and the Cinema of Policing*, 172). Stekl also traces the carceral motif of the film in the flashing red and blue lights during the scene cuts that invokes the flashing lights of the police car ("Queer Times in *Moonlight*," 342).

36. This final scene mirrors the scene on the beach as teenagers, with Chiron resting on Kevin's shoulder as Kevin caresses the top of Chiron's head.[g] The sound of ocean waves plays over this recurrent tableau that undoes us in time. We do not arrive at an end. We do not witness a sexual rekindling of their relationship. There is no climax. There is only this delicate lingering of two bodies resting against one another.

[g] Kameron J. Copeland notes how this scene mirrors an image of Ryan

Coogler (film director known for *Black Panther*) and actor Michael B. Jordan that stirred up controversy after being featured in *Vanity Fair*. There was a lot of homophobic response to the image, but one Twitter user (@know.earth) offered a rejoinder: "If only the black community could praise and applaud the power of solidarity and brotherhood amongst African American men rather than to condemn and emasculate it with labels and ignorance." There are many ways in which Black men can love Black men, and they are all revolutionary. Copeland also argues that "whereas Black men have been urged to normalize themselves through embracing a hegemonic masculinity and anti-Black notions, *Moonlight* presents the failure to create a culturally affirming environment for the traumatized Black male as dangerous. This unique approach serves to normalize Black male sexuality and traditionally stigmatized Black masculinities" ("*Moonlight*," 688–89). When I first presented my thoughts on the film at a conference, a fellow panelist suggested that the film possibly makes Black male masculinity more palatable for a white audience by desexualizing it. First, I think the suggestion is misguided because I do not think the film is at all concerned with making Black masculinity palatable—in other words, consumable—for a white audience. But if I were to consider how a white audience might feel threatened or not by Black masculinity, and how the film helps us think through that dynamic, I might suggest that asexual/nonsexual Black masculinity actually emerges as a threat to whiteness because white supremacy relies on a framing of Black men as hypersexualized in order to hold them in the position of the violent, animal other who must be constrained, consumed, or destroyed to preserve white purity and superiority. The Black male will always be dangerous to those invested in maintaining white supremacy. The film may instead offer ways to honor Black male masculinities, intimacies, and (a)sexualities in its queer embrace of expansive possibilities between men, even within the ongoingness of racist and capitalist violence. See also Ianna Hawkins Owen on asexuality's maintenance of whiteness in "On the Racialization of Asexuality."

37. Maybe we are left with a refusal of categories, with no need to name their sexuality, but to simply value the love between them and the different types of intimacy they share. Here, a head on a shoulder, a hand through the hair. Richard Brody writes in *The New Yorker* on *Moonlight*'s "unbearable intimacy" as discomfiting, but I find it more unbearable (as in, impossible to contain) in its beauty—because it is full of so much joy and capacious love in the face of violence, we should hardly be able to bear that swarm, that overwhelm of so much more than we were told was possible; it must spill out.

38. This final cut brings a flashback to the past that leaves us in an irresolvable, anticlimactic present, dwelling in the temporalities of trauma's

return, reminding us how trauma and silence operate to construct the queer, Black, a/sexual subject suspended in time and place, tethered to a history and an uncertain future. The shape of the intimacy between Kevin and Chiron mirrors the arc of the film narrative itself: anticlimactic and nonlinear, moving through and finding survival in the times of trauma, anti-Blackness, and antiqueerness. This final scene does not culminate in orgasm, just as the film does not resolve itself through a narrative of Chiron's coming of age as some way to move toward a purported healing of trauma. Instead, we are left with the boy on the beach, his skin made "blue" in the moonlight, the horizon of an unknowable future ahead of him.

39. In this refusal to an end lies a reinterpretation of an allegedly stagnant ongoing middle as a vital, interdependent, intertwined, entangled, cyclical formation of queer life. But it also raises existential questions (do we mean *something*?). As Sexton puts it, the pressing questions remain: "What are they, or any of us, doing really when we make the grade or make money, when we make plans or make promises, or meaning or love? Chiron registers, again, the strangeness of our existence, of all existence." *Black Masculinity and the Cinema of Policing*, 181.

40. Erin Manning suggests we "think differently about where 'we' begin and end, and . . . create movements of thought, modes of knowing, that depart from a place that is infested with the legacy of colonialism and the barren imagination it leaves behind" (*For a Pragmatics of the Useless*, 53). The barren imagination, the corpsed and blasted landscape; these are the fallout of colonialism. Yes, this planet is damaged, dying, perhaps always dying and always has been, and we are still here, together even when we feel alone, but also lonely sometimes, making, remaking, and unmaking things into the shapes of a world as if we both anticipate its end and cannot even fathom its end. We are living here on earth; there is no escaping that. We cannot escape being plant or animal or fungus or mineral, molecule of water or air, or inbetween, all or neither, nor, or none. We live in the emptinesses and in the fullnesses, in the ebbs and flows. Until we don't. You remain.

41. Dworkin, *No Medium*, 110.

## "WE ARE GETTING    NOWHERE    AND THAT IS A PLEASURE"

1. Cage, *Silence*, 118, 119, 120, 121, 122, 123.

2. Smilges, *Queer Silence*, 209.

3. I choose the word *neuroqueerness* rather than *neurodivergence* or *neurodiversity* because *neuroqueerness* feels closest to my own existence in the world by which my madness and my queerness are inseparable—not in a pathological way, but in the sense that they intermesh and intersect to shape my worldview and how I act and am perceived in the world. Though less about diction and more about concept, it is worth noting that Matthew J.

Wolf-Meyer points out that a limit of neurodiversity is that it still relies on a "liberal differentiation of kinds of persons" (*Unraveling*, 19). I suppose my hope for neuroqueerness is that, in its queerness, it disavows liberal humanism altogether.

4. Cage, *Silence*, 109.

5. Roland Barthes, again: "Either woe or well-being, sometimes I have a craving *to be engulfed*. . . . I am suffering (from some incident). The notion of suicide occurs to me, pure of any resentment (not blackmailing anyone); an insipid notion; it alters nothing ('breaks' nothing), matches the color (the silence, the desolation) of this morning. . . . The crisis of engulfment can come from a wound, but also a fusion: we die together from loving each other. . . . Therefore, on those occasions when I am engulfed, it is because there is no longer any place for me anywhere, not even in death." *Lover's Discourse*, 10–11.

6. Joseph, *Against the Romance of Community*.

7. Joseph similarly writes of the need to "open a space for creative thinking about the constitution of collective action," especially at the limits of the concept of community, which, Joseph argues, is an operation of capitalism (vii). Compellingly, Joseph suggests that the "fundamental practices of modernity—liberalism, the nation-state, identity political emancipatory movements, and . . . most important, capitalism—depend on and generate community" (xxxi). In some ways, to refuse capitalism's demands, the colonial shape of the nation-state, and modernity's progress narratives is also to refuse community, at least as necessary to happiness, liveliness, action, and social change.

8. I think of how my own silence is not really silent: Though I do not speak, I sometimes play music, or, at this moment of writing, listen to Lake Michigan lapping at the shore outside my window; I hear my own breathing; I occasionally cough or clear my throat; birds sing on my rooftop; I stream a movie; I run the blender. I am surrounded by noise in my quietude.

9. Katz, "John Cage's Queer Silence," 244–45.

10. Owen, "Still, Nothing."

11. Mazzei, *Inhabited Silence in Qualitative Research*, 39.

12. Ruiz and Vourloumis, *Formless Formation*, 39.

13. Cage, *Silence*, 117.

14. Cobb, "Lonely," 449.

15. Cobb, 448.

16. Cage, *Silence*, 119, 120, 121, 122, 123.

17. Florsheim, "Purple Martin Blues."

18. Florsheim.

19. Nancy, *Being Singular Plural*.

20. My invocation of *we* and *us* here and throughout this book manifests

as my way of asking the reader to join me: Can you relate? Do you feel this too? But it is also to acknowledge that even when one feels alone in the *I*, and even when there is a *we* that one does not feel a part of, we are singular plural, we can find "difference without separability." "What if," Denise Ferreira da Silva asks, "instead of The Ordered World, we could image The World as Plenum, an infinite composition in which each existant's singularity is contingent upon its becoming one possible expression of all the other existants, with which it is entangled beyond space and time" ("On Difference Without Separability," 58). Yes, what if, what if, what if.

21. Here, I gesture to Summer Kim Lee's writing on Asian American sociality and the (aesthetic) practice of "staying in" as a way to access the "ambivalent and rich aspects of solitude, of being alone with oneself, that do not suggest lack as much as plenitude of time and space needed for one's protection, comfort, and love" ("Staying In," 28). I am hinting, also, at Stefano Harney and Fred Moten's writing on Black study, how staying committed to the undercommons is to "study without an end" (*Undercommons*, 67).

22. While Kusama's infinity nets contain dots, she is also recognized for her use of the polka dot in her art. She writes, "The red and green and yellow dots might represent the circle of the earth, or of the sun or moon, or whatever you like. Defining them was not important. What I was asserting was that painting polka-dot patterns on a human body caused that person's self to be obliterated and returned him or her to the natural universe" (*Infinity Net*, 102). The polka dot both marks the unit of the singular—a dot, a body—and obliterates that individual in an indistinguishable universe populated with dots upon dots connected to dots (a World as Plenum, perhaps). Again, with a difference, Solmaz Sharif writes about how the Latin root of *obliteration* means "the striking out of text" and that "historically, the striking out of text is the root of obliterating peoples." How, then, does the writer, artist, or performer practice and experience obliteration without replicating state violence? In an incomplete list of "possible political and aesthetic objectives of poetic erasure," Sharif offers a couple that strike me as useful here: "care for what is left behind so that erasure has an additive or highlighting effect" and "render incomplete a text to invite collaboration between reader and text" ("Near Transitive Properties of the Political"). In this obliteration, an act of care and collaboration, an invitation to join in the dissolution into the natural universe.

23. On the role of the diagnosis and treatment of schizophrenia in Martin's life, see Princenthal, *Agnes Martin*. For Kusama's testaments of fear and trauma, see her autobiography *Infinity Net*.

24. Kusama, *Infinity Net*, 109, 42.

25. Przybyło, "Ace and Aro Lesbian Art," 2, 107.

26. In a note that is reprinted in Martin's handwriting and sewn between

the pages of Arne Glimcher's ode to Martin, we find Martin's thoughts on silence in the solitude of her home: "The silence in the floor of my house is all the questions and all the answers that have been known in the world. The sentimental furniture threatens the peace. The reflection of a sunset speaks loudly of days." Glimcher, *Agnes Martin,* placed between pages 24 and 25 of the book.

27. Kusama writes that the revolution of the self is "all about discovering death," which harks back to her ideas about obliteration through the painting of the polka dot. She continues, "My destiny is to make art for my own requiem: art which gives meaning to death, tracing the beauty of colours and space in the silence of death's footsteps and the 'nothingness' it promises." *Infinity Net,* 239.

28. Roland Barthes emerges for me again in the way, ironically, misery loves company: "A cold winter night. I'm warm enough, yet I'm alone. And I realize that I'll *have to* get used to existing quite *naturally* within this solitude, functioning there, working there, accompanied by, *fastened* to the 'presence of absence.'" Barthes, *Mourning Diary,* 69.

29. Michael Cobb writes, "People are pressed to be together in order to eliminate the space between themselves. . . . The individual is crowded, but not in a good way. . . . Closeness has come at the expense of distance." "Lonely," 453.

30. Cobb, "Lonely," 455.

31. Marquis Bey writes, "*Why is there something instead of nothing?* the old philosophical quip goes. The question itself is misleading. There is both. But nothing is something's infinite excess, its vastness that cannot be conceptualized in language, contingent only on the absence of what we have to insufficiently call thingness" (*Them Goon Rules,* 134). To mean nothing is the infinite excess of meaning something; it is just a matter of what we define as the thing to mean. See also Beckett, *Endgame,* 32–33.

32. Cheney, *About That Life,* 51.

33. Deleuze and Guattari, *Thousand Plateaus,* 4–5.

34. Tsing, *Mushroom at the End of the World,* 21.

35. Smilges, *Queer Silence,* 217.

36. Pohl, "Localizing the Void," 296.

37. Manning, *For a Pragmatics of the Useless,* 86.

38. Manning, 16.

39. Ingold, *Being Alive,* 67.

40. Ingold, 64.

41. Bishop, "Bight."

42. Kathleen Stewart's provocation is "to draw theory, through writing, into the compositional attunement through which people and things venture out into reals" ("Studying Unformed Objects," n.p.). Eileen Joy writes

of "modes of weird reading" as antihumanist becoming ("Improbable Manners of Being," 223–24). Kim TallBear writes of the nonsensical distinctions between human, animal, and environment ("Indigenous Reflection on Working," 231).

43. Deleuze and Guattari, *Thousand Plateaus*, 240.

44. Cage, *Silence*, 114.

# Bibliography

Abbasi, Ali, dir. *Border*. META Film, 2018.

Abdelfatah, Rund, and Ramtin Arablouei, hosts. "Public Universal Friend." *Throughline*, podcast. NPR. March 5, 2020. https://www.npr.org/2020/03/04/812092399/public-universal-friend.

Adams, V. "Extravagant Multitudes." *you are here: the journal of creative geography* 23 (2022): 94–99.

Ahmed, Sara. *The Cultural Politics of Emotion*. Routledge, 2004.

Akbar, Kaveh. "Portrait of the Alcoholic with Moths and River." In *Calling a Wolf a Wolf*. Alice James Books, 2017.

Alsous, Zaina. "Translator's Essay." In *A Theory of Birds*. University of Arkansas Press, 2019.

Amin, Kadji. "We Are All Nonbinary: A Brief History of Accidents." *Representations* 158 (2022): 106–19.

Antoine, Katja. "The Swedish Disconnect: Racism, White Supremacy, and Race." *Journal of Critical Mixed Race Studies* 1, no. 2 (2022): 92–104. https://doi.org/10.5070/C81258332.

Apps, Aaron. *Intersex: A Memoir*. Tarpaulin Sky Press, 2015.

Bakhtin, Mikhail. *Rabelais and His World*. Translated by Helene Iswolsky. MIT Press, 1968.

Barad, Karen. *Meeting the Universe Halfway*. Duke University Press, 2007.

Barad, Karen. "No Small Matter: Mushroom Clouds, Ecologies of Nothingness, and Strange Topologies of Spacetimemattering." In *Arts of Living on a Damaged Planet*, edited by Anna Tsing, Heather Swanson, Elaine Gan, and Nils Bubandt. University of Minnesota Press, 2017.

Barad, Karen. "TransMaterialities: Trans*/Matter/Realities and Queer Political Imaginings." *GLQ: A Journal of Lesbian and Gay Studies* 21, no. 2–3 (2015): 387–422. https://doi.org/10.1215/10642684-2843239.

Barker, Adam J. "Locating Settler Colonialism." *Journal of Colonialism and Colonial History* 13, no. 3 (2012). https://doi.org/10.1353/cch.2012.0035.

Barounis, Cynthia. *Vulnerable Constitutions: Queerness, Disability, and the Remaking of American Manhood*. Temple University Press, 2019.

Barthes, Roland. *A Lover's Discourse*. Translated by Richard Miller. Hill and Wang, 1977.

Barthes, Roland. *Mourning Diary*. Edited by Nathalie Léger. Translated by Richard Howard. Hill and Wang, 2009.

Barthes, Roland. *The Pleasure of the Text*. Translated by Richard Miller. Hill and Wang, 1975.

Barzman, Karen-Edis. "The Subject of 'Woman' and the Discipline of Early Modern Studies: Jemima Wilkinson and the Publick Universal Friend." In *Culture and Change: Attending to Early Modern Women*, edited by Margaret Mikesell and Adele Seef. University of Delaware Press, 2003.

Beauchamp, Toby. *Going Stealth: Transgender Politics and U.S. Surveillance Practices*. Duke University Press, 2019.

Beckett, Samuel. *Endgame*. Grove Press, 1958.

Benjamin, Walter. *The Origin of German Tragic Drama*. Translated by John Osborne. Verso, 1985.

Bennett, Jane. *Vibrant Matter: A Political Ecology of Things*. Duke University Press, 2010.

Bennett, Joshua. *Being Property Once Myself: Blackness and the End of Man*. Belknap Press of Harvard University Press, 2020.

Berlant, Lauren. "Intimacy: A Special Issue." *Critical Inquiry* 24, no. 2 (1998): 281–88.

Berlant, Lauren. "Starved." *South Atlantic Quarterly* 106, no. 3 (2007): 433–44. https://doi.org/10.1215/00382876-2007-002.

Bersani, Leo. "Father Knows Best." *Raritan* 29, no. 4 (2010): 92–104.

Bersani, Leo, and Ulysses Dutoit. *Arts of Impoverishment: Beckett, Rothko, Resnais*. Harvard University Press, 1993.

Bersani, Leo, and Adam Phillips. *Intimacies*. University of Chicago Press, 2008.

Bey, Marquis. *Them Goon Rules: Fugitive Essays on Radical Black Feminism*. University of Arizona Press, 2019.

Bhabha, Homi. *The Location of Culture*. Routledge, 1994.

Bierend, Doug. *In Search of Mycotopia: Citizen Science, Fungi Fanatics, and the Untapped Potential of Mushrooms*. Chelsea Green Publishing, 2021.

Bishop, Elizabeth. "The Bight." In *Poems*, edited by Saskia Hamilton. Farrar, Strauss and Giroux, 2011.

Blackston, Dylan McCarthy. "Monkey Business: Trans*, Animacy, and the Boundaries of Kind." *Angelaki* 22, no. 2 (2017): 119–33. https://doi.org /10.1080/0969725X.2017.1322828.

Boully, Jenny. *The Body: An Essay*. Essay Press, 2002.

Brake, Elizabeth. *Minimizing Marriage: Marriage, Morality, and the Law*. Oxford University Press, 2012.

Bray, Alan. "Homosexuality and Signs of Male Friendship in Elizabethan England." *History Workshop Journal* 29 (1990): 1–19.

Brody, Richard. "The Unbearable Intimacy of 'Moonlight.'" *New Yorker*, October 28, 2016. https://www.newyorker.com/culture/richard-brody/the-unbearable-intimacy-of-moonlight.

Bronski, Michael. *A Queer History of the United States*. Beacon Press, 2011.

Brown, Gabrielle. *The New Celibacy: Why More Men and Women Are Abstaining from Sex and Enjoying It*. McGraw-Hill, 1980.

Burik, Steven. "Darkness and Light: Absence and Presence in Heidegger, Derrida, and Daoism." *Dao* 18, no. 3 (2019): 347–70. https://doi.org/10.1007/s11712-019-09670-7.

Cage, John. "Music Lovers' Field Companion." In *A Mycological Foray*. Atelier Éditions, 2020.

Cage, John. *Silence: Lectures and Writings, 50th Anniversary Edition*. Wesleyan University Press, 2013.

Canaday, Margot. *The Straight State: Sexuality and Citizenship in Twentieth-Century America*. Princeton University Press, 2009.

Carotenuto, Aldo. *A Secret Symmetry: Sabina Spielrein Between Jung and Freud*. Pantheon, 1984.

Carrigan, Mark. "There's More to Life than Sex? Difference and Commonality Within the Asexual Community." *Sexualities* 14, no. 4 (2011): 462–78. https://doi.org/10.1177/1363460711406462.

Catanzaro, Mary F. "Masking and the Social Construct of the Body in Beckett's *Endgame*." In *Samuel Beckett's Endgame*, edited by Mark S. Byron. Rodopi Press, 2007.

Cavell, Stanley. "Ending the Waiting Game: A Reading of Beckett's *Endgame*." In *Must We Mean What We Say? A Book of Essays*. Charles Scribner's Sons, 1969.

Cerankowski, KJ. *Suture: Trauma and Trans Becoming*. Punctum Books, 2021.

Chasin, CJ DeLuzio. "Theoretical Issues in the Study of Asexuality." *Archives of Sexual Behavior* 40 (2011): 713–23. https://doi.org/10.1007/s10508-011-9757-x.

Chen, Mel Y. *Animacies: Biopolitics, Racial Mattering, and Queer Affect*. Duke University Press, 2012.

Chen, Mel Y. *Intoxicated: Race, Disability, and Chemical Intimacy Across Empire*. Duke University Press, 2023.

Cheney, Matthew. *About That Life: Barry Lopez and the Art of Community*. Punctum Books, 2023.

Chevigny, Bell Gale, ed. *Twentieth Century Interpretations of Endgame: A Collection of Critical Essays*. Prentice-Hall, 1969.

Chuk, Natasha. *Vanishing Points: Articulations of Death, Fragmentation, and the Unexperienced Experience of Created Objects*. University of Chicago Press, 2015.

Clare, Eli. *Brilliant Imperfection: Grappling with Cure*. Duke University Press, 2017.

Clare, Eli. "Gawking, Gaping, Staring." *GLQ: A Journal of Lesbian and Gay Studies* 9, no. 1–2 (2003): 257–61.

Clifton, Lucille. "the earth is a living thing." Poets.org. https://poets.org /poem/earth-living-thing.

Cobb, Michael. "Lonely." *South Atlantic Quarterly* 106, no. 3 (2007): 445–57.

Cobb, Michael. *Single: Arguments for the Uncoupled*. New York University Press, 2021.

Coelen, Chris, creator. *The Ultimatum: Marry or Move On*. Season 1, episode 1, "The Split." Aired April 6, 2022, on Netflix.

Cohen, Sam. *Sarahland*. Grand Central, 2021.

Copeland, Kameron J. "*Moonlight*, Directed by Barry Jenkins." *Journal of Homosexuality* 65, no. 5 (2018): 687–89. https://doi.org/10.1080/00918369 .2017.1333815.

Cornellier, Bruno, and Michael R. Griffiths. "Globalizing Unsettlement: An Introduction." *Settler Colonial Studies* 6, no. 4 (2016): 305–16. https://doi .org/10.1080/2201473X.2015.1090522.

Coulthard, Glen. *Red Skin, White Masks: Rejecting the Colonial Politics of Recognition*. University of Minnesota Press, 2014.

Currah, Paisley. *Sex Is as Sex Does: Governing Transgender Identity*. New York University Press, 2022.

Currah, Paisley, and Tara Mulqueen. "Securitizing Gender: Identity, Biometrics, and Transgender Bodies at the Airport." *Social Research* 78, no. 2 (2011): 557–82.

Cusick, Suzanne. "On a Lesbian Relationship with Music." In *Queering the Pitch: The New Gay and Lesbian Musicology*, edited by Philip Brett, Elizabeth Wood, and Gary C. Thomas. Routledge, 1994.

Davies, Ben. "Auricular Erotics: Sexual Listening in (and to) Philip Roth's Sabbath's Theater." *Critique: Studies in Contemporary Fiction* 58, no. 4 (2017): 351–64. https://doi.org/10.1080/00111619.2016.1249785.

Deleuze, Gilles, and Félix Guattari. *A Thousand Plateaus: Capitalism and Schizophrenia*. Translated by Brian Massumi. University of Minnesota Press, 1987.

Derrida, Jacques. *Archive Fever: A Freudian Impression*. Translated by Eric Prenowitz. University of Chicago Press, 1996.

de Villiers, Nicholas. *Opacity and the Closet: Queer Tactics in Foucault, Barthes, and Warhol*. University of Minnesota Press, 2012.

Diaz, Natalie. "Fusings." In *Borders, Human Itineraries, and All Our Relation*. Duke University Press, 2024.

Diversi, Marcelo, and Claudio Moreira. *Betweener Talk: Decolonizing Knowledge Production, Pedagogy, and Praxis*. Routledge, 2016.

Driskill, Qwo-Li. "Stolen from Our Bodies: First Nations Two-Spirits/Queers and the Journey to a Sovereign Erotic." *Studies in American Indian Literatures* 16, no. 2 (2004): 50–64.

Dworkin, Craig. *No Medium*. MIT Press, 2013.

Easthope, Antony. "Hamm, Clov, and Dramatic Method in *Endgame*." In *Twentieth Century Interpretations of Endgame: A Collection of Critical Essays*, edited by Bell Gale Chevigny. Prentice-Hall, 1969.

Emens, Elizabeth F. "Compulsory Sexuality." *Stanford Law Review* 66 (2014): 303–86. https://doi.org/10.2139/ssrn.2218783.

Estes, Nick. *Our History Is the Future: Standing Rock Versus the Dakota Access Pipeline, and the Long Tradition of Indigenous Resistance*. Verso, 2019.

Evans, Marc, dir. *Snow Cake*. Alliance Atlantis, 2006.

Faderman, Lillian. *Surpassing the Love of Men: Romantic Friendship and Love between Women from the Renaissance to the Present*. Harper Paperbacks, 1981.

Fahs, Breanne. "Radical Refusals: On the Anarchist Politics of Women Choosing Asexuality." *Sexualities* 13, no. 4 (2010): 445–61. https://doi.org/10.1177/1363460710370650.

Farge, Arlette. *The Allure of the Archives*. Translated by Thomas Scott-Railton. Yale University Press, 2013.

Farrell, Janine, and Thea Cacchioni. "The Medicalization of Women's Sexual Pain." *Journal of Sex Research* 49, no. 4 (2012): 328–36. https://doi.org/10.1080/00224499.2012.688227.

Ferreira da Silva, Denise. "On Difference Without Separability." In *Catalogue of the 32nd Bienal de São Paulo, "Incerteza Viva,"* edited by Jochen Volz and Júlia Rebouças. Fundação Beinal de São Paulo, 2016.

Ferreira da Silva, Denise. "Toward a Black Feminist Poethics: The Quest(ion) of Blackness Toward the End of the World." *Black Scholar* 44, no. 2 (2014): 81–97. https://doi.org/10.1080/00064246.2014.11413690.

"Five Ways to Look at Malevich's Black Square." Tate. Accessed March 17, 2025. https://www.tate.org.uk/art/artists/kazimir-malevich-1561/five-ways-look-malevichs-black-square.

Fleischmann, T. *Time Is the Thing a Body Moves Through*. Coffee House Press, 2019.

Florsheim, Morgan. "Purple Martin Blues." *Entropy*. May 27, 2021.

Foucault, Michel. *The History of Sexuality*, vol. 1, *An Introduction*. Translated by Robert Hurley. Vintage Books, 1990.

Freud, Sigmund. *Three Essays on the Theory of Sexuality*. Translated by James Strachey. Basic Books, 1962.

Frost, Laura. *The Problem with Pleasure: Modernism and Its Discontents*. Columbia University Press, 2013.

Garba, Tapji, and Sara-Maria Sorentino. "Slavery Is a Metaphor: A Critical

Commentary on Eve Tuck and K. Wayne Yang's 'Decolonization Is Not a Metaphor.'" *Antipode* 52, no. 3 (2020): 764–82. https://doi.org/10.1111/anti.12615.

Garland-Thompson, Rosemarie. *Staring: How We Look*. Oxford University Press, 2009.

Gay, Ross. *The Book of Delights*. Algonquin Books, 2019.

Gillespie, Michael Boyce. "One Step Ahead: A Conversation with Barry Jenkins." *Film Quarterly* 70, no. 3 (2017): 52–62.

Glenn, Cheryl. *Unspoken: A Rhetoric of Silence*. Southern Illinois University Press, 2004.

Glimcher, Arne. *Agnes Martin: Paintings, Writings, Remembrances*. Phaidon Press, 2012.

Glissant, Édouard. *Poetics of Relation*. Translated by Betsy Wing. University of Michigan Press, 1997.

Goeman, Mishuana R. "Disrupting a Settler-Colonial Grammar of Place in Hulleah Tsinhnahjinnie's 'Photographic Memoirs of an Aboriginal Savant.'" In *Theorizing Native Studies,* edited by Audra Simpson and Andrea Smith. Duke University Press, 2014.

Gopinath, Gayatri. *Unruly Visions: The Aesthetic Practices of Queer Diaspora*. Duke University Press, 2018.

Gordon, Avery F. *Ghostly Matters: Haunting and the Sociological Imagination*. University of Minnesota Press, 2008.

Greenaway, Peter, dir. *The Cook, the Thief, His Wife & Her Lover*. Miramax, 1990.

Guenther, Lisa. "Abolish the World as We Know It: Notes for a Praxis of Phenomenology Beyond Critique." *Puncta: Journal of Critical Phenomenology* 5, no. 2 (2022): 28–44. https://doi.org/10.5399/pjcp.v5i2.3.

Gupta, Kristina. "Compulsory Sexuality: Evaluating an Emerging Concept." *Signs: Journal of Women in Culture and Society* 41, no. 1 (2015): 131–54. https://doi.org/10.1086/681774.

Gupta, Kristina, and KJ Cerankowski. "Asexualities and Media." In *Routledge Companion to Media, Sex and Sexuality,* edited by Clarissa Smith, Feona Attwood, and Brian McNair. Routledge, 2018.

Haggerty, George E. "Desire and Mourning: The Ideology of the Elegy." In *Ideology and Form in Eighteenth-Century Literature,* edited by David H. Richter. Texas Tech University Press, 1999.

Hammonds, Evelynn. "Black (W)holes and the Geometry of Black Female Sexuality." *Differences* 6, no. 2–3 (1994): 126–45. https://doi.org/10.1215/10407391-6-2-3-126.

Hanson, Elizabeth Hanna. "Toward an Asexual Narrative Structure." In *Asexualities: Feminist and Queer Perspectives,* edited by KJ Cerankowski and Megan Milks. Routledge, 2014.

Haraway, Donna. *Staying with the Trouble: Making Kin in the Chthulucene.* Duke University Press, 2016.

Harney, Stefano, and Fred Moten. *The Undercommons: Fugitive Planning & Black Study.* Minor Compositions, 2013.

Hartman, Saidiya. *Wayward Lives, Beautiful Experiments: Intimate Histories of Social Upheaval.* W. W. Norton & Company, 2019.

Hayward, Eva. "More Lessons from a Starfish: Prefixial Flesh and Trans-speciated Selves." *WSQ: Women's Studies Quarterly* 36, no. 3 & 4 (2008): 64–85.

Hayward, Eva, and Jami Weinstein. "Introduction: Tranimalities in the Age of Trans* Life." *TSQ: Transgender Studies Quarterly* 2, no. 2 (2015): 195–208. https://doi.org/10.1215/23289252-2867446.

Heath, Stephen. *The Sexual Fix.* Schocken, 1984.

Hervik, Peter. "What Is in the Scandinavian Nexus of 'Islamophobia, Multiculturalism, and Muslim-Western Relations'?" *Intersections: East European Journal of Society and Politics* 1, no. 1 (2015): 66–82. https://doi.org /10.17356/ieejsp.v1i1.29.

Heyam, Kit. *Before We Were Trans: A New History of Gender.* Seal Press, 2022.

Hird, Myra J. "Animal Trans." In *The Transgender Studies Reader 2,* edited by Susan Stryker and Aren Z. Aizura. Routledge, 2013.

Hird, Myra J. "From the Culture of Matter to the Matter of Culture: Feminist Explorations of Nature and Science." *Sociological Research Online* 8, no. 1 (2003). https://www.socresonline.org.uk/8/1/hird.html.

Honig, Bonnie. *A Feminist Theory of Refusal.* Harvard University Press, 2021.

hooks, bell. *Black Looks: Race and Representation.* South End Press, 1992.

Howe, Marie. "What the Living Do." In *What the Living Do.* W. W. Norton, 1998.

Hudson, David. *Memoir of Jemima Wilkinson: A Preacheress of the Eighteenth Century: Containing an Authentic Narrative of Her Life and Character and of the Rise, Progress and Conclusion of Her Ministry.* R. L. Underhill, 1844.

Hunt, Mina. "Tracing Transgender Ghosts, Siguiendo el Rastro de los Espectros Trans." *Sociología y Tecnociencia* 11, no. 1 (2021): 91–103.

Hval, Jenny. *Paradise Rot.* Translated by Marjam Idriss. Verso, 2018.

Ingold, Tim. *Being Alive: Essays on Movement, Knowledge, and Description.* Routledge, 2011.

Jackson, Zakiyyah Iman. *Becoming Human: Matter and Meaning in an Antiblack World.* New York University Press, 2020.

Jagose, Annamarie. *Orgasmology.* Duke University Press, 2012.

James, Henry. *The Beast in the Jungle.* Martin Secker, 1915. Transcribed by David Price for Project Gutenberg, February 6, 2005. https://www .gutenberg.org/files/1093/1093-h/1093-h.htm.

Jenkins, Barry, dir. *Moonlight.* A24 Films, 2016.

Jeunet, Jean-Pierre, dir. *Amélie*. Miramax, 2002.

Joseph, Miranda. *Against the Romance of Community*. University of Minnesota Press, 2002.

Joy, Eileen. "Improbable Manners of Being." *GLQ: A Journal of Lesbian and Gay Studies* 21, no. 2–3 (2015): 221–24.

Juster, Susan. *Doomsayers: Anglo-American Prophecy in the Age of Revolution*. University of Pennsylvania Press, 2003.

Juster, Susan. "'Neither Male nor Female': Jemima Wilkinson and the Politics of Gender in Post-Revolutionary America." In *Possible Pasts: Becoming Colonial in Early America*, edited by Robert Blair St. George. Cornell University Press, 2000.

Juster, Susan. "To Slay the Beast: Visionary Women in the Early Republic." In *A Mighty Baptism: Race, Gender, and the Creation of American Protestantism*, edited by Susan Juster and Lisa MacFarlane. Cornell University Press, 1996.

Kahan, Benjamin. *Celibacies: American Modernism and Sexual Life*. Duke University Press, 2013.

Kaishian, Patricia, and Hasmik Djoulakian. "The Science Underground: Mycology as a Queer Discipline." *Catalyst: Feminism, Theory, and Technoscience* 6, no. 2 (2020): 1–26. https://doi.org/10.28968/cftt.v6i2.33523.

Kaler, Amy. "Unreal Women: Sex, Gender, Identity, and the Lived Experience of Vulvar Pain." *Feminist Review* 82, no. 1 (2006): 50–75. https://doi.org/10.1057/palgrave.fr.9400262.

Kang, Han. *The Vegetarian*. Translated by Deborah Smith. Hogarth, 2015.

Kaplan, Robert. *The Nothing That Is: A Natural History of Zero*. Oxford University Press, 1999.

Karkazis, Katrina. *Fixing Sex: Intersex, Medical Authority, and Lived Experience*. Duke University Press, 2008.

Katz, Jonathan D. "John Cage's Queer Silence; Or, How to Avoid Making Matters Worse." *GLQ: A Journal of Lesbian and Gay Studies* 5, no. 2 (1999): 231–52. https://doi.org/10.1215/10642684-5-2-231.

Kellgren-Fozard, Jessica. "Non-Binary and Religious: The Public Universal Friend // Historical Profile // Vlogmas 2019 Day 19." YouTube, December 19, 2019. https://www.youtube.com/watch?v=3vTQE7G648Q.

Key, Amy. *Arrangements in Blue: Notes on Loving and Living Alone*. Liveright Publishing, 2023.

Killjoy, Margaret, host. "The Public Universal Friend: A Non-Binary Icon in Revolutionary-Era America." *Cool People Who Did Cool Stuff*, podcast. June 20, 2022. https://podcasts.apple.com/us/podcast/part-one-the-public-universal-friend-a-non-binary/id1620562792?i=1000567084838.

Kim, Eunjung. *Curative Violence: Rehabilitating Disability, Gender, and Sexuality in Modern Korea*. Duke University Press, 2017.

Kim, Eunjung. "How Much Sex Is Healthy? The Pleasures of Asexuality." In *Against Health: How Health Became the New Morality,* edited by Anna Kirkland and Jonathan Metzl. New York University Press, 2010.

Kim, Eunjung. "Unbecoming Human: An Ethics of Objects." *GLQ: A Journal of Lesbian and Gay Studies* 21, no. 2–3 (2015): 295–320. https://doi.org/10.1215/10642684-2843359.

Kristeva, Julia. *Powers of Horror: An Essay on Abjection.* Translated by Leon S. Roudiez. Columbia University Press, 1982.

Kusama, Yayoi. *Infinity Net: The Autobiography of Yayoi Kusama.* Translated by Ralph McCarthy. Tate Publishing, 2013.

Labuski, Christine. *It Hurts Down There: The Bodily Imaginaries of Female Genital Pain.* State University of New York Press, 2015.

LaFleur, Greta. "Epilogue: Against Consensus." In *Trans Historical: Gender Plurality Before the Modern,* edited by Greta LaFleur, Masha Raskolnikov, and Anna Kłosowska. Cornell University Press, 2021.

la paperson. *A Third University Is Possible.* University of Minnesota Press, 2017.

Larson, Scott. "'Indescribable Being': Theological Performances of Genderlessness in the Society of the Publick Universal Friend, 1776–1819." *Early American Studies* 12, no. 3 (2014): 576–600. https://doi.org/10.1353/eam.2014.0020.

Larson, Scott. "Laid Open: Examining Genders in Early America." In *Trans Historical: Gender Plurality Before the Modern,* edited by Greta LaFleur, Masha Raskolnikov, and Anna Kłosowska. Cornell University Press, 2021.

Lee, Jamie A. "Be/longing in the Archival Body: Eros and the 'Endearing' Value of Material Lives." *Archival Science: International Journal on Recorded Information* 16, no. 1 (2016): 33–51. https://doi.org/10.1007/s10502-016-9264-x.

Lee, Summer Kim. "Staying In: Mitski, Ocean Vuong, and Asian American Asociality." *Social Text* 37, no. 1 (138) (2019): 27–50. https://doi.org/10.1215/01642472-7286252.

Leung, Muriel. "Erasure in Three Acts: An Essay." Poetry Foundation. October 31, 2021. https://www.poetryfoundation.org/harriet-books/2021/11/erasure.

Leuzzi, Tony. "Interview with Robert Glück." *EOAGH,* October 23, 2011. https://eoagh.com/interview-with-robert-gluck/all/1/.

Liboiron. Max. *Pollution Is Colonialism.* Duke University Press, 2021.

Lindqvist, John Ajvide. "The Border." In *Let the Old Dreams Die.* Translated by Marlaine Delargy. Quercus Editions, 2012.

Long, Denis, host. "The Public Universal Friend." *Arch Street Meeting House: Untold Stories in Quaker History,* podcast. May 27, 2021. https://www.historicasmh.org/podcastepisodes/publicuniversalfriend.

Lorde, Audre. "The Uses of the Erotic: The Erotic as Power." In *Sister Outsider: Essays and Speeches*. Crossing Press, 1984.

Love, Heather. *Feeling Backward: Loss and the Politics of Queer History*. Harvard University Press, 2009.

Lugones, María. "Heterosexualism and the Colonial/Modern Gender System." *Hypatia* 22, no. 1 (2007): 186–209.

Malatino, Hil. *Queer Embodiment: Monstrosity, Medical Violence, and Intersex Experience*. University of Nebraska Press, 2019.

Manning, Erin. *For a Pragmatics of the Useless*. Duke University Press, 2020.

Mazzadra, Sandro, and Brett Neilson. *Border as Method, or The Multiplication of Labor*. Duke University Press, 2013.

Mazzei, Lisa A. *Inhabited Silence in Qualitative Research: Putting Poststructural Theory to Work*. Peter Lang AG, 2007.

McCoy, Peter. *The Mycocultural Revolution: Transforming Our World with Mushrooms, Lichens, and Other Fungi*. Microcosm Publishing, 2022.

McCraney, Tarell Alvin. *In Moonlight Black Boys Look Blue*. Unpublished playscript.

Meier, Allison C. "Edward S. Curtis: Romance vs. Reality." *JSTOR Daily*, May 18, 2018. https://daily.jstor.org/edward-s-curtis-romance-vs-reality/.

Meikle, Olivia, and Katie Nelson, hosts. "The Reborn: Jemima Wilkinson & Publick Universal Friend." *What's Her Name*, podcast. June 22, 2020. https://www.whatshernamepodcast.com/jemima-wilkinson-publick-universal-friend/.

Melville, Herman. "Bartleby, the Scrivener." In *Billy Budd, Sailor and Other Stories*. Penguin, 1977.

Meyer, Morgan. "Placing and Tracing Absence: A Material Culture of the Immaterial." *Journal of Material Culture* 17, no. 1 (2012): 103–10. https://doi.org/10.1177/1359183511433259.

Milks, Megan. "Stunted Growth: Asexual Politics and the Rhetoric of Sexual Liberation." In *Asexualities: Feminist and Queer Perspectives*, edited by KJ Cerankowski and Megan Milks. Routledge, 2014.

Mitchell, Joni. *Blue*. Reprise Records, 1971.

Montaigne, Michel de. *On Friendship*. Translated by M. A. Screech. Penguin Books, 1991.

Morgensen, Scott Lauria. "Settler Homonationalism: Theorizing Settler Colonialism Within Queer Modernities." *GLQ: A Journal of Lesbian and Gay Studies* 16, no. 1–2 (2010): 105–31. https://doi.org/10.1215/10642684-2009-015.

Morris, Adam. *American Messiahs: False Prophets of a Damned Nation*. Liveright Publishing, 2019.

Morris, Simon, Forbes Morlock, and Liz Dalton. *Interpretation*. Vol. 1. Printed Matter, 2002.

Morton, Timothy. "Thank Virus for Symbiosis." STRP, April 4, 2020. https://strp.nl/updates/thank-virus-for-symbiosis.

Moyer, Paul B. *The Public Universal Friend: Jemima Wilkinson and Religious Enthusiasm in Revolutionary America.* Cornell University Press, 2015.

Mumford, Stephen. *Absence and Nothing: The Philosophy of What There Is Not.* Oxford University Press, 2021.

Muñoz, José Esteban. *Cruising Utopia: The Then and There of Queer Futurity.* New York University Press, 2009.

Murata, Sayaka. *Earthlings.* Translated by Ginny Tapley Takamori. Grove Press, 2020.

Nancy, Jean Luc. *Being Singular Plural.* Translated by Robert Richardson and Anne O'Byrne. Stanford University Press, 2000.

Nelson, Maggie. *The Argonauts.* Graywolf Press, 2015.

Ngai, Sianne. *Ugly Feelings.* Harvard University Press, 2005.

Ostendorf-Rodríguez, Yasmine. *Let's Become Fungal! Mycelium Teachings and the Arts.* Valiz, 2023.

Owen, Ianna Hawkins. "On the Racialization of Asexuality." In *Asexualities: Feminist and Queer Perspectives,* edited by KJ Cerankowski and Megan Milks. Routledge, 2014.

Owen, Ianna Hawkins. "Still, Nothing: Mammy and Black Asexual Possibility." *Feminist Review* 120 (2018): 70–84. https://doi.org/10.1057/s41305-018-0140-9.

Parks, Suzan-Lori. *Venus.* Theatre Communications Group, 1997.

Perry, Imani. *Black in Blues: How a Color Tells the Story of My People.* Ecco, 2025.

Picard, Max. *The World of Silence.* Translated by Stanley Godwin. Eighth Day Press, 2002.

Plaut, Ethan. "Strategic Illiteracies: The Long Game of Technology Refusal and Disconnection." *Communication Theory* 33, no. 1 (2023): 21–31. https://doi.org/10.1093/ct/qtac014.

Pohl, Lucas. "Localizing the Void: From Material to Immaterial Materialism." In *A Place More Void,* edited by Paul Kingsbury and Anna J. Secor. University of Nebraska Press, 2021.

Preciado, Paul B. *Can the Monster Speak? Report to an Academy of Psychoanalysts.* Translated by Frank Wynne. Semiotext(e), 2021.

Preciado, Paul B. *Testo Junkie: Sex, Drugs, and Biopolitics in the Pharmacopornographic Era.* Translated by Bruce Benderson. Feminist Press, 2013.

Princenthal, Nancy. *Agnes Martin: Her Life and Art.* Thames and Hudson, 2015.

Prins, Harald E. L. "Coming to Light: Edward S. Curtis and the North American Indians." *American Anthropologist* 102, no. 4 (2000): 891–95. https://www.jstor.org/stable/684225.

Prufrock, Animal. "Emotional Boner." Track 4 on *Congratulations; Thank You + I'm Sorry.* Righteous Babe Records, 2010.

Przybyło, Ela. "Ace and Aro Lesbian Art and Theory with Agnes Martin and Yayoi Kusama." *Journal of Lesbian Studies* 26, no. 1 (2022): 89–112. https://doi.org/10.1080/10894160.2021.1958732.

Przybyło, Ela. *Asexual Erotics: Intimate Readings of Compulsory Sexuality.* Ohio State University Press, 2019.

Przybyło, Ela. "Crisis and Safety: The Asexual in Sexusociety." *Sexualities* 14, no. 4 (2011): 444–61. https://doi.org/10.1177/1363460711406461.

Przybyło, Ela, and Danielle Cooper. "Asexual Resonances: Tracing a Queerly Asexual Archive." *GLQ: A Journal of Lesbian and Gay Studies* 20, no. 3 (2014): 297–318. https://doi.org/10.1215/10642684-2422683.

Pugliese, Joseph. "Biometrics, Infrastructural Whiteness, and the Racialized Zero Degree of Nonrepresentation." *boundary 2* 34, no. 2 (2007): 105–33. https://doi.org/10.1215/01903659-2007-005.

Pulsifer, Rebecah. "Trolling Humanism: New Materialist Performativity in *Border.*" *Gender Forum* 71 (2019): 7–22.

Quashie, Kevin. *The Sovereignty of Quiet: Beyond Resistance in Black Culture.* Rutgers University Press, 2012.

Quinan, C. Q., and Mina Hunt. "Non-Binary Gender Markers: Mobility, Migration, and Media Reception in Europe and Beyond." *European Journal of Women's Studies* 30, no. 3 (2023): 380–90. https://doi.org/10.1177/13505068211024891.

Radical Face. *Missing Film.* Bear Machine, 2018.

Rankine, Claudia. *Citizen: An American Lyric.* Graywolf Press, 2014.

Rifkin, Mark. *Beyond Settler Time: Temporal Sovereignty and Indigenous Self-Determination.* Duke University Press, 2017.

Rifkin, Mark. *The Erotics of Sovereignty: Queer Native Writing in the Era of Self-Determination.* University of Minnesota Press, 2012.

Rilke, Rainer Maria. *The Dark Interval: Letters on Loss, Grief, and Transformation.* Translated by Ulrich Baer. Modern Library, 2018.

Rose, Deborah Bird. "Shimmer: When All You Love Is Being Trashed." In *Arts of Living on a Damaged Planet,* edited by Anna Tsing, Heather Swanson, Elaine Gan, and Nils Bubandt. University of Minnesota Press, 2017.

Rosskam, Jules, and Jack Isaac Pryor. *Transfixt: Transgender Aesthetics at the Tipping Point.* Forthcoming. http://www.julesrosskam.com/transfixt-cfp.

Rotman, Brian. *Signifying Nothing: The Semiotics of Zero.* Stanford University Press, 1987.

Rubin, David A. *Intersex Matters: Biomedical Embodiment, Gender Regulation, and Transnational Activism.* State University of New York Press, 2017.

Ruiz, Sandra, and Hypatia Vourloumis. *Formless Formation: Vignettes for the End of This World.* Minor Compositions, 2021.

Russo, Vito. *The Celluloid Closet.* Harper and Row, 1981.

Savarese, D. J. "Passive Plants." *Iowa Review* 47, no. 1 (2017). https://iowareview.org/from-the-issue/volume-47-issue-1-%E2%80%94-spring -2017/passive-plants.

Schmidt, Samantha. "A Genderless Prophet Drew Hundreds of Followers Long Before the Age of Nonbinary Pronouns." *Washington Post,* January 5, 2020. https://www.washingtonpost.com/history/2020/01/05 /long-before-theythem-pronouns-genderless-prophet-drew-hundreds -followers/.

Sedgwick, Eve Kosofsky. *Between Men: English Literature and Male Homosocial Desire.* Columbia University Press, 1985.

Sedgwick, Eve Kosofsky. *Epistemology of the Closet.* University of California Press, 1990.

Seigworth, Gregory J., and Melissa Gregg. "An Inventory of Shimmers." In *The Affect Theory Reader,* edited by Gregory J. Seigworth and Melissa Gregg. Duke University Press, 2010.

Sexton, Jared. *Black Masculinity and the Cinema of Policing.* Palgrave Macmillan, 2017.

Sharif, Solmaz. "The Near Transitive Properties of the Political and Poetical: Erasure." *Evening Will Come: A Monthly Journal of Poetics* 28 (2013): https://thevolta.org/ewc28-ssharif-p1.html (website discontinued).

Sharpe, Christina. *Ordinary Notes.* Farrar, Straus and Giroux, 2023.

Sheldrake, Merlin. *Entangled Life: How Fungi Make Our Worlds, Change Our Minds & Shape Our Futures.* Random House, 2021.

Shimizu, Celine Parreñas. *The Hypersexuality of Race: Performing Asian/ American Women on Screen and Scene.* Duke University Press, 2007.

Sigvardsdotter, Erika. "Presenting Absent Bodies: Undocumented Persons Coping and Resisting in Sweden." *Cultural Geographies* 20, no. 4 (2012): 523–39. https://doi.org/10.1177/1474474012465845.

Simpson, Audra. *Mohawk Interruptus: Political Life Across the Borders of Settler States.* Duke University Press, 2014.

Singh, Julietta. "Errands for the Wild." *South Atlantic Quarterly* 117, no. 3 (2018): 567–80. https://doi.org/10.1215/00382876-6942159.

Singh, Julietta. *Unthinking Mastery: Dehumanism and Decolonial Entanglements.* Duke University Press, 2018.

Siobhan. "The Public Universal Friend: A Deep Dive on a Story of Nonbinary Identity, Quakerism, and Near-Death Experiences." Autostraddle, April 7, 2020. https://www.autostraddle.com/the-public-universal-friend/.

Smilges, J. Logan. *Queer Silence: On Disability and Rhetorical Absence.* University of Minnesota Press, 2022.

Smith, Justin. "'[T]he Happiest, Well-Feddest Wolf in Harlem': Asexuality as Resistance to Social Reproduction in Claude McKay's *Home to Harlem.*"

*Feminist Formations* 32, no. 3 (2020): 51–74. https://dx.doi.org/10.1353/ff
.2020.0040.

Smith, Linda Tuhiwai. *Decolonizing Methodologies: Research and Indigenous
Peoples.* Zed Books, 1999.

Snaza, Nathan. *Animate Literacies: Literature, Affect, and the Politics of Humanism.* Duke University Press, 2019.

Snaza, Nathan. "Asexuality and Erotic Biopolitics." *Feminist Formations* 32,
no. 3 (2020): 121–44.

Snaza, Nathan. *Tendings: Feminist Esoterisms and the Abolition of Man.* Duke
University Press, 2024.

Sontag, Susan. *Styles of Radical Will.* Picador, 2002.

Sorensen, Roy. *Seeing Dark Things: The Philosophy of Shadows.* Oxford University Press, 2008.

Spoerri, Daniel. *Topographie anécdotée du hasard.* Éditions Galerie Lawrence,
1962.

Spurgas, Alyson K. *Diagnosing Desire: Biopolitics and Femininity into the Twenty-
First Century.* Ohio State University Press, 2020.

Steedman, Carolyn. *Dust: The Archive and Cultural History.* Rutgers University Press, 2002.

Stallings, L. H. *Funk the Erotic: Transaesthetics and Black Sexual Culture.* University of Illinois Press, 2015.

Stekl, Míša. "Queer Times in *Moonlight.*" *New Review of Film and Television
Studies* 21, no. 2 (2023): 338–62. https://doi.org/10.1080/17400309.2023
.2206391.

Stewart, Kathleen. "Studying Unformed Objects: The Provocation of a Compositional Mode." *Fieldsights,* June 30, 2013. https://culanth.org/fieldsights
/studying-unformed-objects-the-provocation-of-a-compositional-mode.

Stryker, Susan, and Aren Z. Aizura. "Introduction: Transgender Studies 2.0."
In *The Transgender Studies Reader 2,* edited by Susan Stryker and Aren Z.
Aizura. Routledge, 2013.

Szymborska, Wisława. "Compulsion." In *Map: Collected and Last Poems,*
edited by Clare Cavanagh, translated by Clare Cavanagh and Stanisław
Barańczak. Mariner Books, 2015.

TallBear, Kim. "Critical Poly 100s." In *Shapes of Native Nonfiction: Collected
Essays by Contemporary Writers,* edited by Elissa Washuta and Theresa
Warburton. University of Washington Press, 2019.

TallBear, Kim. "An Indigenous Reflection on Working Beyond the Human/
Not Human." *GLQ: A Journal of Lesbian and Gay Studies* 21, no. 2–3
(2015): 230–35.

TallBear, Kim. "Making Love and Relations Beyond Settler Sex and Family."

In *Making Kin Not Population,* edited by Adele Clark and Donna Haraway. Prickly Paradigm Press, 2018.

Tavakoli, Mina. "In 'Paradise Rot,' Jenny Hval Traces a Surrealistic Sexual Awakening." *NPR,* October 25, 2018. https://www.npr.org/2018/10/25 /660242476/in-paradise-rot-jenny-hval-traces-a-surrealistic-sexual -awakening.

Taylor, Jodie. "Taking It in the Ear: On Musico-Sexual Synergies and the (Queer) Possibility That Music Is Sex." *Continuum: Journal of Media and Cultural Studies* 26, no. 4 (2012): 603–14.

Teitelbaum, Benjamin R. "Implicitly White: Right-Wing Nihilism and the Politicizing of Ethnocentrism in Multiracial Sweden." *Scandinavian Studies* 89, no. 2 (2017): 159–78.

Tippett, Krista, host. "Ross Gay: On the Insistence of Joy." *On Being,* podcast. July 25, 2019. https://onbeing.org/programs/ross-gay-on-the-insistence -of-joy/.

Tompkins, Kyla Wazana. *Deviant Matter: Ferment, Intoxicants, Jelly, Rot.* New York University Press, 2024.

Tortorici, Zeb. "Archival Seduction: Indexical Absences and Historiographical Ghosts." *Archive Journal* (November 2015): http://www.archivejournal .net/essays/archival-seduction/.

Tracy, Maurice. "Moving Through Trauma: Black Queer Vulnerability in *Moonlight.*" *QED: A Journal in GLBTQ Worldmaking* 9, no. 1 (2022): 43–58. https://doi.org/10.14321/qed.9.issue-1.0043.

Trinder, Kingston. "Where the Whippoorwill Sound and Morel Lay." In *A Mycological Foray.* Atelier Éditions, 2020.

Tsing, Anna Lowenhaupt. *The Mushroom at the End of the World: On the Possibility of Life in Capitalist Ruins.* Princeton University Press, 2015.

Tuck, Eve, and C. Ree. "A Glossary of Haunting." In *Handbook of Autoethnography,* edited by Stacy Homan Jones, Tony E. Adams, and Carolyn Ellis. Left Coast Press, 2013.

Tuck, Eve, and K. Wayne Yang. "Decolonization Is Not a Metaphor." *Decolonization: Indigeneity, Education & Society* 1, no. 1 (2012): 1–40.

Waite, Stacey. "Cultivating the Scavenger: A Queer Feminist Future for Composition and Rhetoric." *Peitho* 18, no. 1 (2015): 51–71.

Warren, Calvin L. *Ontological Terror: Blackness, Nihilism, and Emancipation.* Duke University Press, 2018.

Wendell, Susan. *The Rejected Body: Feminist Philosophical Reflections on Disability.* Routledge, 1996.

Wendell, Susan. "Unhealthy Disabled: Treating Chronic Illnesses as Disabilities." *Hypatia* 16, no. 4 (Autumn 2001): 17–33. https://doi.org/10.1111 /j.1527-2001.2001.tb00751.x.

Whyte, David. *Everything Is Waiting for You*. Many Rivers Press, 2003.

Whyte, David. "The Well of Grief." All Poetry. https://allpoetry.com/poem/15379848-The-well-of-grief-by-David-Whyte.

Whyte, Kyle Powys. "Indigenous Science (Fiction) for the Anthropocene: Ancestral Dystopias and Fantasies of Climate Change Crisis." *Environment and Planning E: Nature and Space* 1, no. 1–2 (2018): 224–42. https://doi.org/10.1177/2514848618777621.

Williams, H. Herukhuti Sharif. "Believing Is Seeing: *Moonlight*, Asexuality, and Bisexuality." Center for Culture, Sexuality, and Spirituality blog post, March 1, 2017. https://sacredsexualities.org (site discontinued).

Wills, David. *Inanimation: Theories of Inorganic Life*. University of Minnesota Press, 2016.

Wisbey, Herbert Jr. *Pioneer Prophetess: Jemima Wilkinson, the Publick Universal Friend*. Cornell University Press, 1964.

Wolf-Meyer, Matthew J. *Unraveling: Remaking Personhood in a Neurodiverse Age*. University of Minnesota Press, 2020.

Wolfe, Patrick. "Settler Colonialism and the Elimination of the Native." *Journal of Genocide Research* 8, no. 4 (2006): 387–409. https://doi.org/10.1080/14623520601056240.

Yaitanes, Greg, dir. *House*. Season 8, episode 9, "Better Half." Aired January 23, 2012, on Fox.

Yates, Julian. *Of Sheep, Oranges, and Yeast: A Multispecies Impression*. University of Minnesota Press, 2017.

Yergeau, M. Remi. *Authoring Autism: On Rhetoric and Neurological Queerness*. Duke University Press, 2018.

# Index

**KJ CERANKOWSKI** is the author of *Suture: Trauma and Trans Becoming* and coeditor of two editions of *Asexualities: Feminist and Queer Perspectives.* He is associate professor of comparative American studies and gender, sexuality, and feminist studies at Oberlin College.